WHERE NO DOCTOR HAS GONE BEFORE

WHERE NO DOCTOR HAS GONE BEFORE

CUBA'S PLACE IN THE

GLOBAL HEALTH LANDSCAPE

Robert Huish

**WILFRID LAURIER
UNIVERSITY PRESS**

This book has been published with the help of a grant from the Canadian Federation for the Humanities and Social Sciences, through the Awards to Scholarly Publications Program, using funds provided by the Social Sciences and Humanities Research Council of Canada. Wilfrid Laurier University Press acknowledges the financial support of the Government of Canada through the Canada Book Fund for its publishing activities.

Library and Archives Canada Cataloguing in Publication

Huish, Robert, 1978–
    Where no doctor has gone before: Cuba's place in the global health landscape / Robert Huish.

Includes bibliographical references and index.
Also issued in electronic format.
ISBN 978-1-55458-833-6

    1. Medical care—Cuba. 2. Medical education—Cuba. 3. Medical care—Cuba—International cooperation. I. Title.

RA456.C7H84 2013   362.1097291   C2012-904276-5

——

Electronic monograph issued in multiple formats.
Also issued in print format.
ISBN 978-1-55458-860-2 (PDF).—ISBN 978-1-55458-861-9 (EPUB)

    1. Medical care—Cuba. 2. Medical education—Cuba. 3. Medical care—Cuba—International cooperation. I. Title.

RA456.C7H84 2013   362.1097291   C2012-904277-3

Cover design by Sandra Friesen. Front-cover image by Piet den Blanken/Panos. Text design by Brenda Prangley.

© 2013 Wilfrid Laurier University Press
Waterloo, Ontario, Canada
www.wlupress.wlu.ca

RECYCLED
Paper made from recycled material
FSC
www.fsc.org   FSC® C103567

This book is printed on FSC recycled paper and is certified Ecologo. It is made from 100% post-consumer fibre, processed chlorine free, and manufactured using biogas energy.

Printed in Canada

The Delivery

After three days of labour, the baby still hadn't been born.

"He's stuck. The little guy's stuck," the man said.

He had come from a remote farm in the country.

The doctor went with him.

Valise in hand, the doctor walked under the noonday sun, towards the horizon, into that desolate world where everything seems born of accursed fate. When he got there he understood.

Later, he told Gloria Galvín: *"The woman was at death's door but was still panting and sweating, and her eyes were wide open. I had no experience with situations like that. I was shaking; I hadn't the faintest idea what to do. And then, as I drew back the blanket, I saw a tiny arm sticking out from between the woman's spread legs."*

The doctor realized that the man had been pulling on it. The little arm was rubbed raw and lifeless: a flap of skin, black with dried blood. And the doctor thought: *There is nothing to be done.*

And yet, for whatever reason, he caressed the arm. He rubbed the inert limb with his index finger, and when he got to the hand, it suddenly closed, clutching his finger for dear life.

Then the doctor asked for boiling water and rolled up his sleeves.

Eduardo Galeano, *The Book of Embraces*

CONTENTS

PREFACE

On any beach, in any language, a red flag erected in the sand means "stay out of the water!" On April 29, 2001, while swimming at Playa Santa Maria, just east of Havana, I missed that message and ran full speed into an angry sea. A wave came up on me, threw my feet in the air, and drove my head into the ground, shredding my shoulder to pieces. A bloody mess, I dragged myself out of the water and collapsed on the sand. Within no time, two locals put me in the back of their old American car, a 1956 Oldsmobile, and we were driving to Calixto Garcia Hospital in the Vedado section of Havana. I kept telling them that I needed my insurance card, "¡Necesito mi tarjeta de seguro!"

"Never mind that," the driver said.

We arrived at the hospital. A doctor was lounging by the main entrance reading the daily issue of *Granma*. He took me, along with another unfortunate Canadian, who had sliced open his foot having trod on a broken beer bottle, into the surgery, and two nurses and another doctor appeared immediately. They put the man with the wounded foot on the table, cleaned him up, and then, with catgut suture, sowed him up. Then they turned to me. They cleaned my shoulder and treated it.

We were both treated and out the door in less than twenty-five minutes. I had $50[1] with me, and I offered the doctors and the nurses the full amount. They refused it and laughed. It took longer to get a cab back to the hotel than it did to receive excellent medical treatment. At the very same time in Canada, newspapers were reporting that hospitals in the province of Ontario were turning away ambulances, physician wait times had never been worse, and Canada suffered from a chronic lack of doctors. And yet, in Havana, the capital of an economically hobbled country, I received first-rate care for absolutely no cost. Two days later, a nurse even came by the hotel looking for me: "How is the guy with the shoulder?" she asked the front desk.

Thanks to that wave, I was thrown into the world of Cuban medical internationalism. At the time, I knew nothing of health care, medicine, or even foreign policy. A few days after the visit to Calixto Garcia Hospital, however, I, along with a group of Canadian students, visited the Latin American School of Medicine. I met with the staff and students and discussed why the school was built and for whom it was built. During this first trip to Cuba, while the pundits and politicians back home were screaming for greater privatization of medical services, I came to realize that Cuba, an economically modest nation, could make a difference by showing other nations an example of a radical and badly needed approach to affordable health care and universal well-being.

I offer this book as a means to build understanding of Cuban medical internationalism. This work explains how a service ethic embracing compassion and altruism developed as normative practice within Cuba, and how it is making its way to the world's most vulnerable communities around the world. The lessons Cuba has to offer the world are not necessarily about how to design a health-care system or how to structure an economy to support universal public health care. The real lesson is that which comes from the experiences and stories of individuals who want to care for the poor. They seek opportunities to go where no doctor has gone before, and with the right social and political support, their efforts can be a powerful force in bringing greater equity to our global health landscape.

ACKNOWLEDGEMENTS

While I hold that fateful wave fully responsible for setting this project in motion, I, too, hold responsible all those who have provided their support throughout this project. Without them, this could never have succeeded the way that it did. As the author of this book, my role was actually minimal. Those who have invested financial support, provided supervision, built networks, gave their warm beds, or gave their not-so-warm couches, and who always encouraged this project to move forward are the ones who have truly made this study possible. I will take a moment here to give them all well-deserved acknowledgements and thanks and to explicitly state that I hold them accountable for seeing this through.

To the Pierre Elliott Trudeau Foundation: thank you. This foundation offers financial and networking assistance to scholars to engage Canadians about pressing social issues. Its support, dedication, and encouragement are refreshing ingredients in how to approach international research. There is simply no way that I could have completed this study without the Foundation, and I will be forever grateful to them for it. Foundation President P. G. Forest, former President Stephen Toope, and interim President Fred Lowry have done so much for the Foundation and its members, and they have been personally involved in helping me to develop and initiate this project. I sincerely thank them for their time and encouragement. A very, very special thanks goes to Josée St-Martin, who has gone above and beyond the call of duty in handling my travels, untangling confusion, and always offering her support. Et plus, je veux donner un merci à Bettina Cenerelli, Stéphanie Forest, et Michel Hardy-Vallée pour leur assistances dévouées. As well, I thank my fellow scholars, notably William Tayeebwa, David Mendelsohn, Karen Rideout, and Anna-Liisa Aunio. They are friends and colleagues alike, and I am extremely grateful to have worked and grown with them.

I thank the Social Science and Humanities Research Council for its substantial financial assistance throughout this project. As well, the Faculty of Arts and Social Sciences at Dalhousie University has offered generous support for the production of this book.

Dr. John Brohman has been a dedicated and encouraging mentor throughout this process, and I greatly appreciate his efforts in helping to prepare grants, build theoretical frameworks, and wade through mountains of edits and typos. Dr. Jerry Spiegel has played a consummate supervisory and mentorship role throughout this process. Jerry has gone above and beyond the call of duty to provide workspace in Vancouver and valuable professional development and networking in Ecuador and Cuba. I also extend thanks to Dr. Robert Woollard and Dr. Eric Hershberg for their comments on this work.

I sincerely thank Dr. John Kirk of Dalhousie University for his dedicated mentorship over the years and for moving the idea of Cuban medical internationalism into the forefront of Cuban studies. His advice and support for this research project and his assistance with publications has been exceptional. Dr. W. George Lovell of Queen's University has continued to be a close ally, offering assistance and advice throughout. Dr. Susan Babbitt of Queen's University has also been very supportive in helping me overcome some of the conceptual roadblocks to this study. Thanks also go to Dr. Gregory Marchildon, Dr. William Coleman, Dr. James Tully, Dr. Michael Erisman, and Dr. Daniel Weinstock. Also, the late Honourable Jacques Hébert played an important role in opening doors for this project in Cuba. I am very thankful for his personal encouragement, which helped to bring the idea of this study into action, and I extend my condolences to his family for losing him at the end of 2007.

A big thanks also goes to the staff of the Canadian embassy in Havana, particularly Simon Cridland, Ram Kimini, and Alexandra Bugailiskis. Thanks also to Diane Applebaum and MEDICC for their outstanding work in Cuba, and for bringing me on board with their 2007 delegation to Havana. I would also like to thank Duncan and Nora Etches for their assistance in introducing me to the medical world in the early days of this project.

Big thanks go to my colleagues in International Development Studies at Dalhousie University: John Cameron, Nissim Manathukkaren, Theresa Ulicki, Matt Schnurr, and Owen Willis. I give a very special thanks to Marian MacKinnon and Nicole Drysdale for their selfless support, and also kudos go to Ms. MacKinnon for her dedication to bringing students to Havana through an excellent Cuba study program. And to the hundreds of students that I have had the pleasure of teaching, thank you so much for being engaged, curious, and committed in the class. It is all very much appreciated.

En Cuba, gracias a Alberto Velázquez Lopez, Ada Bertha Frómeta Fernández Javier Cabrera, Sonia Catasus Cervera, y Dr. Alfredo Espinoza para sus asistencias y colaboraciones. I must extend a large thanks to Cedric Edwards and Dania Suarez, two ELAM graduates who helped to put the fieldwork into motion in both Cuba and Ecuador. I most certainly give thanks to each of the ELAM students and graduates that I met. Every one of them is, to me, a true "fugitive of compassion."

I give enormous thanks to my two sets of parents who, in addition to keeping my old beds reserved for times needed, have offered their full and unbridled support for this and many other scholastic pursuits since day one. More recently, Simon Darnell and Sandy Wells offered great insights and conversations throughout this process. And, of course, Rachel Brickner has offered tremendous support in seeing this book through.

For most of this study, I have lived out of two knapsacks and a post-office box, and I have slept on a lot of couches. I owe so many people tremendous thanks for their hospitality in putting me up and putting up with me during this long globetrotting process. Without your support, I could not have physically managed this. All of the people mentioned here have come through once or, in some cases, dozens of times with a warm bed and a good breakfast, and not one single time has anyone left me to sleep out in the mud. Thanks goes to Ira and Linda Matthews, Paul Biln and Brenda Tang, Hugh Barnett and Sarah Moyle, Dan Carney and Anita Schreiber, Daniel and Kerith Stevens, Sean and Kim Connelly, B-Jae Kelly, Annalee Yassi, Louis-Joseph Saucier, Samuel Spiegel, Kunle Owalabi, Robyn Atkinson, Jason Luckeroff, James Milner, Michael Ananny, Joseph Irwin, Tom Blair, Jessica Everet, Julio Canas, Alexis García, Juan Alberto Gaibor, Georgina Muñozo, and Fany Guamán.

To all of these people, I am guilty of dirtying their sheets, cleaning out their fridges, and stealing their toothpaste, and yet not one of them had the common sense to call the authorities on such transient behaviour. In thanks, I want you all to know that clean sheets, a full fridge, and plenty of toothpaste await you wherever I am, whenever you are ready.

LIST OF ACRONYMS

ALBA	The Bolivarian Alliance for the Peoples of Our America (Alianza Bolivariana para los Pueblos de Nuestra América)
BHT	basic health team
CARICOM	Caribbean Community
CENIRMED	International Centre for Medical Reference (Centro Internacional de Referencia Médica)
CDR	Committees for the Defense of the Revolution (Comités de Defensa de la Revolución)
CME	continuing medical education
CMPP	Cuban Medical Professional Parole Program
ELAM	The Latin American School of Medicine (La Escuela Latinoamericana de Ciencias Médicas)
ENSAP	The National School of Public Health (La Escuela National de Salud Pública)
FIS	Internationalist Federation of Health (Federación Internacionalista de Salud)
FMC	Cuban Women's Federation (Federación de Mujeres Cubana)
GME	General Medical Exam
IFCO	Interreligious Foundation for Community Organization
IMF	International Monetary Fund
IMG	international medical graduate
LMIC	lower- and middle-income country
MEDICC	Medical Education Cooperation with Cuba
MINREX	Ministry of Foreign Affairs (Ministerio de Relaciones Exterior)
MINSAP	Ministry of Public Health (Ministerio de Salud Publica)
MSF	Doctors Without Borders (Médecins Sans Frontières)
NSAP	National Service to Eradicate Malaria (Servicio Nacional de Erradicación de la Malaria)
OECD	Organization for Economic Co-operation and Development
OFW	overseas foreign worker
PAHO	Pan American Health Organizations
RPSM	Residency Program in Social Medicine (Motefiore Medical Centre)
RSMS	Rural Social Medical Service
TNM	traditional and natural medicine (*medicina verde*)
USMLE	United States Medical Licensing Exam
WHO	World Health Organization

A NOTE ON SOURCES

Primary research for this study took place between 2004 and 2010 with forty-seven first-person interviews. Participants included ELAM students, graduates, teachers, and administrators, members of MINSAP and MINREX, and villagers in rural Ecuador. I also collected interview data through multiple field site visits coordinated through MEDICC. Multiple method research was used for interviews, but data tended to weigh heavily on the use of descriptive analysis by participants. Open-ended interviews took place using a semi-structured interview guide that was given to each group of participants. The goal of the methodology sought multiple perspectives of Cuban medical internationalism by those who participated in it and those who were affected by it.

CHAPTER 1

AGAINST THE GARDEN PATH THAT JUSTIFIES

HEALTH INEQUITY: MAKING THE CASE FOR

HEALTH CARE AS A HUMAN RIGHT

Just at dusk, I stood on the rooftop of the public clinic in La Joya de los Sachas,[1] a small town in Ecuador's Amazon, with Cuban-trained doctor Dania Suarez. We watched the gas flares from the petroleum developments shoot up above the rain forest. This clinic, surrounded by thick jungle and standing pools of water ripe with mosquitoes—the kind that make you burn alive with dengue or go mad with malaria (Ribeiro Galardo et al., 2007; Sideridis, Canario, & Cunha, 2003)—had received a fourteen-year-old girl who had gone into labour while we were in the village dining on the indigenous delicacy of *gusanos al carbon*. The physicians who were on duty received her in the emergency room. Holding back tears, Dania said, "I remember treating her nine months ago after she was raped."

"She'll be okay, yeah? I mean Jacqueline is taking care of her, and the others are there," I said.

Sure enough, the skilled attendants on staff helped the girl give birth to her child safely. It was the end of another day in the La Joya de los Sachas clinic. While working with locally trained Ecuadorian health-care workers, Dania and Jacqueline, both Cuban-trained doctors, see days and nights of disasters and miracles. In the only public clinic for eighty kilometres, these doctors, trained at Cuba's Latin American School of Medicine (ELAM), serve on the front lines of primary care for the poor. The clinic is severely underfunded and resources are always scarce. Still, the patients who come to the humble clinic have most, but not all, of their primary care needs met. Some men come in injured from working in the petroleum developments (Sawyer, 2004). Many women and children visit these doctors, sick from the effects of poverty (Farrow, Larrea, Hyman, & Lema, 2005).

In 2006, the clinic had six *consultorios* (consultation rooms), three of which had been flooded out because of a lack of a foundation that consequently let in water from a nearby standing cesspool. With the floodwater came mosquitoes, and with them dengue and malaria. In the three functioning *consultorios*, everything was in short supply. The examining table was bare, sanitation was a miracle, and the medicine ancient. We tore cotton balls into smaller cotton balls, and those pieces were torn into even smaller pieces because there were no others. The examination equipment needed repair, as did the diagnostic equipment, worn out from much usage and not enough maintenance.

The story of La Joya de los Sachas could be story of countless communities in the global South, ones that sit on top of a wealth of resources but suffer a paucity of public health service. This book is about understanding the role of committed health workers like Dania who are part of a Cuban-trained global health workforce that aims to serve the poor in communities like La Joya de los Sachas. Since 1960, Cuba has sent over 135,000 of its own health workers to 101 different countries. In addition, the country has trained tens of thousands of foreigners, like Dania, as health professionals in the hopes that they will return to their homes and practise where they are needed the most. In addition to this program are other Cuban initiatives that pursue international cooperation through disaster relief, free eye surgeries, pharmaceutical development, and public health campaigns. Some have called this medical diplomacy (Feinsilver, 1993), others label it soft power (Kirk & Erisman, 2009). In 2007, John Kirk and I first referred to this as "Cuban medical internationalism" because the impacts of these health campaigns go well beyond strategic foreign policy (Huish & Kirk, 2007). Alongside political gains for Cuba, these interventions are saving the lives and easing the suffering of millions.

This book is about understanding Cuba's place in the global health landscape. There are several objectives. One is to take notice of the political rationale for a small and relatively poor nation to make enormous investments in health, especially in an era when some of the wealthiest countries in the world call for greater cuts to public health. Another is to understand the actual impacts Cuban medical internationalism[2] makes on the ground. But the main goals of the book are

- to recognize the transformative impacts of Cuban medical internationalism
- to acknowledge Cuba's efforts as a global health power and as a state-sponsored counter-hegemonic alternative of comprehensive primary health care to the numerous philanthropic global health projects that focus on specific diseases

- to acknowledge the challenges Cuban-trained health workers go up against in the field
- to demonstrate that it is not only practical, but also in the best interest of nation states, to engage in health outreach on a global scale. As Joseph Nyes' (2004) theory of soft power states, political, moral, ethical, and practical benefits exist for a nation state to engage in health outreach and cooperation that serves the broad interests of the poor
- to suggest that the transformative merits of Cuban medical internationalism is a work-in-progress. Additional cooperation and structural support by the international community for marginalized communities is necessary to facilitate the ethics of service that Cuba has brought to the global health landscape.

I suggest that Cuba pursues medical internationalism because it is in its own interests to assist other countries in overcoming structures of underdevelopment. Moreover, the success of Cuban medical internationalism in fulfilling foreign policy objectives is a result of the positive impacts the programs actually have on the ground with the appropriate social and political support. Cuba's international health programs are not just symbolic; they are addressing a broad range of health calamities throughout the global South by encouraging primary care at the community level. They have made impressive gains in countries such as Venezuela, Guatemala, and The Gambia thanks to the moral commitment of their own workers and to supportive local governments. For many places in the world, however, there is still a need for increased support to ensure that these health workers can effectively serve the poor.

For a country with a humble economy and only 11.5 million inhabitants, Cuba has an unmatched global health workforce of over thirty-eight thousand health workers in sixty-six countries as of 2011. While these numbers are impressive and worthy of discussion, the purpose of this book is to explain how this global health workforce fits into the larger global health landscape. As Samb et al. (2009) show, billions of dollars are committed each year by wealthy nations and private philanthropists for global health causes. In some cases there are gains, and in others only repeated defeat on some of the most basic health challenges (World Health Organization [WHO], 2006). In most cases, Cuban medical internationalism makes a noticeable impact on pressing health challenges and often with considerably less cost than some of the more narrowly focused and disease-specific initiatives from the global North. In other cases, serious challenges exist to facilitating the goals of the programs, but the example of a state-backed global health workforce committed to the service of, and training of, the poor stands out as a unique global force. This book aims to position various Cuban programs against broader trends in global health in order to expose its unique importance.

So what makes Cuba different? At the heart of the Cuban approach is a belief that health cannot be compartmentalized into specific diseases. In order to improve global health, resources—notably human resources—must be directed at meeting primary care demands at the community level rather than raising enormous budgets for disease-specific interventions. Cuba's approach aims to treat people over the long term, and is part of its international agenda that values comprehensive development rather than merely waging war on various diseases. Cuba's commitment to the basics of primary care, public health, and education are making a world of difference in thousands of communities around the world. For this reason, the Cuban experience occupies a unique and vitally important place in the global health landscape.

Is Cuba merely a Marxist oddity sporadically sending its doctors all around the world? One Canadian physician remarked to me recently, "Are they doing this to spread communism?" I responded to him, as ELAM students had put it to me, "Cuban doctors are too busy taking care of people to hold seminars on Marx." Positioning Cuban medical internationalism as a carefully planned strategy of international outreach that reflects Cuba's own domestic strengths is a far more fitting lens through which to see and understand their efforts (Nye, 2004). If Cuban medical internationalism is understood as a means to strategic cooperation that aims to help the poor, then important comparisons can be drawn to the broader global health landscape. There are Cuban medical brigades working in over thirty African nations. Cuban eye surgeons have restored sight to over 2 million people in the Americas. After the devastating 2010 earthquake in Haiti, Cuba committed two thousand medical professionals to Haiti's public health system. These health workers go to Haiti on a rotating basis and will return to Cuba for good when Haitian health professionals are trained to take their places (Six months after the earthquake, 2010). Even though there are recognizable tenets of solidarity at work, this is not symbolic theatrics. In each program, Cuban health workers go to the root of poverty and make long-term commitments to assist the marginalized. These programs are transformative in communities where no doctor has gone before.

The following chapters discuss broad challenges currently unfolding in global health, such as the increased privatization of health services, reduced accessibility of services for the poor, the rise of medical tourism in resource-poor settings, the ethics of medical education, and the role of the biomedical industrial complex. Against these broad challenges, the book discusses how Cuba's various campaigns, such as disaster relief medicine, free medical education for foreigners, free eye surgery for foreigners, and the provision of hundreds of comprehensive health brigades across Latin America, Asia, and Africa, are filling important gaps that other efforts and international health policy often miss.

Around the world, underserviced public health centres like the one in La Joya de los Sachas abound. Crumbling infrastructure, burned-out doctors, and deep poverty are the norm for public health services (WHO, 2006). However, in other, more ravaged places of this planet, the idea of a well-functioning public health centre is rarely a reality, and often only an idea. For 2 of the 7 billion people who live in this world in absolute poverty, too many die without ever receiving access to health care (Pogge, 2008). The overwhelming majority of the poor live in the global South, although there are thousands of people in the global North who are systematically denied health care because of an inability to pay or to be insured (Reinhardt, 2006). By no means can Cuban-trained physicians like Dania overcome these enormous health-care challenges on their own. Health workers who are dedicated to serving the poor require support at multiple levels. How that support is organized and implemented matters enormously (Gaye & Nelson, 2009), but what matters most is to realize that it is possible to offer such support, and facilitating processes that allow health-care workers to serve the poor can lead to enormous progress in development. How Cuba has attempted to support such health-care workers, at home and abroad, is a lesson on how it can be in a nation's best interest to provide care for its own citizens while meeting the needs of others.

The Global Health Landscape

Today, in an era when there is more money, attention, and knowledge dedicated towards global health than ever before, the inequities between the best off and the worst off have never been worse (People's Health Movement, Medact, & Global Equity Gauge Alliance, 2008). Notable philanthropic organizations, such as the Bill & Melinda Gates Foundation and the William J. Clinton Foundation, are spending billions on health programs for the global poor (McCoy, Chand, & Sridhar, 2009). Despite this enormous financial contribution dedicated to global health, enormous challenges remain to preventing suffering and death from basic infections, easily treatable parasites, and childbirth (Farmer, 2005). For example, a hospital in sub-Saharan Africa may be well funded for HIV/AIDS anti-retrovirals, yet, could have a complete lack of basic medicines, such as penicillin and painkillers. While donors give generously for the prevention and treatment of HIV/AIDS, basic infections receive little philanthropic attention. As many poor countries rely heavily on philanthropic support, the focus on high-profile diseases creates massive distortions in the level of care between health issues. Simple, yet often lethal, health issues that affect the poor could best be handled through strong, comprehensive programs that could address the broad structural causes of suffering, rather than react to a select collection of internationally acknowledged health issues.

The stark contrast of health indicators between wealthy and poor nations is extreme and the result of a broad range of historical, political, and colonial processes that have resulted in strong economies often being able to establish quality health-care systems that can meet the health-care needs of their populations. The contrasts are alarming: almost everyone in Japan is born with the assistance of a health professional, while in Ethiopia only 5.6 percent of the population are born with a skilled attendant (York, 2010). In 2010, maternal mortality in Iceland was zero (Indrayan, 2008), and in Canada, one mother dies for every 16,600 live births (WHO, 2007), but in Afghanistan—a country that receives ample official military assistance and humanitarian aid from countries like Canada—one mother died for every 53 live births in 2006 (WHO, 2007). Further, Canadians can expect to live for eighty years, while in Afghanistan people can count on making it only to their forty-first birthday. In Swaziland, a country ravaged by HIV/AIDS, tuberculosis, and rampant poverty, thirty-nine years is the estimated life expectancy.

The reasons for such inequity are vast and complex. In Afghanistan, the lack of gender equality and education contributes to poor maternal health outcomes. Swaziland has a unique history that has shaped the social developments that created an enormous vulnerability to the HIV/AIDS epidemic. As well, the political decisions of regional powers like South Africa have affected Swaziland's ability to cope with its HIV/AIDS crisis. The answer as to why these health inequities exist is enormously complex, and perhaps it is not entirely fair to juxtapose the current health outcomes of affluent nations on the expectations of poorer ones. Rather, the question is why are inequities continuing in an era when there is an enormous commitment to global health? Scientific knowledge has advanced medicine in terms of clinical procedures, pharmaceuticals, and treatments for diseases that twenty years ago were all but fatal. In the past five years, thanks to enormous investments in biomedical science, there is more knowledge about the workings of the human brain than ever before. Yet, knowledge of how to overcome unnecessary suffering through affordable health-care access to the most desperate places on the planet has not kept pace.

Over 4.3 million health-care workers are needed right away to beat these gross health and health-care inequities (WHO, 2006). That is to say that these workers are needed for the most marginalized communities in the global North and the global South alike. In Canada and the United States, there is one physician for every 450 people, but Malawi has only 266 physicians for its population of 13 million people. That is a doctor-to-patient ratio of one physician for every 49,000 people. The comparison is extreme, but it should be noted that increasing physician numbers is not the whole answer. Despite the number of physicians to people in the United States, many citizens go without health care. In Ecuador, there is one physician for every 730 people, but many doctors dedicate their time to the private sector and other activities. In the mornings, an Ecuadorian physician could work in a public hospital for five hours and be responsible for three hundred people. In the afternoon, the same doctor could work in a private clinic, be paid more money for the same amount of time, and spend that time with only fifteen people. In Ecuador, 30 percent of the people go without affordable health-care services. Further, wealthy nations often poach health workers from poor nations (Labonte et al., 2006). Notably, African and Caribbean nations are left reeling from the flight of their doctors, and all too often, the global North gives little back in official development assistance to build local health workforces (Bourgeault, Parpia, Oryeme, & Gulamhusein, 2010). In Canada, Australia, and the US, one-quarter of the physician workforce was originally trained somewhere else (Labonte et al., 2006).

These stark figures reveal that the global North, while dedicating resources for health issues in the global South, has benefited from the receipt of health-care professionals from countries that likely experience suffering as a result of poorly funded health-care systems. While resource-rich countries cannot be blamed for the entirety of global health inequity, the positioning of global health outreach to address big-scale diseases and remain uninvolved with basic care services is morally questionable. Even more troubling is the lack of attention to building up human resources for health care in the global South. The pressing dilemma of the lack of 4.3 million health-care workers is not so much a problem of where to find them but how to allow those willing to serve the poor the opportunity to do so. To actively encourage the disinvestment in human resources in health care in struggling nations without offering any compensation to improve primary care capacity for the marginalized is morally troubling.

On a global scale, the failure to take care of the poor is alarming. Martin Luther King, Jr. (1966) said that, "of all the forms of injustice, inequality in health care is the most shocking and inhumane." Considering that fifty thousand people are lost each day due to preventable causes, and considering that most of the world is in dire need of health-care workers, should there not be a focus within global health outreach towards access to quality health care in what have been traditionally marginalized communities (WHO, 2006)? Why are there not greater efforts to train health-care workers so that there is no greater risk of falling ill in sub-Saharan Africa than there is in southern Canada? This is not an impossible goal. Some argue that it is possible for everyone to have access to health care if there is political will and dedicated attention to local needs (Pogge, 2008). The first step in overcoming the acceptance of health-care inequity and in overcoming the reluctance to make health care a human right starts by asking how to invest effectively in people as agents and actors of global health. It is time to invest in people rather than just invest in material things.

There are amazing benefits to having committed health-care workers and the communities they serve embrace health and well-being (Mullan & Epstein, 2002). In Jamkhed, India, local doctors trained thousands of poor women to be village health workers, and, as a result, they were able to turn the tide on health challenges ranging from high infant mortality to leprosy (Parikh, Antoniello, Arole, & Thakkar, 2008). This is why the story of three Cuban-trained doctors working in La Joya de los Sachas and, indeed, the stories of the over 135,000 other Cuban-trained doctors who have worked abroad since 1960 may shed light on new and innovative ways to deliver health care to some of the most vulnerable places on the planet. The realist school of thought in foreign policy suggests that foreign influence is best exercised through military and economic power (Morgenthau, 1985; Schweller, 1996). But what if a country's strength is in caring for others? Is it possible for a nation to feel inclined to work for the humanitarian needs of others while fulfilling its own national interests? Is it possible to for a nation to see the investment in comprehensive public health care as a foreign policy that furthers its own interests? Is it possible for a nation to fulfill its own interests by taking care of others (Nye, 2004)?

If it can be assumed that Nye's (2004) theory of soft power is a viable alternative to the realist approach to foreign influence, it might help to explain why one small, poor country is trying to make a difference by offering health services on a global scale. Cuba, a country that has a history of realist interventions, notably with a sixteen-year military presence in Angola (Gleijeses, 1996), has, more recently, made enormous efforts to position its foreign influence through primary health care for marginalized communities around the world. The Cuban approach deserves attention; it is a country that comprehensively practises health as a human right, and it is working to take this philosophy beyond its own borders and address basic health issues that have been long overlooked. From training physicians to work in Ecuador's Amazon to operating the largest free eye surgery program in the world, Cuba's commitment to global health is large, impressive, evolving, and meeting the needs of some of the world's poorest communities (Kirk & Erisman, 2009). The history of and the reasons for Cuban medical internationalism are important to understand, as these policies evolved through a unique blend of historical circumstance, political will, and economic necessity (Saney, 2004). Cuba's example offers the chance to move towards a much-needed paradigm shift that will address current global health inequity and understand what is needed to create a global health workforce for the twenty-first century.

Cuban Medical Internationalism

Struggling through a fifty-year US embargo and one of the most devastating economic collapses in modern history, Cubans have had to innovate a great deal, from food security to public transit. Parking lots were converted into community gardens to ensure access to fresh food during the economic collapse, and public transit in Havana includes the *camello*, a makeshift bus pulled by a tractor-trailer that could easily have two hundred people stuffed into it. During this time, when the country lacked material resources and many ad hoc coping mechanisms were put into place, the government made a well-planned effort to strategically invest in human resources. That investment has resulted in a global health workforce. At times, the Cuban government has deployed health workers abroad to serve countries, such as Qatar, in exchange for hard currency. In other times, Cuba has secured bilateral trade agreements for access to resources, notably oil from Venezuela. In other cases, the government has scaled up cooperation with ideologically akin countries, such as those participating in The Bolivarian Alliance for the Peoples of Our America (ALBA). Medical internationalism has also warmed politically cool relations with Guatemala, Honduras, and Uruguay. Although, there are cases, such as in The Gambia and Uganda, where the Cuban government has received very little in return for helping to establish national medical education programs. Cuban medical internationalism evolved over a forty-year period from a small brigade of workers to help earthquake ravaged Chile in 1960 to a permanent global workforce. It has expanded from simply sending health workers abroad to receiving students from around the world for free medical education. By 2009, Cuba's ELAM had received twenty-four thousand students from fifty-four different countries under the moral obligation that they would go home to serve where they were needed the most. This is an enormous global outreach that deserves recognition and scholastic investigation. For the purposes of this book, the focus will be upon the professional experiences of the Ecuadorian graduates whom I interviewed in the field between 2006 and 2007. Cuba, a country of modest economic means, boasts twenty-three medical schools and annually graduates between three and four thousand doctors (Cuba Health Profile, 2007). While attempting to scale up its human resources for health for its own needs and the needs of others, Cuba has not let slide scientific advancements in medicine and pharmacology (Huergo, 2007). Even though so many Cuban doctors have committed to serve abroad, the country has maintained the best doctor-to-patient ratio in the world with one physician for every 179 people (WHO, 2007). Family doctors are distributed across the country so that citizens in rural and urban areas have full access to public health services.

Since 2003, medical internationalism has scaled up considerably; there are nineteen thousand Cuban health-care workers practising in urban slums and rural villages in Venezuela and the result has been that Cuba's doctor-to-patient ratio has slipped from one physician for every 159 people in 2002 to one physician for every 179 people (WHO, 2007). It is still the best national doctor-to-patient ratio in the world, and although Cuba received much-needed oil in trade, it has caused challenges and grumblings among Cubans who have grown used to a health-care system par excellence (Huish & Spiegel, 2008). Instead of having a doctor and nurse on every other block, more citizens have to go a bit further to access polyclinics, which are still free and abundant. But another tension comes from health workers who remain in Cuba's domestic service, as colleagues who travel abroad in brigades subsequently acquire additional revenue. The economic challenges in Cuba cannot be underestimated, as they cause enormous hardship across the country. As Eckstein (2009) suggests, many Cuban professionals, including health workers, leave to seek out remittances to help alleviate economic hardships within their families. Roughly 3 percent of Cuban health-care workers reject both domestic and international service and leave the country to pursue monetary gains. Yet despite the income inequity between Cuban physicians practising at home and abroad and those who leave the system altogether, the overwhelming majority—97 percent—of health-care workers continue practising medicine within Cuban programs.

Aside from the enormous commitment to human resources for health, Cuba's Finlay Institute is developing a pharmaceutical industry aimed at producing affordable medicines for poor communities in the global South. The institute, located just outside of Havana, works towards the development of vaccines and low-cost generic medicine. In the 1980s, the Finlay Institute made breakthroughs with the forward innovation of a vaccine against Group B Neisseria Meningitidis (Sierra et al., 1991).[3] More recently, Labiofam, a Cuban commercial pharmaceutical operation, has begun preparing to release a homeo-therapeutic cancer drug to the international market (Multari, Gallo, & Fiorentini, 2011). These pharmaceutical developments are notable; a forward innovation of pharmaceuticals has been rare in countries with a centralized economy. Typically, countries without a private sector pharmaceutical industry focus their research efforts on backward innovation, meaning the pharmaceutical already exists and the recipe is deconstructed for generic copying and distribution. Resource shortfalls in the 1990s brought Cuba to the point where the country had run out of necessary medicines. For this reason, Cuba explored backward innovation on a panoply of medicines in order to develop low-cost generics for domestic use and international sales. Cuba's forward and backward innovation demonstrates a commitment to health for a broad range of illnesses. The country is committed to developing oncology therapy alongside generic aspirin.

Some have discussed the motivations for Cuba's medical internationalism in detail. Both Feinsilver (1993) and Kirk and Erisman (2009) discuss the size and scope of Cuba's medical projects, and they explain the rationale behind an economically hobbled country pursuing a massive international health campaign: it produces goodwill and social capital and it is in its own best interests.

These authors have demonstrated the benefits of Cuban medical internationalism for foreign policy. Still, many continue to ask why Cuba is so dedicated to global health equity when they have enormous economic and social challenges at home (Millman, 2011). Feinsilver (1993) and Kirk and Erisman (2009) conclude that Cuba invests heavily in global health in order to receive the benefits of international goodwill. It would seem perplexing for a country to pursue intentionally a foreign policy that goes against its own perceived interests, but Cuba's international efforts are not simply politically symbolic. As these scholars attest, Cuba's internationalism to other countries that are working to overcome underdevelopment creates political and economic benefits that can be measured and valued.

Rather than ask why Cuba does it, one could ask a more challenging moral question: In this era of global health inequity, why would Cuba and other nations not make efforts towards global health equity? If a person or a nation has the ability to save lives, why would they not?

In order to answer this question, this book discusses Cuba's medical internationalism not just in terms of geopolitical strategy, but also from the point of view of those working within and impacted by this worldwide movement. Efforts in Cuban medical internationalism, universal public health care, international-medical humanitarianism, and international solidarity do not directly correlate to immediate or obvious economic benefit. These efforts need political will, proper management, and public support over the long term in order to succeed in the short term and to garner broader socioeconomic benefits in the long term.

The reason to pay attention to Cuba's experience goes well beyond gains in global politics. It saves lives and livelihoods. It restores vision to those who have lost their livelihood after being blinded with cataracts. It offers the chance for medical education, regardless of race or gender or financial resources, to those willing to serve the needs of the poor rather than simply meet the demands of the rich. It emphasizes training the next generation of health workers at the local level to take over where the current *brigadistas* (volunteers) leave off. It demonstrates that the borders of geography can be overcome so that health workers can help the marginalized regardless of their location.

Cuba's medical internationalism considers advancements in health-care accessibility just as important as any scientific advancement in clinical medicine.

The country dedicates enormous efforts to improvements in social accessibility. Cuba's mission of global health equity demonstrates that commitment to social accessibility is not an accident of economic fortune or geographic location; it is a product of careful management and development, just as is any medical advancement (Farmer, 2005). This stems from a long-standing ethic of Cuban medicine. Charitable interventions and short-term medical brigades are not enough to treat all the needs of the world's poor (Castro, 1999; Orbinski, 2008). Long-term interventions are necessary in order to address the most pressing, albeit basic, conditions of suffering. Cuba's internationalism is not short-course programs. The programs are often lengthy, in some cases lasting over ten years, and they aim to provide the basics first. For this system, serving the poor is not a side project; it is its very essence.

The result is that those who participate in Cuba's many global health initiatives become much-needed agents working to overcome massive inequities. Their examples, their experiences, and the results of some of their projects could greatly inform other nations and global financial institutions, such as the International Monetary Fund (IMF) and the World Bank, to embrace a commitment to advance global health equity through improved accessibility with the same moral convictions as investing in scientific advancements for biomedicine.

Cuba manages accessibility in a way that brings well-being to some of the most vulnerable people on the planet. All the while, its own health-care system continues to flourish through commitments to Alma-Ata:[4] health for all. Cuba's example of commitment to accessibility can be explored by rich and poor nations alike, but it will require political support and imagination, two things that many nation states and international financial institutions—that largely regulate health care in the global South—lack as they fail to see the benefits of taking care of each other.

Cuba's Refusal to Acquiesce

Pogge (2008) suggests that there are two general excuses used by nations to avoid addressing the pressing needs of the poor. The first comes from those who suggest that the needs of the poor are not really of concern to the affluent. As Pogge (2008) notes, this is an easy excuse to dismiss. There are both moral and rational reasons to ensure that human beings do not suffer in poverty. Moral reasons to tackle poverty date back to antiquity. Recently, aid dependency, the lack of autonomy, laggard economies, poor efficiency, and endemic pestilence have all been cited as obvious and practical reasons to address poverty as they dampen a broader global economy (Moyo, 2009). Morally or rationally, it is difficult to argue that poverty is not of concern. The second excuse suggests that the normal behaviour, decisions, and daily operations of governments and institutions are not directly causing harm to the poor and marginalized. This argument, often defended by world leaders and captains of industry, implies that while poverty is an unfortunate condition, it cannot all be tied to the actions of prosperous nations. Besides, nations are supposedly thought to have a preferred interest in meeting the needs of their own citizens before the needs of others, according to Pogge (2008). If a nation protects the health of its citizens through a single-payer health system, and if that nation supports international trade policies to stimulate its economy and effectively pay for that system, some may ask what harm is done? If another, poorer nation, does not fare as well in the same trade agreement—by, say, allowing for resource extraction that does not see substantive revenue remain in the country—then is it the responsibility of the benefiting nation or the citizens of that nation to pursue more equitable relations? Why is it that it is easier to say that a nation should meet the needs of its own people than it is to say it should be equally concerned with the health of others? The excuse that nations are not actively causing harm, or, if they are, that it can be justified, does not explain the cause of all health inequities, but it is at the heart of the matter in explaining why health care inequities persist within poorer countries.

Investing directly in health and health care is one of the best means for a society to flourish, but under neoliberal doctrine, robust public health care is widely perceived as a social burden rather than a means to flourish (Steger & Roy, 2010; Steinbrook, 2006). The ongoing IMF austerity measures reflect this. In 2011, the IMF expected Greece to slash spending for public health and to pursue more fee-for-service options. Economic austerity demands fast results, and cutting public spending on health care can deliver such economic results while it can take a lifetime to see the benefits of investing in good health (Martin, 2009). Yet, the economic benefits of maintaining a healthy population are not difficult to assume. Even in the narrowest sense, individuals who are not financially ruined from excessive health-care costs can do more to contribute to gross domestic product by having the capital to invest in the economy. The person who is bankrupt from having his or her savings sunk into health expenses can be a burden to a country's economy. This scenario affects fragile economies as much as affluent ones. When a person falls ill in conditions where no insurance is available and that person loses income while accumulating medical costs, the broader socioeconomic consequences can be dire. Two billion people need quality health care right away, and yet there is a labour deficit of 4.3 million health-care workers to service that market (WHO, 2006). Despite the obvious demand to increase service capacity, addressing global health-care inequity remains a tough sell. Too often, the suffering that comes as a result of deep poverty is positioned as bad luck and not a direct consequence of particular policies. Poor health from grinding poverty lands on a different moral grounding than more overt threats. War, terrorism, and nuclear proliferation are seen as urgent risks to global society, and yet childbirth is a far greater risk to millions of women around the world than are any of these factors (Indrayan, 2008; York, 2010). Is there a difference between the suffering that occurs through violence and that from a lack of health-care resources? Some may say that the structural violence (Farmer, 2005) that comes from the broad conditions of endemic poverty rather than from bombs and bullets is too messy for the public imagination to consider addressing.

Are governments and global institutions so disorganized as to be unable to handle the complexity of improving health care? No, they are not. A military intervention into an overtly violent scenario often occurs under complex political circumstances: governments manage to organize the material and human resources to go to war into Afghanistan, Iraq, Somalia, Libya, and elsewhere. What is more, many governments are able to muster enormous political support for overseas conflicts. With the exception of the Iraq war, the twenty-first century has seen widespread public support for military action in places such as Afghanistan and Libya. The real crisis for addressing global health equity is to challenge two dominant narratives addressing the needs of others.

- Going to war can fulfill one's own national best interests, especially its economic interests.
- Providing health care and aid to others is a burden on one's own national interests, as it will stymie economic growth.

As Cuba's medical internationalism makes clear, these realist narratives deserve to be challenged and dismissed.

The choice to see global health inequity as an issue of little concern stems from a belief that health care is a strenuous social burden that does not require as urgent attention as, perhaps, an overtly violent scenario would, and a tacit assumption that national and global institutions have little relation to, or impact in, health-care services abroad.

On top of this, nationalist discourses tend to value health care as a national issue rather than a universal human right. Nationalist culture often encourages citizens to join together as part of a common history and embrace a shared heritage even though not every citizen can get to know each other on a personal level. The need to help a fellow citizen is a normative process; realist narratives, however, understand the action of helping an international neighbour in health and well-being as exceptional. International assistance is widely understood as something that is above and beyond the call of duty. Even the term "aid" implies something temporary and out of the norm. The act of helping others is widely positioned as a product of generosity rather than a normative commitment to human rights. Anderson (2006), Hobsbawm (1990), and others discuss how nationalist logic is able to construct clear boundaries of responsibility where one can be normatively compassionate to a fellow citizen but partially indifferent to a foreign national. Combined with writings on neocolonialism, institutionalized racism, Eurocentrism, and Orientalism as explained by Said (1979), the power of nationalist rhetoric to distance the real needs of others from the perceived needs of fellow citizens is clearly seen. The Orientalism argument, which understands the construction of the orient as an antithesis to Occidentalism, influences perceptions about the place of health care in the global South. This is to say, the platform of public health in the global North is based on solid foundations of science and modernity, which are supposedly lacking in the global South, and the notion of care in societies that have not equally participated in the processes of modernity is unrealistic. Notably, Cuba's medical internationalism is strongly grounded in nationalist rhetoric that plays heavily on the idea of international solidarity throughout the global South. The story of the formation of ELAM claims that it began within "the tradition of solidarity of Cuban people to others in the world" (Escuela latinoamericana de medicina, n.d.). Moreover, the school's stated goal is to teach medical science with an ethics of humanitarianism and solidarity. So how does its story work to include international assistance as a morally justified action that fulfills national goals?

Three Moral Reasons to Change the Discourse: Cuba's Contribution

Cuba's commitment to medical internationalism provides three moral reasons as to why the pursuit of global health equity can be within a nation's own best interest. First, international financial institutions do not always act in a nation's best interests, but they have enormous impacts within the fabric of a national society, especially when it comes to the management of health-care spending. Austerity plans—often the prescription for economic betterment—usually involve privatization, and, consequently, the limiting of access to services (Peet & Hartwick, 2009). As international financial institutions discourage, or prohibit, nations in the global South from spending more on public health, the solution to access is supposed to come from increased philanthropy from the North. Donors often pursue a narrow approach to aid. The focus is on specific, manageable, and highly popular diseases or health issues in select places, rather than working to build broader primary care systems (People's Health Movement, Medact, & Global Equity Gauge Alliance, 2005). Often what happens is that donor money can work to constrict a health system's strengths to only a few key diseases (Atun, Pothapregada, Kwansah, Degboste, & Lazarus, 2011). A hospital in Malawi may enjoy the placement of a surgery centre established by international aid, but there may be no penicillin or painkillers in the maternity ward. A hospital may do well to provide an HIV drug regimen, but it may fall short of providing care for the most basic infections and illnesses. I have seen this first hand in Uganda and Burundi where hospitals are designed so that the morgue is as close as possible to the maternity ward, where patients most often die. Without a direct focus on primary care, as in the Cuban model, accessibility and equity challenges will always be encountered.

The second moral reason for action is to influence neighbours through solidarity and cooperation. Cuba's Ministry of Foreign Affairs have an innovative yet simple approach to international relations: invest in the well-being of other systems and it will benefit your own interests (Kirk & Erisman, 2009). The migration of health workers between countries in the global South and from the global South to the global North creates devastating impacts on the source country's health-care system. Instead of taking health-care workers from other countries in the Caribbean, Cuba reverses the trend and trains workers for the areas that are losing personnel. Canada, the United States, and Australia all rely on international medical graduates (IMGs) for 25 to 27 percent of their health-care workforces (Bourgeault et al., 2010). As long as working conditions in foreign health-care sectors remain difficult, and as long as health professionals in those countries cannot find opportunities to work in sustainable and rewarding conditions within their country, they will continue to find migration opportunities in wealthy nations. Even in South America, there is a push for Ecuadorian medical graduates to seek opportunities in Chile, just as in South Africa, a nation ravaged by the flight of its doctors to wealthy countries, receives health-care workers from other African nations (Migration resources, n.d.; Pena, Ramirez, Becerra, Carabantes, & Arteaga, 2010). As long as there is minimal investment in sustainable public health-care systems in the global South, health professionals will continue to seek options elsewhere, and as long as they do, wealthy countries will not invest in medical training spaces within their own borders, as it is cheaper and easier to recruit international graduates.

The third moral reason to pursue global health equity is to realize a new era of foreign policy. Nationalist motivations to avoid international solidarity and to "other" one's neighbour are based on a tired, nineteenth-century assumption that the global international order needs to be competitive rather than cooperative (Scott, 2004). Many governments in the North have expressed interest in pursuing soft power strategies that would involve cooperation, collaboration, and capacity building. But such strategies have to go beyond the symbolic. They need to work on the ground. Soft power, as discussed by Nye (2004), is truly effective only when the policies practised make actual impacts to improve people's lives. The symbolic capital of soft power will wane quickly if marginalized communities are not experiencing transformative development. Cuba's extensive medical internationalism, while a symbol of soft power, has made real life changes for millions who have received care and been awarded opportunities to further their professional education.

Cuba's Compelling Example: Discontent for Global Health Inequity

To challenge the status quo of global health inequity and national institutions that fall short of meeting the needs of the poor, it is important to focus on working alternatives that lead to health equity. Canada's *National Collaborating Centre for Determinants of Health* (http://www.healthequityclicks.ca) argues as much. Here is where Cuba's experience, from the success of its revolution in 1959 to its place as a global health power, offers a compelling lesson in how to position health equity as a soft power strategy. There are three key lessons to draw from Cuban medical internationalism to challenge moral acquiescence:

- Cuba views the struggle against underdevelopment and health-care inequity as worthy of concern.
- Cuba sees the provision of health care and the establishment of medical cooperation as imperative to its own national interests.
- Cuba's approach to medical internationalism aims to establish cooperative, not competitive, relationships of solidarity with other countries struggling to overcome underdevelopment.

Through the exchange and collaboration of medical care and material resources, both Cuba and its partners make gains.

Even Michael Leavitt, the former Secretary for Health and Human Services under the George W. Bush administration acknowledged the importance of a soft power approach:

> our nation supports a lot of different things. We develop water, we do economic development, we do education all over the world, we do joint research, we train soldiers, we provide weapons, and we even give money. But there is nothing more powerful that we do than to administer to the health of people who are in need. Why? Because, the language of health is really heard in the heart ... health diplomacy is the highest octane fuel that a soft power machine has. (Leavitt, 2008)

However, there is a crucial factor to medical internationalism that stands apart from the classic medical tokenism that many developed countries have practised in the past.[5] Cuban medical internationalism works to provide effective and accessible comprehensive primary care that has transformative benefits for the poor. In 2008, Canadian Prime Minister Stephen Harper was praised for a donation of medical supplies to an urban Haitian clinic ("Harper arrives," 2010). The one-time donation represents a token gesture towards health provision in Haiti that would have little long-term benefit to the clinic. At the same time the prime minister was in Haiti, Cuba had over six hundred health-care workers providing services to 80 percent of that country in rural areas (Burnett, 2010). After the devastating earthquake in 2010, Cuba sent in over two thousand health-care workers to cope with the aftermath and to help with the construction of a comprehensive medical system. While Canada sent some medical personnel and supplies, the majority of aid went to operations involving food imports, debt relief, police training, technical assistance, and prison construction (Aid Facts on Haiti, 2011). This clearly shows that despite Canada's wealth and its own national commitment to universal public health outreach to poor, albeit earthquake ravaged, countries involves a limited commitment to public health.[6]

Primary care comes first in the Cuban approach. Even with the program Operación (or Misión) Milagro (Operation Miracle), which has provided free ophthalmological surgeries to over 2 million people, primary care is an included part of the program. Such programs address the most basic needs of communities because they are often the most urgent needs for the global poor. Further, the programs adhere to the needs of patients and not the capacity of donors. They are rooted in Alma-Ata—health care for all—rather than the mission statements of philanthropic charities or the specified mandates of civil society organizations. By focusing on primary care first, Cuban health workers address a broad range of health concerns.

Cuban doctors, trained to work in remote and difficult areas, deal with the most basic health problems that arise, from non-potable water, mosquito bites, poor nutrition, and a lack of sanitation. Community-based, comprehensive primary care is tremendously important for addressing such basic health indicators, and it is vital in building broader health-care networks. The world's toughest health challenges, including HIV/AIDS and multi-drug-resistant tuberculosis, cannot be effectively managed, let alone prevented, without a comprehensive primary care framework in place.

The Commitment to Alma-Ata

In an April 19, 2009, press conference at the Summit of the Americas in Port of Spain, US President Barack Obama said that there was a common theme among the leaders: "One thing that I thought was interesting ... hearing from these leaders who, when they spoke about Cuba, talked very specifically about the thousands of Cuban doctors that are dispersed all throughout the region, and upon which many of these countries heavily depend" (Stephens, 2012). Considering that members of the preceding administration, under George W. Bush, also realized the value of soft power, the political motivations for Cuba sending health-care workers around the world can be well understood. What seems odd to many in the global North is that there is not always a clear economic determinant. But with Cuba, the economic determinants tend to unfold as the cooperation evolves. In some cases, it might be a windfall of oil, in others only beans. In some cases, Cuba receives next to nothing at all.

The motivations for medical internationalism have made for tremendously good political support from other nations in the global South even though the United States continues to maintain its embargo. The political reasons are obvious, but the humanitarian reasons for doing so may be harder to grasp simply because they go against popular health economics that assume that a physician's interest is in seeking lucrative gains. As Rodwin (1995) points out, health systems assume that most physicians seek wealth, which presents a conflict between the physician being a pursuer of profit and being a healer of the sick. The health profession balances this moral conundrum through fee-for-service practice and third-party insurance companies, which allows the patient access but ensures lucrative gains for the physician. Rodwin (1995) suggests that this does not excuse financial conflicts of interest, and the medical profession tends to centre its ethical dilemmas on simple doctor–patient interactions rather than the governing economic structures of the relationship.

Globally, the centres where health care is profitable are rarely the same places where health care is needed the most. In Malawi, a country where 65 percent of the population lives in desperate poverty and where there is only one physician for every 49,000 people, former president Bingu wa Mutharika said that people should take more individual responsibility for their health, and use market advantages to find care. In Honduras, the post-2009 coup by Roberto Micheletti Baín resulted in the army closing down public health centres, seeing them as incongruous to efficiency and market norms (Anderson, 2009). In Venezuela, private sector doctors swarmed the streets in protest against nineteen thousand Cuban health-care workers offering free care in parts of the country where no Venezuelan doctor had ever worked before ("Venezuelan doctors," 1999). Some enthusiasts, consumed by nationalist pride and free-market passion, went as far as to lob tear gas and concussion grenades at the Cuban embassy in Caracas in protest of the presence of medical workers.

But is the craft of medicine ultimately a business (Rodwin, 1995)? Rising health-care costs, the selective nature of private insurance companies, and the continual critique against state-run medicine in the United States and around the world have seen many countries abandon the key principles of the Alma-Ata declaration, which proclaimed that

- Health is a fundamental human right and the attainment of the highest possible level of health is a most important worldwide social goal whose realization requires the action of many other social and economic sectors in addition to the health sector.
- The existing gross inequality in the health status of people, particularly between developed and developing countries as well as within countries, is politically, socially, and economically unacceptable and is, therefore, of common concern to all countries.
- The promotion and protection of the health of people is essential to sustained economic and social development and contributes to a better quality of life and to world peace.
- A main social target of governments, international organizations, and the whole world community in the coming decades should be the attainment by the year 2000 by all peoples of the world a level of health that will permit them to lead socially and economically productive lives. Primary health care is the key to attaining this target.
- Primary health care is essential health care based on practical, scientifically sound, and socially acceptable methods and technology made universally accessible to individuals and families through their full participation and at a cost that the community and country can afford to maintain at every stage of development.
- Primary health care addresses the main health issues in a community, providing preventive, curative, and rehabilitative services accordingly; it should be sustained by integrated, functional, and mutually supportive referral systems leading to the progressive improvement of comprehensive health care for all; it relies at local and referral levels on health workers, including physicians, nurses, midwives, auxiliaries, and community workers, as well as traditional practitioners as needed, suitably trained socially and technically to work as a health-care team and to respond to the expressed health needs of the community (*Declaration of Alma-Ata*, 1978).

Rich and poor countries alike have moved away from these goals, assuming that preventative primary care is less desired than reactive specialized procedures and believing in the myth that health comes from the choice of the individual consumer. Against the global abandonment of Alma-Ata, Cuba continues to hold on to the declaration that health is a human right.

Making Health and Health Care a Human Right

For the global North, accessibility to universal health-care services in the global South is thought of as an outcome benefit from other development projects aimed at improving economic growth. In liberal societies, the state has gotten a bad reputation for being inefficient and at times less qualified in providing essential services than the free market supposedly can. In the 1980s and 1990s, neoliberal policies fuelled by structural adjustment plans from the World Bank and the IMF embraced liberal values and the market distribution of services approach to a more extreme level than liberal societies in the North had ever experienced (Harvey, 2005). The doctrine states that a market-based health-care system would be able to distribute services in an efficient manner. This resulted in the construction of a narrative that government-sponsored care is inefficient and harmful, and that private insurers and providers really have the individual's best interests at heart. The reality was that market-based health-care systems allowed for private owners to organize the services towards the consumer tendencies of those able to pay instead of the ones who could not. In health care, as with other social goods, neoliberalism unfolded as a well-organized political project of redistributing maximum amounts of wealth and power to the elite while increasing inequity between members of society (Harvey, 2005). The rich got richer and poor got poorer, and the rich received better access to health care while the poor went without. And all the while, the poor were told that the private sector could better handle their needs than a well-funded public sector.

Country by country, and case by case, the story of for-profit doctors practising in urban areas to cater to the needs of rich while vulnerable communities are left without any reliable or affordable services is all too common (Evans, Whitehead, Diderichsen, Bhuiya, & Wirth, 2001). The neoliberal creed—that is, the political reorganization of a nation's social spending so that private capital is engaged while less public funding is spent on necessary services—was advertised under banners of individualism, freedom, and assurance that the market would offer universal social prosperity for all. Such market-based liberal values became entrenched in the behaviour of nations around the world, and the nations managed their social safety nets accordingly. Malawi's former president Bingu wa Mutharika stated on billboards throughout the country that health was the responsibility of the individual and not anyone else's burden.

Health is viewed as something earned, not doled out. In Canada, citizenship gives you that privilege: under the Canada Health Act, every citizen is entitled to health-care services without charge. Canadians do a fairly good job at looking out for one another before foreigners, although First Nations and recent immigrants tend to fare poorly. But Canada does not extend that right to health care beyond its own borders. Why is it that citizenship to a country can permit or deny access to a human right?

In many other countries there is far less of a national guarantee to health care. Almost all Latin American countries declare health a right in their national constitutions, but in practice health care is the responsibility of the individual.

For the wealthy, there is no limit on the innovative options of meeting your health needs. One afternoon in 2006 on the music-video channel in Ecuador, I noticed a banner scrolling along the bottom of the TV pleading for type A+ blood donations for Sra. Rodriguéz: "If you have type A+ blood, contact her cell phone right away to arrange a transfusion." In between advertisements for Pepsi and Dentyne gum, the elite have resorted to paying for ads for blood donations. However, this is hardly a public request when one considers how many people in Ecuador can spend their days watching MTV, or can afford satellite TV, or can afford a TV at all.

The poorest of the poor live and work in unhealthy conditions that bungle health and break down hope. Poor housing, poor nutrition, non-potable water, and faulty sanitation all lead to a plethora of health consequences. For the global poor who have the chance to work only in unsafe working conditions, be it picking out recyclables in dumps in Brazil, breaking down ships in Bangladesh, or selling gum in traffic anywhere, health problems—from pollutants to accidents—abound.

In the United States, the responsibility for good health comes down to the individual, who must choose the right insurance provider, choose an affordable service option, and ensure that there is money to cover high deductibles. In the United States, it is not necessarily the poorest part of society that has traditionally gone without health care but, rather, the middle class and low-middle class who do not qualify for state-supported assistance and who must shoulder the costs on their own. In an affluent country that spends more on health care than any other nation, and where 47 million people (15 percent) have no health insurance as of 2011, and where 4,400 people die unnecessarily every month, publicly funded health care is seen as a weighty burden that is reluctantly handed out (Gever, 2011).

Society speaks of health as a right but health care as a privilege because the tenets of liberalism conceptualize socialized, or public, health care as a burden. With liberalism valuing the individual good over the societal good, there is little compassion for the needs of others who are deemed to have equal opportunity to succeed as any other citizen of the nation state. That field may include fellow citizens, regardless of their economic or social backgrounds, and the view can be extended to other nation states regardless of their economic or social backgrounds. In such a political culture, the following question might come from someone who is living in relative comfort and feels that they owe society little for their good fortunes: "I've done well to keep healthy and I've never smoked, so why should I pay for your cancer treatments or your coronary bypass?"

Liberal society considers all persons equal under the governance of the nation state. It demands that individuals be responsible for their own life, liberty, and security, of which health is a part. The health-care needs of citizens of other nations are just that: the concern of other nations. The argument is "We've got enough problems here, without worrying about problems somewhere else" (Pogge, 2008). However, for authoritarian countries, such as Zimbabwe, that fail to meet the needs of their population, the case for intervention becomes compelling because those individuals do not have basic equity. Still, the number of times when this prompts outside action for broad public health interventions remains limited.

This understanding of societal interactions does not account for the power and dependency relationships that give clear advantages to some members of global society while stripping others of those privileges. In a liberal society, citizens may be tasked with the pursuit of their own health, but the wealthy will always enjoy a wider range of options to achieve it over those of the poor, from advertisements on MTV to flying overseas to take advantage of the latest medical tourism package.

In cases where visible inequity and discrimination occur, the response from liberal society is to act with philanthropic charity and extraordinary interventions, but giving aid is an act that goes beyond the normative actions of society. It takes effort, time, and goodwill. Those who give their time to the poor are not considered to be just helping their fellow being. Global society illuminates them as exceptional figures who are going well out of their way to bring justice to unjust situations. Society idolizes people who give their careers to humanitarian interventions. Physicians who journey around the world and the wealthy elites who donate millions to notable causes are widely perceived as being exceptional, but only because their commitment stands out against a general culture of acquiescence.

Not everyone can act exceptionally, but thanks to those who do, it is assumed that any visible discriminations and acts of injustice will be addressed by the good efforts of these volunteers. From this perspective, the message is that individuals need not worry about changing the behaviours of global institutions that lead to discriminations in the first place. The humanitarians will handle it. The Red Cross will be there, and if not them, Doctors Without Borders (MSF), and if not them, UNICEF, and if not them, someone else.

When Others Have Tried to Make Health Care a Human Right

The true challenge is to position global health interventions as a normative reflection of a society's commitment to universal health at home. Some political leaders have considered health care as something other than a burden that can be left to sporadic humanitarian interventions. Canadian politician Tommy Douglas, who served as the province of Saskatchewan's premier and later a federal member of parliament in the mid-twentieth century, thought the concept of universal public care was not a burden at all but a means for society to prosper (Stewart, 2004). Douglas was a key architect in bringing universal single-payer health insurance to Saskatchewan and then to all of Canada. He believed that no one should be financially ruined as a result of medical costs and that no one should be denied the opportunity to access health-care services because of too much distance or too little money. In 1947, his government established a publicly funded hospital insurance plan that covered the costs of any hospital visits.

In 1962, at the very same time that Cuba passed laws requiring doctors to bill the state for services rather than patients, Canada began to pursue a similar law. In 1961, the Canadian government partnered with the provinces to cover hospital insurance costs across the country. Although Douglas had moved on to federal politics by this time, the province of Saskatchewan, with his support from Ottawa, implemented an innovative insurance plan to see allotted federal dollars used to cover the costs of physician care in addition to hospitalization. The plan demanded that doctors bill the government for most health-care services. Douglas endorsed the plan as he thought that it would encourage citizens to access primary care services routinely and not only in states of emergency that required hospitalization. With no cost burden to individuals, the health-care system would move towards an arrangement that kept people healthy, as he put it, and not just "patch them up" when they got ill (Douglas, 1982).

Other provinces had their own ideas of health insurance. Alberta and British Columbia demanded a premium to be paid by each citizen regardless of income or employment, and Ontario offered only a voluntary enrolment into public insurance (Marchildon, 2005). There was fierce resistance to the Saskatchewan model. The province's physicians went on strike to protest government control of the plan. Initially, they positioned their labour action as a protest of the inability to collectively bargain with the province, but the veneer gave way, and many residents of Saskatchewan sided with the government. Other provinces exercised caution in adopting the Saskatchewan model for fear of similar physician responses and for worry of the cost involved in covering such a wide range of medical services (Stevenson, Williams, & Vayda, 1988; Warren & Carlisle, 2004). Still, the federal government under the Pearson Liberals moved towards passing the Medical Care Act that would see the federal government share costs with the provinces to ensure hospitalization and physician visits for all, although it would be up to the provinces to determine how the insurance would be granted to each resident. Nationally, ophthalmologists and dentists wanted no part of it, and the proposal for a pharmacare plan was met with fierce resistance (Houston, 2002).

The Canadian Medical Association decried the Medical Care Act as well, but popular opinion thought otherwise (Houston, 2002). The Canadian public backed the Saskatchewan politicians and demanded that citizens not be sent into bankruptcy over medical costs. In 1967, universal insurance for hospitalization and doctors' visits was passed in the House of Commons by a vote of 177 to 2. In 1984, it was reworked under the Trudeau Liberals as the Canada Health Act, and was meant to give greater agency to the provinces as to how services were managed while ensuring that the tenets of universal care remained intact. Today, poll after poll shows that Canadians agree that universal public health care is one of the nation's greatest assets. Global business agrees, too: Toyota, Honda, Ford, and other automobile manufacturers benefit in Canada in order to avoid paying employees private health-care benefits, as they would have to in the United States (Joint letter on publicly funded health care, n.d.).

While Douglas believed that medicare would ensure that citizens would engage with their system and with their primary care practitioners to prevent the onset of severe disease, the health-care system failed to adopt practices of health promotion and disease prevention in day-to-day practice. Physicians continued to practise in reactive rather than preventative manners, and many Canadians continued to seek treatment in costly hospital settings. As an insurance system, the Medical Care Act and the Canada Health Act did well to prevent financial ruin for patients, but it did not embrace the management necessary to shift health care towards a system of disease prevention and health promotion.

Because the insurance acts allowed physicians to continue billing for services rather than receive a fixed salary, many began over billing and/or ordering costly exams that may not have been necessary to a patient's needs, according to the Auditor General in Ontario. In one case, a doctor billed the public system for prenatal services on a patient who had a hysterectomy (Tomlinson, 2008). In recent decades, Canada's health-care costs have skyrocketed. It is largely due to the operation costs of hospitals and the rising costs of pharmaceuticals, but generous physician billing is also part of the picture. There are countless anecdotes of gynecologists requesting unnecessary pap smears for a few extra dollars, or specialists requesting bone density tests on patients who would never need them, or private travel clinics double-billing the public system and the patients. In 2005, family doctors and generalists billed the provincial governments Cdn $4.7 billion in services (Physician Database, 2009). Approximately Cdn $2 billion came from "other services" that are not checkups, consultations, or services along these lines. The leadership of the Canadian Medical Association under former Presidents Brian Day and Robert Oullet have campaigned tirelessly for a greater introduction of for-profit services so that they could take their billing expectations even higher under the pretence that it would reduce public costs and create better efficiency for the health-care system.[7]

Many provincial and federal politicians, citizens, and physicians continue to put pressure on Canada's universal, single-payer health insurance. They view public insurance as costly, inefficient, bulky, and unable to meet consumer demands for efficiency and practitioner demands for higher profit. Advocates for increased private care must feel that they are removed from the consequences of economic ruin that could result from health-care costs. It is as if to assume that poverty, illness, and misfortune are all accidents that are not tied to the social fabric of society.

Douglas's vision of health care was that of a benefit not a burden to society. It mirrored the epistemology of health care that Cuba employs today. The system was a means for citizens to be free of the financial and health burdens that kept them from flourishing, which are the very burdens that are so prevalent in the global South today. Keeping people healthy was the goal because a system that just patches people up would be a burden. While Canada's system managed to stave off bankruptcies brought on by personal health-care costs, the Medical Insurance Act, which sought to ensure that Canadians were healthy, was never fully realized.

The Canadian experience shows that political energy was mobilized and then challenged to make health care a right. Canada's journey towards universal single-payer health care offers two important points about framing health care as a social benefit rather than as a burden. First, the attempt to frame health care as a social good met with ferocious opposition by physicians to the point where they organized labour disruptions to deny patients care. The same opposition to public health occurs around the world today, and any attempt to expand public health care will be met with equally vicious resistance. Second, when the legislation did pass, it brought with it a political discourse that clearly valued public health care as a benefit, rather than a burden, to society. If Cuba's model of providing affordable primary care on an international scale were to be repeated or scaled up, enormous political resistance should be expected at the start but then a new discourse would emerge that would see the benefit of affordable quality care.

Cuban Medical Internationalism: Health Care as a Global Human Right

About the same time that Tommy Douglas was bringing health insurance to Saskatchewan, and a short while before Canada enacted it at the federal level, Dr. Ernesto "Che" Guevara, an Argentinean doctor turned revolutionary guerrilla and icon of the Cuban revolution, figured it best to see that individuals, regardless of their economic status, have the right to health care. He also figured, while fighting as a leader in the Cuban revolution, that the health of individuals should come from the whole social collectively. He was not convinced that poverty, illness, illiteracy, and other damnations were just accidents. He believed that such misfortunes were the fault of an inequitable society, which is why he dedicated his life to make it otherwise (Guevara, 1997).

In Cuba in 1961, just months before the Saskatchewan doctors went on strike, the government enacted a single-payer system for health-care services. As in the Saskatchewan proposal, Cuban doctors were told that they could no longer bill patients for services and that they had to bill the government. In response to this, half of Cuba's 6,912 physicians and almost all of the some 260 medical professors at the University of Havana left the country between 1961 and 1965. Many went to Miami (*Gapminder*, n.d.; Kirk & Erisman, 2009). Just as the fight for universal health care was met with resistance in Canada, so too was it met with resistance in Cuba.

It is troubling to think that the ethical foundations of medicine are to relieve suffering, disease, and to promote quality of life, and yet when practitioners are offered the chance to participate in a system that expands universal coverage in promotion of these ethics, there is resistance, as seen in Saskatchewan or Cuba in the 1960s. Plato wrote, "Is it not also true that no physician, in so far as he is a physician, considers or enjoins what is for the physician's interest, but that all seek the good of their patients? For we have agreed that a physician strictly so-called, is a healer of the sick, and not a maker of money, have we not?" (Plato, 1987, pp. 342b–43a).

In Saskatchewan and in Cuba, the government did not tell doctors that they would take a pay cut. They did not even suggest for doctors to go on salary, just that they could no longer bill patients directly.[8] Indeed, ethical tensions arise when physicians are positioned as pursuers of profit on lucrative fee-for-service schedules.

Despite the mass exodus of health-care workers, Cuba planned accessibility strategies for its entire population. The plan involved training the remaining physicians as medical instructors and establishing medical schools across the entire country. Every province built a medical school, and students would spend just as much time training in clinics as they would in the lecture hall. In the early stages of the revolution, the majority of doctors were trained specifically for primary care at the community level. The emphasis in the 1960s was to get access to health care resources established and to address the high levels of vector-borne diseases associated with poverty. In 1961, Cuba had a doctor-to-patient ratio of one physician for every 1,100 people. Using this approach of managed accessibility though progressive medical education strategies, Cuba's doctor-to-patient ratio did not go higher than one physician for every 1,200 people, and by 1976, there was one physician for every 886 people across all provinces. Cuba's 1976 ratio of doctors to patients, despite the economic and infrastructural challenges, was equal to that of Japan and the United Kingdom, and above all Soviet bloc nations (*Gapminder*, n.d.).

In the 1990s, after the collapse of the Soviet Union, when Cuba's GDP declined by 35 percent and when it lost 87 percent of its exports, the Ministry of Public Health (MINSAP) did not close a single hospital or medical school (Huish & Kirk, 2007). It created more space to train more health-care workers. Economists said that by all rights the economic collapse should have wiped Cuba off the map (Cole, 1998). But the country defied all economic logic by investing heavily in human capital and health care resources. In contrast, during a mild recession in the 1990s in Canada, the province of Alberta demolished hospitals and centralized public services. By 2010, thanks in large part to an oil boom, the Alberta government has scaled up public spending for health services. The question then is if governments only expand capacity to health services in eras of prosperity, how did Cuba manage to expand its service provision in an era of economic crisis?

There are two quick explanations. First, Cuba did not and does not experience the same level of structural costs, from physical plant to human resources that Canadian provinces do. According to the Canadian Institute for Health Information, the average annual amounts that Canadian family doctors billed the public systems are Cdn \$237,492 (Physician Database, 2009). Cuban doctors are paid about Cdn \$432 per year on average. Simply speaking, the cost of one Canadian physician is equivalent to 549 Cuban physicians. Obviously, this is a huge savings in human resources for health, and it raises difficult ethical questions for Cuba to justify paltry salaries when highly trained doctors in the global North make much more income. The second reason is that Cuba's centralized economy absorbs the cost of physical plant operations, supplies, and technology. In the Canadian system, these services are handled on the basis of costly contracts, most through third parties. In sum, the Canadian model is designed to meet the market expectations of physicians, hospitals, and medical suppliers. The result is that costs become very difficult to contain in such a system. Cuba's centralized economy absorbs these costs.

Cuba's quest for domestic and global health equity is grounded in a belief— one that many nations hold—that health is a human right. But unlike many nations, Cuba disagrees with the positions that the market is an appropriate system to govern an individual's means to that right. And Cuba disagrees with the position that the state has a responsibility only to alleviate gross social calamities through insurance programs. Instead, Cuba has ensured that its citizens and the citizens of other nations have a better means to achieve health as a human right.

In Cuba health care is granted from the state; it is not a privilege that can be retracted, nor is it a product of chance that is tied to good economic fortune. Despite economic collapse, political hostility with the most powerful nation in the world, and an interminable embargo, the right to health has never waned for three reasons:

- The Cuban government believes that for individuals and society to flourish, advancements in accessibility to health care should be combined with advancements in pure medical science.
- Cuba maintains a moral commitment to ensuring that knowledge and technology overcome most health challenges without enduring crippling expenditure to individuals or economies.
- Cuba directs attention to the urgent health-care needs of the poor; it does not leave citizen's health-care needs to the chance of trickle-down economics. The government sees this as the best way to form cooperative international relationships aimed at advancing the equity and prosperity of the human condition.

These fundamental beliefs in Cuban society are practised by the sixty-six thousand Cuban doctors serving at home and in sixty-six other countries, the over twenty-four thousand international medical students who have come to ELAM to study free of charge, and the millions of people around the world who have received Cuban health care, and this is testimony that another health-care paradigm exists.

Cuba chooses to overlook traditional Market theory to regulate health-care provision. The maintenance of a health-care system guarantees a universal standard of equity that states that despite economic and material inequality in Cuban society no one will fall victim to ill health or avoidable mortality. And Cuba negotiates these values against a backdrop of increasing financial hardship. Is it possible to reproduce the Cuban case in each and every country? It is possible to revisit these values in order to find ways of addressing global health inequity. And while it may be futile to try to find ways to repeat the Cuban revolution, it is important to understand how universal accessibility to health-care services and investment in the health-care needs of others are means that can advance broader comprehensive development.

The Case for Health Care as a Human Right

It might seem that global society has all but given up on the idea that public health systems can be a means to individual and societal empowerment. By continuing to see public health care as a social burden, neo-liberal governments continue to search for reactive solutions to service inequity within costly systems that do little for quality health promotion and disease prevention. In such systems, be it fully market driven or with a social security net, serving the vulnerable on a national or on a global scale requires health-care workers to be exceptional and go beyond the norms of existing structural deficiencies. As willing as the health-care workers who dedicate their time to the indigent are, the broad goal for health care in the twenty-first century should be to make the job of the exceptional physician go away. There should be enough health workers providing care through their normative routines. The goal for global health equity should be an assurance that the needs of the vulnerable are fulfilled through the normative day-to-day operations of health-care systems.

In Cuba's pursuit of health as a human right, there have been setbacks. Sceptics tend to focus on them, as do those who are politically charged to find faults with Cuban society and its political processes. Certainly, some Cuban doctors have sought ways out of domestic and international service commitments. Some have become bartenders in resort hotels. There are Cuban doctors working in the lucrative private health-care sector in South Africa because they tired of the cooperation campaigns. Based on first-person interviews at ELAM, it was noted that there are international medical students who dropped out of Cuba's training programs because it was too tough.

These stories are the minority, and yet global media and popular narratives have focused on them as if these stories were all the stories. In fact, these stories are of only 3 percent of Cuban doctors. The story of flight from Cuba is well chronicled in the international media and in publications arguing that such factors are undermining the revolution, but this book provides an understanding of the 97 percent of Cuban health-care workers who undeniably face challenges but who indisputably believe in the right to health care.

Stories of rough working conditions and venturing out to work in difficult conditions such as those found in the La Joya de los Sachas clinic make it is easy to understand why 3 percent abandon the programs (World Bank, 2012). It is tough, the pay is poor, and you watch fellow human beings perish because of the vices of preventable poverty. It is more difficult to say why 97 percent stay and why they want to make places like La Joya de los Sachas better. The stories that come from Cuban medical internationalism may make no immediate economic sense, but such stories of humanism and compassion demonstrate that it is possible to make the exceptional normal. Despite the overwhelming perils of poverty and inequality, with social and political support and a little imagination, people can behave magnificently to one another.

CHAPTER 2

SOWING THE SEEDS OF HEALTH AS A RIGHT: THE ORIGINS OF HEALTH CARE IN CUBA

There are so many stories of structural and economic hardships coming out of Cuba, from overcrowded buses to faulty water systems (Ritter, 2010). In rural areas, there are outspoken complaints about the distribution of certain resources and sporadic transportation. There are critiques against the freedom of expression of political opposition movements and the nature of political representation ("Cuban ladies," 2010). Other critiques focus on how many university-trained graduates wind up with mid-level jobs in government ministries. There are plenty of points of critique regarding the Cuban economy and its political institutions just as there are plenty of points to critique any political system.

In Canada, for example, there is no shortage of sociopolitical critiques to be made on the increase in child poverty, the marginalization of First Nations peoples, urban homelessness, and democratic transparency (Russell & Sossin, 2009). Public transit in Toronto is in crisis, as are the waterworks in Montreal. Access to health-care resources in northern Canada are often lacking, and transit from the Arctic to major urban centres is enormously expensive. How many university graduates in Canada find only low-paying jobs outside of their desired fields? Some observers even question whether to maintain our archaic political system that appoints, rather than elects, senators.

So if Cuba, despite its own social problems and political challenges, puts attention to global health, why is it that other nations do not? When considering the numerous social and economic problems faced by wealthy countries, liberal societies, or emerging economies in the global South, why is there not a solid commitment to health care as a right?

This chapter explains the internal organization of Cuba's health-care system against internal economic chaos. The focus is on the post-revolution period and the fall of the Soviet Union in 1991, which threw Cuba into the *Periodo Especial*. The message here is that in both economic periods Cuba faced enormous crises, but with political will and with social mobilization the country emerged from crisis by investing in their strongest natural resource: each other.

Two Common Prejudices against Learning from Cuba

Why would a resource-flush country take pointers from Cuba be it in global health or in any other matter? After all, Canada enjoys universal public health care and dedicates significant attention towards international aid and humanitarian interventions. While Canada makes generous contributions to global health causes, Canada's humanitarian efforts to deliver primary care to the global poor fall short of Cuba's medical internationalism, and even at home, Canadian medicare continues to struggle with rising costs and wait times for elective non-life-threatening treatments. Moreover, the geographies of the two countries are radically different and the economies cannot be easily compared; Canada is dependent upon the United States for 81 percent of its exports while Cuba lives under an embargo. There are also differences in democratic processes and principles between the two countries. These are all fair points when discussing economic geography, but when it comes to taking lessons from Cuban approaches to health care, the conversation rarely gets far because of two common prejudices:

- Cuba is a communist country.
- It is not within the thinking of a liberal market, multi-party democracy to invest in the long-term capacity as Cuba did.

The first bias is easily overcome through an understanding that Cuba is a complex society where people do exercise personal agency on a daily basis. Roman (2003) and Saney (2004) have written extensively on this. Simply put no one-man, green suit or not, is an island. The maintenance and expansion of Cuba's health-care system was managed centrally, but it relied on popular participation at the local level across the country (Feinsilver, 1993). There are stories of Cuban doctors finding their way to resorts and others taking to the United States for better salary (Millman, 2011). While some resort workers do carry medical degrees, today the majority of workers in the tourist trade are graduates from Cuba's hospitality and tourism training institutes.

Still, official US policy largely views Cuba as repressive and destructive to human capabilities. The US Department of State's Commission for Assistance to a Free Cuba notes that, "The physical, mental, and emotional health of the

Cuban people is directly linked to their level of empowerment. Healthy individuals are better able to make informed decisions about their own well-being and that of their community. This ability to be involved in the decision-making process leads, in and of itself, to a sense of empowerment" (Powell, 2004, p. 8). Empowerment does lead to better health. Although, in the State Department's focus on empowerment as having "free multi-party elections" (Powell, 2004, p. 8), the report overlooks the fact that many Cubans do enjoy physical, mental, and emotional health in their current system. The State Department overlooks any potential benefits that Cuba's health-care system produces. The report states that "the Castro dictatorship had been able to maintain its grip on the Cuban people by repressing the development of independent civil society and keeping the Cuban people on a desperate hunt for dollars and basic necessities" (Powell, 2004, p. 7). The report misses the fact that Cuba constructed a participatory community-based health-care system that relies on individuals' knowledge of their own well-being and their ability to be involved in personal and community health initiatives. This system, contrary to what the US State Department believes, has fostered one of the most equitable and healthy societies in the world.

Thanks to popular participation in the public health system, Cubans enjoy impressive health figures, such as having the best doctor-to-patient ratio in the world, one of the lowest infant mortality rates in the hemisphere, a life expectancy on par with the United States (seventy-seven years), and the lowest HIV incidence rate in the Americas (WHO, 2007). Moreover, unlike many countries in the Americas, Cuba does not suffer from drastic inequalities in the provision of care between the urban and the rural (Rojas Ochoal, 2004). The collective participation of Cubans in their health-care system gives it both strength and sustainability. Community-level public health campaigns are routinely organized to target specific diseases, such as dengue or HIV, or certain lifestyle choices, such as smoking or overeating, or local resource problems with potable water. Physicians and nurses routinely make house and workplace calls, monitor community-level health trends, and collect data for broader epidemiological analysis. Health-care workers have open and regular contact with their communities, and, of course, many members of that population are also health-care workers (Spiegel & Yassi, 2004).

Cuba's participatory framework succeeds exactly because citizens have the chance to engage with their system and to become actors within it. Is it possible for other health-care systems to enjoy such a widespread level of participation? The answer lies in how public health care manages illness or maintains the health of society. If health care is perceived as a social service rather than a human right, then the management of health-care services is often organized in a way to mitigate costs while providing care. If health care is approached as an integral right, then the discussion moves towards assuring the maintenance of health and well-being rather than simply repairing its faults.

The Inspiration

Many of the Cuban government's domestic and international projects are grounded not within Marxist doctrine but in a broader idealism of pan-American solidarity that is often symbolized through the teachings, legends, and iconography of José Martí. The nineteenth-century philosopher has held an important place in Cuban narrative since the early part of the twentieth century. He dedicated his life to the creation of an independent Cuba and to developing unity south of the Rio Grande in what he titled, *Nuestra América* (Martí, 1963, 1999). He is an important moral inspiration behind past government projects such as the campaign to eradicate illiteracy (Keeble, 2000), and now he plays a role as a philosophical guardian of medical internationalism. Martí iconography abounds in Cuba, and his identity commands a major place in Cuba's landscape (Mayor Lorán, 2007). While there is a statue or painting of him in every school, library, and hospital including ELAM and Operación Mílagro, it is important to go beyond the visualisation to identify connections of Martí's thought to Cuba's foreign policy. Martí's concepts of solidarity and humanism are rooted in the understanding that individuals should be able to control Nature, rather than be controlled by it (Martí, 1961). This means that conditions of poverty, neocolonialism, or other sorts of repression often hinder the development of the individual to their full potential. These values are all at the heart of Cuban solidarity movements.

Many of Cuba's foreign interventions are, in some way, rooted in Martí's thought, or, as Cubans say, *Martiano*. Two major themes are apparent in *Martiano*. First, is the emphasis on individual well-being and the respect for meeting an individual's needs in "Nature" (Martí, 1961).[1] Second, is the call for Latin American solidarity against imperialism (Martí, 1963). In order to truly build solidarity, as it was understood in the early days of the 1959 Cuban revolution, the most marginalized communities require control of Nature and resources (Castro, 2000; Saney, 2004). This is a later departure from Martí's earlier writing on society where he adhered to liberalism and argued for the mixing of races in Latin America through liberal reforms (Huish & Lovell, 2008). But the elder, more radical Martí thought individuals without basic needs, including health and education, remain displaced by Nature, and because of this displacement, they could not enjoy a meaningful role within society. Solidarity, as resistance to imperialism, would occur only if and when all members of a society had a sense of control over their needs through health, education, and, most importantly, access to resources.

Much literature overlooks the ideological affinity Cubans have for Martí and instead attribute most of Cuba's policies solely to former President Fidel Castro's individual will. Some had said that without Fidel Castro and his personal charisma, the Cuban paradox would collapse, but well after Fidel Castro left office, Cuba continues to march to its own drum with new and innovative economic reforms coming into play. The former president's image and character account for a great deal of nationalist sentiment, but even with Fidel Castro well out of the political leadership, Cuba has hardly disappeared. As Montaner and Ramonet (2007) argue, "Castro has not been on the job since July [2006] ... and yet nothing has happened. The regime has not collapsed ... the system is showing that it can operate normally under these conditions, and the legal institutions are withstanding the shock of Fidel's withdrawal" (p. 58). Still, some critics refuse to move past Castro idolatry (Golden, 2003; Ritter, 2006). Doing so limits a broader appreciation of Cuban nationalist culture and narrows the complexity of medical internationalism. Close to twenty years after the economic collapse of the Soviet Union, Cuba's former preferred trading partner, much scholarship remains focused on the inevitable transition into a post-Soviet-bloc economic framework (Font & Larson, 2006; Pérez López, 2006; Ritter, 2006; Roy, 2006). Many of these critics miss the point that Cuban policies and reforms are nationalist inspirations, deeply rooted in Martí's ideology and are not the result of "foreign ideas driven by foreign troops in Soviet-armoured vehicles" (Montaner & Ramonet, 2007, p. 58).

Since the earliest stages of the revolution, the Cuban medical system has been governed by the philosophy of providing equitable care and by the reality of coping with an anemic supply of material resources. These two forces shaped the Cuban health-care experience into a unique system that relies heavily upon human resources for primary care and does well by lessening its dependency on high-tech and costly procedures. Doing so places the control of health away from the forces of Nature, as Martí believed, and into the participatory dimensions of society. Franco, Kennelly, Cooper, and Ordúñez-Garcia (2007) see Cuba's "better than expected" (p. 239) health indicators for a developing nation to be the result of a well-defined strategy using public health principles to reduce major risk factors.

The origin of Cuban health care and physician education goes back over two hundred years. The University of Havana has one of the oldest medical schools in the hemisphere. Even in the nineteenth century, doctors in Havana practised medicine in the community with the weekly doctors venturing to poorer communities that were without regular care. According to Delgado Garcia, "They offered free medical care to all the sick and injured people among the indigent poor. They administered treatment in their patients' own houses, sending them to charity hospitals when necessary. They also acted as forensic doctors, inspected hygienic conditions in public places, and were responsible for food hygiene in the city's markets" (Delgado García, 1993 as translated in Rojas Ochoa, 2004). These altruistic physicians were the frontline of early primary care in Cuba: they offered their services for free and relied heavily on the missionary hospitals to treat their patients. Certainly, the methods, illnesses, and social conditions were of a unique time and place, but it is important to recognize that a heritage of primary care for the desperate and poor extends into the colonial history of the country, a time during which Martí lived.

By the 1950s, Cuba boasted the highest number of doctors per capita in the Americas, with about 1,078 patients per physician in 1958 (Oficina Nacional de Estadísticas, 2007). However, accessibility to physicians and health-care resources was desperate across the island. In 1959, 65 percent of physicians and 62 percent of hospital beds were located in Havana while most Cubans lived outside of the capital and half of Cuba's population lived in rural areas. The country had only one rural hospital with ten beds (The priority given to health, n.d.). MINSAP estimates that 36 percent of the population suffered parasites, 14 percent suffered from tuberculosis, and 30 percent carried malaria (The priority given to health, n.d.).

Before the 1959 revolution, there were small organizations of socialized health care. The transport unions of Havana had its own socialized clinic for workers. Other "mutual-aid" or insurance programs had been established by Spanish ethnic societies closer to the turn of the twentieth century to ensure medical coverage for paid members. In pre-revolutionary Cuba, according to Feinsilver (1993), the mutualist clinics provided service to approximately half of habaneros. Outside of the capital, their services were non-existent.

The revolution furthered these altruistic currents by building more capacity for more accessible medical services on a national scale. Instead of simply expanding services through the traditional rubric of health-care provision, the government adopted the progressive World Health Organization's (WHO) approach to health as being much more than merely the absence of disease or infirmity. To achieve a complete state of health, Cuba needed to bring citizens to a state of good health and keep them there.

It was no easy task, as the state of health for most Cubans was dire. Fidel Castro described the health landscape in his famous speech "History Will Absolve Me":

> Ninety percent of rural children are consumed by parasites, which filter through their bare feet from the earth. Society is moved to compassion upon hearing of the kidnapping or murder of one child, but they are criminally indifferent to the mass murder of so many thousands of

children who die every year from lack of facilities.... They will grow up with rickets, with not a single good tooth in their mouths, and will finally die of misery and deception. Public hospitals, which are always full, accept only patients recommended by some powerful politician who in turn demands electoral votes. (Castro, 1967)

Che Guevara described the same sort of conditions as he treated *campesinos* (farmers) during the 1957 guerrilla invasion into Cuba. Guevara wrote about treating peasants who had plenty of births but very little food, and who were needlessly losing their children to diarrhoea and treatable fevers. Speaking to medical students in 1960, Guevara told them about children consumed by hunger and poverty "who by their physical stature would appear eight or nine years old, but who nevertheless are almost 13 or 14.... [W]hen those children arrived at school at night for the first time and saw the electric lights, they exclaimed that the stars were very low that night" (Guevara, 1997)

On February 23, 1959, The Department of Technical, Material and Cultural Assistance to the Farmers of the Rebel Army was created in order to, among its many operations, offer health care for the underserved rural *campesinos*. However, the infrastructure and human resources of this department fell far short of delivering universal care across the island (Rojas Ochoa, 2004). In 1960, the Rural Social Medical Service (RSMS) developed a strategy to increase human resources for health in outlying areas. It offered contracts to recent medical graduates for a six-month posting to a rural medical clinic (Rojas Ochoa, 2004). Medical graduates prior to 1959 were permitted to maintain private clinical practice if they chose to do so. However, more than 300 of the 330 medical school graduates from 1960 signed up for the rural program. The number of volunteers increased the following year to 386, and fell slightly to 346 in 1962. That year, 46 dentists joined the cause. By 1973, 1,265 graduates were enrolled in the service, which evolved from a six-month contract to a two-year commitment. According to Rojas Ochoa (2004), all of the country's medical graduates enrolled for the program by the 1970s because since 1965 it had become "tradition to renounce private practice in the graduate's oath." Despite the exodus of more than three thousand Cuban physicians to Miami during this time, the expansion of medical education as part of the RSMS not only allowed Cuba to maintain its human resources for health to 1959 levels but also to go well beyond those levels to match countries such as the United Kingdom and Japan in their doctor-to-patient ratios (*Gapminder*, n.d.).

This human resource expansion fostered the establishment of rural clinics in every municipality in the country. In the early stages, the clinics were geared towards treating many of the communicable ailments and at-risk conditions afflicting the Cuban population, such as tuberculosis, leprosy, venereal diseases, pregnancy (which is of course not a disease in itself, but when combined with conditions of poverty can be lethal), children's acute diarrhoea, and malnutrition in children (Rojas Ochoa, 2004). The clinics also offered general primary care, waste disposal instruction, and health condition inspections within the community. In order to deliver primary care to the community, the RSMS health units coordinated with community-based organizations such as the National Service to Eradicate Malaria (NSAP), the Health Coordinators of the Committees for the Defense of the Revolution (CDR), the Health Brigades of the Cuban Women's Federation (FMC), and social workers from the Ministry of Welfare (Feinsilver, 1993). These organizations assisted in facilitating inter-action and supervision among physicians when the development of transporta-tion networks and other infrastructure was still in its infancy.

From the onset, the expansion of health-care services came through a commitment to medicine in the community. This involved routine engage-ments with community members to provide targeted services and to gather data to monitor health challenges locally. Attention was given to basic health areas. The first basic health area concerns the health of women, and focuses on extensive prenatal care and education. Even today, ultrasounds are given after the eighteenth week and health-care workers go to the homes of women to follow progress throughout the pregnancy. Pregnant women have oppor-tunities to attend public lectures on prenatal and postnatal care, and feeding guidelines are given to new mothers. Breastfeeding is strongly encouraged. As well, women at high risk are offered accommodation in maternity homes that provide around-the-clock medical attention. MINSAP insists on institutional childbirth, as the ministry claims that hygiene and guaranteed access to water can be a challenge if births were to take place in homes (Feinsilver, 1993).

The second basic health area focuses on children. Health-care workers visit kindergartens and daycare centres to offer checkups and to give lessons to students. Vaccinations and assessments of mental and physical health are offered along with exams for oratory and speech development issues. Thanks to an extensive vaccination effort, Cuba eradicated polio and tuberculosis by the 1970s.

The third basic health area targets adults. This is a more general area that relies heavily on the monitoring of chronic conditions. Diet, exercise, and men-tal health are given particular attention. Persons who have identifiable chronic conditions are given special attention, and in such cases monitoring takes place frequently.

Many infrastructure developments unfolded alongside these human resource driven expansions. Perhaps the most significant of these was the development of the *policlinicos* (specialty clinics). These centres offer comprehensive health care provision for up to forty-five thousand inhabitants within a maximum nine-kilometre radius (Feinsilver, 1993). They offer advanced services beyond primary care and diagnostics, while remaining focused on community medicine. *Policlinicos* are responsible for community health initiatives, such as keeping family records, constructing population groups, implementing disease prevention and health promotion programs, encouraging community participation, and administering vaccination programs (Hernández, 1971; Rojas Ochoa, 2004).

As much as the development of *policlinicos* advanced the quality of care on the island, building a healthy population was rooted in other social programs that sought to increase education, public sanitation, and infrastructure (Danielson, 1985; Feinsilver, 1993). Despite their ingenuity, many shortcomings were identified by the mid-1970s with the *policlinicos*. Rojas Ochoa (2004) claims that *policlinicos* suffered from poor integration; overemphasis on curative rather than preventative care; inadequate teamwork between health workers; transient physicians; the referral of too many patients for secondary care; and health-care professionals trained in hospitals not *policlinicos*, which affected their proficiency in the field.

The 1974 evaluation of *policlinicos* concluded that they were not having sufficient community health impact. Curative care and basic clinical practices continued to consume the majority of activities. A new model of *medicina en la comunidad con los policlinicos comunidades* (medicine in the community with the community *policlinicos*) evolved from this critique. To increase the role of disease prevention and health promotion, five major innovations were proposed, initially tested at the Alamar polyclinic located in old Havana. These involved

- programs giving special attention to women and children's health and epidemiology,
- programs for the care of the environment emphasizing food hygiene and home and workplace safety,
- service optimization, involving the dispersal of health-care duties through a health team,
- a management program to track and record shortcomings and successes within programs, and
- a teaching and research program to be carried out with students and graduates from the country's numerous medical schools (Rojas Ochoa, 2004).

In 1984, the family doctor program began as a pilot project to put "a doc on every block." The government literally sought to have a doctor and a nurse for every eighty households. This was meant to expand the number of health-care workers to incredibly high levels and to ensure that they would be regularly accessible in communities. Increased monitoring and prevention programs were part of the plan. Between 1984 and 1990, Cuba's doctor-to-patient ratio quickly rose and surpassed that of most countries, rich or poor. Putting doctors and nurses outside of the *policlinico* had major advantages for accessibility as it helped to monitor population health, not just the health of those at risk or coming into the *policlinico* ill. Doctor–nurse teams actively engaged the healthy as much as the ill, which allowed them to put a clinical spin and prognosis on fitness, diet, and risk factors. Doctors worked about four to five hours a day in their *consultorios* and then made house calls in the afternoon.

By the 1980s, Cubans were suffering from chronic and degenerative diseases much more than diseases of poverty, and this prevention framework became the new dominant model for health in Cuba. Not only did this approach keep people healthy, it greatly reduced costs from the overdependence on advanced and costly forms of treatment.

With this said, encouraging good health did not come at the cost of over-looking scientific medical advancements. Cuba put tremendous resources into the establishment of advanced medical research facilities ranging from pharmaceutical development to surgery. In 1985, Cuba's Hospital Hermanos Ameijeiras performed its first heart transplant surgery. By the time the hospital had performed its tenth transplant, the Yale Medical School's Hospital in New Haven had performed only five (Feinsilver, 1993). In 1988, as Feinsilver (1993) notes, the entire state of Connecticut was without extracorporeal shock wave lithotripsy devices to non-invasively crush kidney stones, while Cuba had been using this technology since 1986.

Cuba Faces the Special Period

Friedman (1962) argued that great changes in a society come only through cri-sis, real or imagined. Without having to imagine anything, Cuba faced a real crisis after the collapse of the Soviet Union. The country lost 87 percent of its exports and food imports were cut by half (Cole, 1998). The country, despite its own agricultural potential, had come to depend on importing everything; even fruit was imported in cans. When the imports dried up overnight, a public health emergency followed. And yet, this event led to the enhancement of a sus-tainable primary care system, a global health workforce, and advancements in accessibility to medicine. After the fall of the Soviet Union, Cuba's economy all but collapsed, but, as Cole (1998) suggests, it left economists baffled, as the col-lapse should have meant the downfall of the society, but it did not. A multitude of health crises broke out during this time: the average Cuban male lost thirty pounds between 1992 and 1993 and over sixty thousand people suffered from ophthalmological degeneracy due to a lack of vitamins (Huish & Kirk, 2007). Deplorable sanitation problems became the new norm in urban areas, and low birth rates increased to 9 percent as mothers were eating less.

Cuba's agricultural sector was in peril as well, which greatly impacted the upstream determinants of health. With the majority of land used for sugar production, urban centres suffered serious shortages of foodstuffs. A lack of fuel also complicated matters. Transportation systems buckled, and twenty-four-hour power outages became a regular occurrence. In Havana, the city's water delivery system worsened, and sanitation systems became intermittent and unreliable. These factors made for a desperate public health scenario.

The collapse ravaged medical supplies. Disposable supplies, from gloves to syringes, had to be washed and recycled. Doctors could continue to diagnose patients, but they could not always treat them due to a lack of supplies. Many doctors left the profession during this time, and some of them sought positions in the tourism sector (Kirk & Erisman, 2009). Even though Cuba continued to train more and more doctors each year, many health-care workers left the system frustrated by the inability to practise medicine with a near total absence of resources.

In this desperate time, the state put what meagre resources it had into public health, primary care, and universal accessibility. The health-care system increased attention on community-based early detection strategies. Such methods helped to lessen demands on expensive and desperately scarce material resources by treating patients at the community level rather than in hospitals or centralized institutions where physical plant conditions were deteriorating.

While the government increased its commitment to train physicians during the period, infrastructure was still hard to come by. No materials were available to build or repair *policlinicos* or *consultorios*; MINSAP suffered from shortages of medicines, equipment, and advanced diagnostic tools; therapeutic alternatives were limited; and access to new medical literature was restricted as a result of the embargo (Person Labrador, 2004). However, despite inadequate material supplies to service the entire Cuban population, MINSAP nevertheless geared its policies towards ensuring universal accessibility to health-care practitioners, encouraging holistic diagnosis and analysis, and promoting education at the community level in order to sustain and improve national public health.

Brotherton (2012) argues that the resource shortfall faced during the special period spelled the abandonment of health as a human right in Cuba. As Brotherton (2012) sees it, reliance on the market, in many cases the black market, to acquire certain medicines in times of state supply shortage is demonstrative of Cuba's surrender of the right to health. Indeed, the lack of material resources caused tensions and various levels of inequity in Cuban society, but the physical absence of material resources should not be equated with a moral abandonment of health as a human right. While the material resources were in short supply, the human resources never waned. The working conditions were difficult, but the Cuban government continued to take action in response to resource shortfalls rather than integrate more market-based coping responses into service provision. MINSAP worked to ensure that citizens had access to the system and that community-level health data was tracked and acted upon. The material shortages were a result of the US embargo that restricted exports of medicine to Cuba and Cuba's feeble internal resource distribution networks. The shortages thus forced a greater focus on the early detection of disease, disease prevention, and health promotion. Had the Cuban government failed to provide human resources for health, or had it installed more market-oriented mechanisms for service provision throughout the system, then it could be taken as a moral abandonment of the Alma-Ata principles, but MINSAP worked to evolve the system to meet needs around the extraordinary resource shortfalls. It was not easy and it caused additional strain, but it was in no way an admission of defeat or a rejection of Cuba's commitment to universal health care.

An abandonment of health as a human right would occur if an affluent nation with ample resources failed to invest in health care provision. But for an economically crippled nation like Cuba to adopt and respond to economic structures by orienting care is a refusal to acquiesce to broader economic conditions that impact the right to health.

Cuba's commitment to community-level access was an important strategy in ensuring public health, but it required two key elements for success. First, it emphasized a less technical approach to downstream (reactive) health care. Instead, it focused far more on addressing upstream determinants through disease prevention and health promotion. This required collaborative intersectoral work involving public health workers, social workers, epidemiologists, biological and agri-food scientists, teachers, coaches, and municipal CDRs to work in teams to identify community-level health issues. Collaborations in the preparation of community health maps and campaigns to eradicate specific vector diseases involved frequent exchanges of information among professionals.

Resource allocation and community-level assistance in maintaining foodstuffs and potable water needed professional coordination, but it also required popular participation at the local level. One example of this is the numerous *huertos privados* and *huertos populares*, urban-based privately and community-run gardens that grew fresh organic produce for private and market consumption. Community members participated in small-scale community produce gardens to provide for their needs and to sell either to the state or to non-community members. State-run *organiponicos* were also established to provide affordable produce throughout urban centres. This popular participation in nutrition was an important element to maintaining public health.

The second element for success during this special period was the expansion of medical and health-service training schools. Despite the economic chaos, Cuba did not close a single hospital or university. In fact, it expanded enrolment for higher education. During this same time, the province of Ontario in Canada, coping with a mild recession, restricted the number of medical school spaces.

MINSAP realized that ensuring universal, public access to health-care personnel could only happen if the personnel existed in the first place. Cuba went into the special period with a decent doctor-to-patient ratio of one physician for every 264 people. Still, the demands of working extensively at the community level and spending extensive time working on community-based rounds taxed doctors and other health-care workers extensively. MINSAP, therefore, expanded medical school spaces, as well as spaces for nurses, social workers, and health technicians. By 1999, the country had twenty-three medical schools, 66,000 practising doctors, and 2,200 medical school graduates entering the system each year. The doctor-to-patient ratio improved to one physician for every 169 people, which made it the best doctor-to-patient ratio anywhere in the world. By 2001, community-based physicians had returned to working six-hour days.

Without this committed focus to human resources for health, health indicators would have most certainly deteriorated. Thanks to these measures, life expectancy increased and infant mortality drastically declined. In 1980, the infant mortality rate was 27.5 deaths per 1,000 live births; in 1990, it was 10.7 per 1,000 live births; and by the end of the economic crunch in 1995, it was 6.4 per 1,000 live births (Reed, 2000). In 2012, the infant mortality rate was under 4.0 per 1,000 live births (Reed, 2000). A multitude of factors led to these improvements. Some may argue that these improvements are not particularly surprising because of worldwide advances in procedural obstetrics and technology. Certainly, technology and best-practice methods did improve during the 1990s, but during a time of complete economic disaster, during a time when common logic would assume that society would fall to pieces, and during a time when advances in public health were thought to be direct products of economic prosperity, Cuba managed to improve its core health indicators significantly by ensuring access. No other health-care system, let alone one in the developing world, has been able to advance our understanding of access to medicine as much as Cuba. Other countries such as Liberia, Malawi, and Angola suffered economic chaos during this time as well, and despite advances in the global knowledge of obstetrics, their infant mortality rates worsened substantially

(*Gapminder*, n.d.). For these countries, economic adversity ruined accessibility and with it the health outcomes of their populations. The fact that Cuba made enormous health gains cannot be accredited to general global knowledge of maternal health and public health procedures. Rather, the gains that occurred in an era of enormous economic chaos speak to the merits of intersectoral management of public health and care.

Revisiting the *Policlinico:* Community Access and Intersectoral Care

With sporadic public transit, few running cars, and a continuing fuel crisis during the special period, people could not easily travel far for health-care services. So, the services travelled to them. Since the 1970s, Cuba's health-care system has had three tiers:

1 national and provincial hospitals,
2 community-level *policlinicos*, and
3 community family practice through basic health teams (BHTs) based on medicine in the community model

Before the special period, the system focused heavily on the first and third tiers. Hospitals were responsible for advanced care, most diagnostics, screening, and various other advanced routines. BHTs were responsible for the first stage of primary care, basic diagnostics, and minor ambulatory treatments. BHT clinics were established in rural and urban areas alike and were responsible for eighty households each. The BHT units each had one doctor–nurse team who lived on site, performed house calls, and did rounds at the hospitals.

When the crisis hit, the hospitals suffered a lack of resources, and physical plant conditions worsened. At the community level, the BHTs suffered serious resource shortfalls as well. With resources strapped at the provincial and local level, MINSAP revisited the idea of *policlinicos* as a way to merge advanced and tertiary care at the community level.

Policlinicos undertook community health initiatives, such as keeping family records, constructing population groups, implementing disease-oriented prevention and health promotion programs, encouraging community participation, and administering vaccination programs (Hernández, 1971; Rojas Ochoa, 2004).

The special period reforms included the development of integrated health teams within the *policlinico*. For example, the *policlinico* Plaza de la Revolución, which served a population of 27,000 people, had 114 physicians, 86 nurses, 136 technicians, and 106 social workers. As Presno Labrador (2004) suggests, "the [traditional] splintering" of care among medical personnel did not provide truly comprehensive care for families. But as a team of various specialists, nurses and nurses' aides, pediatricians, sanitation brigades, epidemiologists, and family doctors, they could collectively provide comprehensive attention to the health of individuals and families, rather than just repairing the "damage or illness" of a person. Teams could be responsible for developing sensitive health promotion strategies for families in their serviced areas based on personal, family, and constructed risk assessment.

The *policlinicos* have become important training centres for Cuba's healthcare workers. Medical students, Cuban and foreign, work and train with *policlinico* health teams. *Policlinicos* are an ideal centre for medical education with close mentorship relations, extensive patient contact, and the ability to work in a multisectoral environment. *Policlinicos* are equipped with lecture theatres, small libraries, Internet, and audiovisual instructional equipment. The *policlinico* Plaza de la Revolución had seventy-one medical students training there in December 2008.

Today, the *policlinico* has an important role in community health-care provision in Cuba. More advanced procedures beyond basic treatment and diagnosis are finding their way into *policlinicos*, taking pressure off hospitals. They are responsible for electrocardiograms, X-rays, ultrasounds, vector disease analyses, minor surgeries, obstetrics, gynecological exams, and often offer allergy clinics.

With increases in the number of family physicians travelling abroad to work in places such as Venezuela, more and more primary care is being conducted within the *policlinico* rather than at the local *consultorio*. This is a relatively new development; for over thirty years, the initial entry point for patients into the health-care system came from consultations with family physicians or the BHTs at their community *consultorios*.

While Cuba continues to maintain an outstanding doctor-to-patient ratio across the entire island, the US Department of State sees this as "an over-surplus of physicians" (Powell, 2004, pp. 83–84). Even so, the reduction of this so-called "over-surplus" has created some discontent within the country among patients who have to travel further or wait a little longer for service. Many of the doctors employed in the BHT have joined international missions abroad, and this has caused some grumbling about access to health-care personnel, and a thirty-minute wait time at a *policlinico* is a new phenomenon compared to just walking into the BHT office. However, the increase in distance from a BHT centre to a *policlinico* would be no more than a couple of kilometres. Indeed, Cubans have grown used to having physicians nearby. Another sore point is that physicians who remain in the country do not receive salary bonuses in foreign currency as international physicians do. This has created some resentment and envy among doctors who have chosen the lower-paying domestic service.

Accessibility to physicians and nurses remains relatively equitable in rural and urban areas alike, with 99.4 percent of the population having regular accessibility to physicians. There are, however, some regional discrepancies. For example, in Havana there is one physician for every one hundred people, while in Havana province there is one physician for every two hundred people (Cuba Health Profile, 2007). This ratio is still better than the national ratio of any G8 nation (WHO, 2006). According to MINSAP, no province experiences less than one nurse for every 144 people (Rojas Ochoa, 2003).

Building Medical Internationalism

Cuba made it out of the special period through a number of economic strategies that attracted more foreign currency. This scenario is certainly not uncommon to any nation in the global South that has sought out economic prosperity through foreign investment to bolster the national economy. Unlike many countries, however, that cut social spending in order to produce more attractive investment climates, Cuba heavily committed to strengthening its domestic health-care system and invested in the training of thousands of health-care workers. In addition to noticeable public health gains, Cuba made considerable economic progress with a steady 8 percent annual GDP growth thanks largely to the close to 2 million tourists passing through the island each year. Still, despite such gains, MINSAP remained strapped for resources under the US embargo of medical supplies, even if they were shipped from third-party countries that had economic relations with both Cuba and the United States.[2] Despite such persistent difficulties at home, Cuba continued to scale up its long-standing international health-care service during and after the special period. While doctors worked overseas in health brigades, and while human resources and medical equipment were needed at home, the special period witnessed a bolstering of international health-care workers on a scale the world has never seen before.

While the reasons that Cuba invests in a robust health-care system at home seems obvious, it has remained a riddle for many scholars as to why Cuba sends its doctors abroad. Some have developed appreciative reasons for the country's international altruism: an expression of President Fidel Castro's leadership (Macintyre & Hadad, 2002), an act of pan-American solidarity (Huish & Kirk, 2007), a building of "symbolic capital" (Feinsilver, 1993, p. 24), or a paradox outside of neoliberal globalization (Spiegel & Yassi, 2004). Certainly, all of these factors play a role in understanding medical internationalism. However, some critics label Cuba's medical diplomacy as a practice done for political influence (Falcoff, 2003, p. 234) or just to earn hard currency (Montaner & Ramonet, 2007). Of course, all countries construct their foreign policies to meet their national interests and Cuba is no different. Its medical internationalism, while benefiting the lives of the poor and destitute, has warmed political and economic relations with nations around the world. The recent inclusion of Cuba into the Organization of American States is testimony to this. Even US President Barack Obama has said that he had "heard much" about Cuba's "soft-diplomacy," and called it a reminder of the positive benefits of doing more than military intervention (Huish & Kirk, 2009).

The political and economic gains that Cuba receives from its medical internationalism are noteworthy and range from significant (the inclusion of Cuba in Venezuela's ALBA agreement) to minor (The Gambia lobbying for the inclusion of Cuba on select trade agreements with Europe). It is important to note that Cuba's commitment to medical internationalism was in sync with the capacity-building projects going on within the country during the special period. In essence, medical internationalism is not an attempt to pursue exceptional humanitarianism; rather, it is an international reflection of normative national values.

By building this capacity at home, Cuba is in a strategic position to offer cooperation abroad. With certain countries, such as Venezuela and South Africa, Cuba receives direct economic and political benefits. But consider that The Gambia, a country whose economy consists of little more than peanut exports, has received generous Cuban cooperation that has cut the malaria incidence rate in half, helped control the spread of HIV/AIDS, improved the doctor-to-patient ratio from one physician for every fifty thousand people to one physician for every nine thousand people, and set up a community-oriented medical school in the capital. There is little political payment Cuba receives for this work with The Gambia, let alone any economic gain, and yet it continues to develop strong internal capacity efforts in The Gambia.

A sense of capability, more than lucrative gains, drives Cuban medical internationalism. By examining the development of international medical campaigns and taking note of official state discourses, it is clear that Cuban medical internationalism evolved in accordance with two processes. First, it expanded from a long-standing foreign policy devoted to pan-American and pan-Southern solidarity. Second, it mirrored developments of community-based primary care at home. As Cuban health authorities witnessed the tremendous benefits that came from having doctors attend to their own underserved communities, they realized that it was possible for physicians to create positive health impacts in other poor countries. This policy would evolve from its origin as a small medical brigade in Chile into the creation of the largest medical school in the world.

Cuba emerged out of a brutal socioeconomic disaster to become a world leader in global health because it embraced health care as a moral good that could address an immediate crisis and achieve long-term benefits. There are, then, five lessons that Cuba can offer:

- Cuba survived the collapse of the Soviet Union by investing in human resources, rather than just material resources.
- Building health-care capacity and intersectoral partnerships, from national to community levels, can allow health to flourish, even in resource-poor settings.
- Building capacity does not have to stop during the management of a national crisis. It can also address much broader global crises and still act within the nation's own interest.
- The decision to not close a single university or hospital during an economic disaster is grounded in an epistemology that views health as a human right and not as a social burden.
- With political leadership that values health and with popular support to address upstream determinants, immediate and long-term health needs in the global South can be addressed. This is to say that with the appropriate political leadership, many global health challenges related to access could be remedied.

In order for these lessons to be received, nation states must address the current global health crisis as a worthy cause rather than a nuisance. It requires a framework of cooperation rather than competition between rich and poor nations in order to make it happen. Most importantly, the positive examples of building capacity out of crisis that Cuba has shown suggest that health as a right can be loaded into normative processes of foreign and domestic policy. But to move forward requires overcoming common prejudices against Cuba's communism and the belief that our public institutions do not have the capacity to be strengthened, and careful thinking about how it is possible to flourish during calamities rather than just manage them.

Cuba continues to have resource shortfalls, money is scarce, and there are numerous social challenges that continue. No one denies that. Because of the control of certain patented medicines in the United States, there are serious shortages in Cuba. Still, Cuba invests its limited foreign exchange in purchasing needed drugs through third countries at often elevated prices. And despite all of the social problems from overcrowded buses, a lack of international travel opportunities, and purchasing costly medicine through secondary markets, no one is denied the right to health care. Everyone is entitled.

Considering this, one must ask why, despite all of the social challenges, does Cuba pursue global health equity? As mentioned earlier in this chapter, they do it because they can. They do it because it is in their best interest, and they do it because of a belief that it is virtuous to pursue health-care as a right. Perhaps, then, the harder question to ask is why wealthy nations do not pursue global health equity with the same enthusiasm and moral fervour they use to engage in war?

Why do many wealthy societies stop short of objecting to the behaviour of nation states and global institutions that do little to ensure even the most basic access to health-care resources? Why do wealthy societies make considerable efforts to help the poor only in times of natural disasters? And when they do make the effort, as in Haiti in 2010, why does society place such value on the amount of money raised and equipment sent, and not on the number of lives saved? No one denies that the global North faces pressing social challenges, and that there is a lot of work to do in the areas of global justice and human rights around the world, but why does it turn its moral attention away from the overwhelming demand for health care? Why are citizens not constantly asking their leaders why, if the knowledge, money, and resources to save lives exist, is nothing being done?

CHAPTER 3

GROWING ALTERNATIVES THROUGH FOREIGN

POLICY: FOREIGN POLICY AND PERSPECTIVES

ON INTERNATIONAL HEALTH

A Grim Hundred Years

The twentieth century was one of the most violent periods in human history. Humanity mastered its ability and efficiency for war and violence at an alarming rate. On a global scale, the twentieth century will be remembered as a time when governments raised armies and invested in innovative ways to break bones than ways to heal them. Military weapons have been advanced with ruthless efficiency in the past one hundred years, and today, in many parts of the world, it is easier to get access to a weapon than it is to receive affordable medical care (Fleshman, 2001). In Burundi, there is a government ministry dedicated to pulling small calibre weapons out of the general population, but directly across the road, the ministry tasked with public health has barely enough resources to keep the lights on. Why do governments defend the continued investment in military stockpiles and dangerous devices but fall short of investing in better public education or public health care?

While governments spent most of the twentieth century investing in new means of destruction, global health gaps grew to new levels of inequity. Clearly, there have been tremendous advancements in medicine in the twentieth century, and thanks to these technologies, many people live longer, healthier lives than they would have a hundred years ago. Notably, many affluent countries have spent enormous sums on social medicine programs in order to grant health care access to all citizens. European countries invested heavily in their social health care programs following World War II. Canada continues to maintain universal public health care, and under the Obama administration, the United States has made attempts to move towards universal coverage. But in the global South, the vast majority of citizens have a greater chance of witnessing innovations in weaponry through war, local conflicts, or the crimes that poverty breeds, than they have of receiving even basic medical care.

In the twentieth century, the distance in life expectancy between poor nations and rich nations stretched out to new heights. In the 1830s, the average Indian lived to twenty-five and a Norwegian forty-five years. In 1900, the gap in life expectancy between all nations was about twenty-three years. In Bangladesh, a person could expect to live to twenty-three while Norway had the best life expectancy of fifty-five years. Today, people of Bangladesh have the same life expectancy that Norwegians and Swedes enjoyed in 1920. For Bangladeshis who work in the dangerous shipbreaking industry, they can expect a life expectancy that is on par with what life expectancy was for the entire country in 1870: twenty-nine years (*Gapminder*, n.d.). Life expectancy for some in Bangladesh has hardly budged in six generations.

It is not possible to correlate every war or violent conflict in the twentieth century to the shape of life expectancies. The calculation for life expectancy is far too complex for that. There have also been times when life expectancy actually improved in times of war, such as in the United Kingdom during World War II and in Vietnam during the war with the United States as these governments lessened inequities in health access by increasing social services in times of crisis (Wilkinson, 1996).

Physicians in the global South often feel helpless trying to overcome suffering and illness in countries that have had their public health sector gutted to the core (Ogilvie, Mill, Astle, Fanning, & Opare, 2007). In Uganda, the national referral hospitals swell with patients while the medicines deplete. Because access to primary care in the rural areas is extremely limited, the inflow of severe emergencies easily overwhelms the national referral hospitals. On a daily basis, in the city of Mbarara, where hospital beds are in short supply, the poor camp outside of the wards waiting for care and with little means to pay for their medicine. These conditions of inequity are unfortunate and unnecessary, and medical science in itself cannot overcome such global health challenges. Only as a part of a broad socioeconomic fabric where health-care workers are empowered at the local level and access to medicine can be guaranteed for the poor, can global health equity be sought.

There has never been more in-depth knowledge, resources, and advancements in communication and travel for global health. There are generous donors—the Bill & Melinda Gates Foundation, the William J. Clinton Foundation, and the Millennium Development Goals Fund—and thanks to these organizations and programs millions of lives are being saved. However, the lives saved are the ones that fall into the specific categories of assistance that the particular organization is targeting. Sometimes it is HIV, other times it is tuberculosis. At the 2010 G8 Summit held in Muskoka, Ontario, the theme was maternal mortality. But why stop with there? What about the hundreds of waterborne and vector-borne infections that can cut life short? What about death that occurs from infections because antibiotics cannot be found or the incredibly high mortality that occurs on unsafe roads in the global South? Even the unnecessary suffering of non-life-threatening conditions that millions of people endure because of a lack of basic medical care is something that musters little political enthusiasm. There are almost no donation schemes set up for poor countries to receive chemotherapy treatment for cancer, despite the fact that the prevalence of cancer in the global South is just as common as it is in the North (Filou, 2011).

Simply put, health systems in the global South are not given the same public support as are systems in the global North. The IMF and World Bank have long opposed the expansion of public expenditure in health care (Lema et al., 2007). The World Trade Organization insists that markets in health care be opened up for business (Lipson, 2001). In Mbarara, Uganda a community clinic has a sign that reads, "Your health is our business." When health care is approached as a business, it becomes enormously difficult to establish a system that addresses all health needs. Private systems work on a transactional basis, and the system often offers interventions that are curative, narrow, and specific. Based on the ability to pay, a patient may be able to receive certain treatment and have to forgo others because of the costs of treatment and resources. Health care does not work well when treatment is compartmentalized into pay-as-you-go services. Consumer choice has its benefits when it comes to purchasing automobiles or mobile phone packages, but choice in treatment can be dangerous. To choose not to include a particular drug in a treatment regimen or an extra unit of blood during surgery because the patient cannot afford it, can be lethal.

Universal public health that covers the entirety of health services is one way to ensure that market logic does not hinder an individual's health. In North America, there are constant attacks from conservatives about the inefficiency of public health, and complaints about how it violates one's rights to prevent one from paying for medical service if they so choose. In Canada and the United Kingdom, the majority of the populations tend to reject such logic ("Canadians favour," 2009). In Canada, Canadian Doctors for Medicare continues to show that doctors and patients fare much better with public health care than they would with private (Resources, 2010). Numerous scholars discuss how societies fare better with public health care (Campbell & Marchildon, 2007; Lewis, Donaldson, Mitton, & Currie, 2001). So, instead of tolerating more space for the private sector, there should be efforts to bolster the public sector to ensure that it is well resourced, robust, and efficient. Still, such good advice tends to fall far from elite ears. If the elite cannot pay for speedy treatments at home, then why not look for them abroad?

Enter Medical Tourism

Increasingly, the global elite seek health care across borders and often in areas where health services for locals are anemic. Costa Rica, Singapore, Jamaica, Thailand, and India (despite the desperate state of its rural health services) all boast advanced medical facilities. Knowing that imaging scans, elective surgeries, and organ transplants can occur quickly and often more cheaply than they can in the global North, tens of thousands of people with the ability to pay for treatment seek medical treatments in the global South. This growing trend holds enormous dangers for the sustainability of health-care systems in the North and South alike. Wait times for certain procedures in some places in the global North are bothersome and the equipment is standing idly by in the South. So what if India has a critical physician shortage? If a physician can make good money treating wealthy medical tourists using high-tech equipment, and if the Indian health system offers no incentive to put doctors in rural areas, what is the problem? Market logic would suggest that this is a measured response.

If it is normative to accept the redirection of human resources for health and to train future health-care workers for the business demands of the elite rather than for the humanitarian needs of the poor, the poor will continue to suffer and die at current if not worse levels. From this point of view, medical tourism is the latest incarnation of the rich stomping on the needs of the poor to fulfill their own self-interest. The creation of the medical tourism market, which is encouraged by the World Bank, presents complex market dynamics (Ramírez de Arellano, 2007). Doctors tend to go where there is money, and airlines can get people just about anywhere to find those doctors. Is medical tourism a new norm? All the tools and resources of globalization ensure that it can be. If the worry is that the wealthy will take human resources away from the poor, an ethical response may not be found in an attempt to halt or reverse the broader processes of globalization. There are ways to make medical tourism ethical in order to promote health equity rather than exacerbate inequity. If it were possible to see ethical medical tourism that meets the interests of the poor while ensuring national interests, it would be possible to create similar programs. Cuba's Operación Milagro may be an important example for this.

An Example of Unethical Medical Tourism

The danger of medical tourism is perhaps best illuminated by a position of a report from McKinsey & Company aimed at measuring the corporate feasibility of medical tourism. The report suggests that the number of global medical travellers is only about eighty-five thousand people (Ehrbeck, Guevara, & Mango, 2008). Certainly, there are tens of thousands more people than this who travel internationally for medical services each year, either from the North to the South or between countries in the global South. The report arrives at this number by offering a narrow definition of a medical traveller as an individual who seeks care abroad even though he or she has access to care within their home health-care system. The aim of the report was to estimate the potential growth of the medical tourism market specifically by North Americans who might travel abroad for health care even though they could receive similar services at home in a timely manner through government or private insurance provision. The report was aimed at investment firms to propose increased insurability of medical tourists in the global North in order to encourage medical tourism destinations in poor countries that would lower the operating costs of insurance companies. The report called for a goal of at least 15 percent cheaper than that of normal operating costs in the United States (Ehrbeck et al., 2008).

The report suggests that the medical tourism market could explode by ten times, and 850,000 medical tourists from North America alone would potentially seek services abroad even though such services would be available at home. That is good news for those who invest in the stocks of medical tourism operators or who want to invest in insurance or medical tourism facilities that might see a ten-fold increase in clients, but it spells trouble if you are a poor citizen of Thailand seeking basic care or if you are a citizen of Canada who needs specialized treatment and have no interest in flying to India from Newfoundland. Through this lens, medical tourism is understood as a comparative advantage against domestic services in the global North. If the market were to grow as McKinsey & Company suggests it might, it would desperately undermine community-oriented primary care in countries receiving medical tourists, as more health workers would migrate to this burgeoning sector. Moreover, it would encourage disinvestment of advanced resources for public care in the global North in favour of more cost-effective treatment abroad. In the global South, there would be greater motivation to train health workers and to relocate existing health workers into exclusive medical tourism centres. This is already under way in the Caribbean and India. In the global North, government and private insurance providers could offer discounts to patients who would seek health care abroad rather than the more costly care at home. If discounts were found abroad, then what advantage would there be in investing greater resources to improve efficiency at home?

But how did the report manage to limit the number of medical tourists? First, it excluded travellers seeking holistic and spa-like therapy. McKinsey & Company excluded those who were not in-patients in hospitals as they said that no reliable data existed on persons seeking minor and boutique treatment world-wide (Ehrbeck et al., 2008). Second, current patients that were sent to another country under the insurance of a national health coverage plan were excluded. This would include patients in Ontario who were sent to Michigan to receive care under the province's insurance plan. While these patients were occupying space in a foreign country as medical travellers, they did not willingly elect to travel for care; the insurer made the decision. Third, patients who had accidents abroad were excluded, as they did not intentionally travel to seek out care. Fourth, McKinsey & Company excluded expatriates returning home for care as questions of remittances and national insurance coverage strategies complicated the picture. Indeed, this group accounts for a large share of medical tourists to Thailand and Singapore. In the end, the report focused only on the market potential of patients who would willingly elect to seek treatment abroad.

The report narrows the definition of the medical traveller purposefully so that it can compare the direct and indirect costs of medical tourism services that compete against a nation's primary care and specialized services. The narrow definition is done in order to encourage health insurance (both public and private) to embrace medical tourism for certain procedures over nationally based care in the global North. The medical tourists defined in this report are those who could easily access care at home, but who, if the costs were low enough or if their insurance fully embraced it, would travel for medical services. Medical tourism then becomes a cost saving mechanism, and one that has the potential to further exacerbate health care inequities in the global North and the global South alike.

If medical tourism were to continue to flourish and expand, then one could assume that an increasing number of trained doctors in the global South would compete for placement and specialization in the medical tourism sector rather than in less lucrative public sectors. Travellers seeking therapeutic massage do not directly take away from the place of doctors and nurses serving poor populations, but demand for cosmetic surgery and organ transplants in countries with poor medical coverage clearly does.

McKinsey & Company estimate that of the 8 million elected procedures that are paid for in the United States, only up to 700,000 of these patients would choose medical tourism with appropriate insurance support, as many would be unlikely to travel if the costs were comparable or if they were only to break even (Ehrbeck et al., 2008). If the savings were $10,000 or greater per case, more patients would likely travel for care. If insurance policies in the global

North supported medical tourism, then the number would grow faster still. With most countries struggling with a lack of human resources for health, the increased service demand in the global South from medical tourism would certainly see more health-care workers in poor places catering their services to foreign tourists rather than local, primary care needs (Ehrbeck et al., 2008).

Knowing that the dominant medical tourism model intentionally redirects resources away from the poor, it becomes all the more important to question the ethical framework. In order to act, society must not abandon the key tools that make medical tourism possible: technology, knowledge, communication, travel, and building capacity. These elements possess the ability to do enormous good for global health equity; it is just the manner in which they are controlled and implemented that causes harm. And this harm is caused by systematically excluding the needs of the poor for the needs of the rich. The solution, then, would be to find a way to ensure that the needs of the poor are not forgotten while a country pursues desired capital from medical travellers.

An Example of Ethical Medical Tourism

Cuba participates in revenue generating medical tourism aimed at affluent clientele from wealthy countries. Wilkinson (2008) estimates the revenue figure at about $40 million per year, often in hard currency. No doubt, this is an important and growing revenue stream for Cuba, as it takes advantage of market demand from other countries. But this high revenue generator receives only a fraction of the low-income foreign patients who come to Cuba to receive medical care at absolutely no charge.

Operación Milagro is an initiative by Cuba and Venezuela that has restored eyesight to over 1 million people since 2004. Established through the ALBA agreement, Cuba provides ophthalmologists and Venezuela provides hard currency through nationalized petroleum revenues to transport, treat, and accommodate hundreds of thousands of ophthalmological patients from Latin America and Africa in Cuba. The governments charge patients nothing. The program has now expanded, and Cuban doctors have set up clinics in other countries. In St. Lucia, the only ophthalmologist in the country is Cuban working under this program. Today, those Cubans working abroad are also working to train local ophthalmologists.

The program is one of several Cuban–Venezuelan missions that capitalize on Venezuelan fiscal resources and Cuban medical expertise to provide free services for the poor. Operación Milagro emerged after the 2003 literacy campaigns in Venezuela identified that many of the rural poor suffered from vision-impairing illnesses that created barriers to learning and to pursuing livelihoods (Muntaner et al., 2008). Persons suffering from ophthalmological impairments in Venezuela and neighbouring Caribbean countries are invited to travel to Cuba to receive treatment and then undergo post-surgery treatment in Cuba, all for no charge. Of the some 1.6 million patients that have been treated, over 113,000 of these have been Cubans who have also received free eye surgery (Huish & Kirk, 2007). While many of the foreign patients are flown to Cuba, the program has expanded to thirty-seven ophthalmological centres in eight countries in Latin America and Africa. Indeed, centres outside of Cuba are now providing the majority of the program's services as of 2009, which demonstrates the sensible preference to have patients treated locally rather than using medical tourism as a permanent foundation for care.

Participating as part of a medical delegation to Cuba in 2007 with the group Medical Education Cooperation with Cuba (MEDICC),[1] I surveyed Operación Milagro. Through field visits, roundtables with members of the program, and engagements with several doctors, various groups of patients, and their social worker teams, I can offer a brief overview of the program.

Patients destined to travel to Cuba are screened in their home countries either by Cuban doctors working there or by local health authorities. Cuban social workers receive them in Havana and assist them throughout their stay. These workers ensure that basic needs are met and help coordinate communication with the patient's family in their home country.

All patients are given a comprehensive evaluation both for vision and for general health. Some patients are too ill to be treated, such as those experiencing complications from diabetes. Patients who are too ill to receive ophthalmological surgery are referred to Cuban doctors for additional treatment. Surgeons use modern Zeiss surgical laser equipment, and the maximum time for cataract surgery is twenty-five minutes per eye operation. Post-surgery, some patients are accommodated at a seaside community east of Havana for about fifteen days or up to two months if there are complications and any need for follow-up work. Others are housed in various hotels in Havana. Accommodations at the post-surgery centres are immaculate: there are two patients per air-conditioned room and a team of nurses and social workers dedicated to each house.

I, along with a group of fifteen physicians from the United States, visited one such house that accommodated a group of taxi drivers from St. Martin. The taxi drivers all suffered from cataracts and because of it, they could not drive their cars.

"Who wants to ride with a blind taxi driver?" one told us.

In St. Martin, there is no social security for cab drivers who go blind, just as in most parts of the Caribbean and Latin America there is no compensation for trade workers who have to give up their profession because they cannot see.

"If we can see, we can work and keep a roof over our families. No one else has offered us anything this gracious. We could never afford this sort of surgery at home," said one patient of Operación Milagro.

While relieving cataracts is just a small step in overcoming underdevelopment, it is an important step in ensuring that the vulnerable have the right to sight so that they can live their lives and maintain their livelihoods.

With the expansion of thirty-seven clinics operating outside of Cuba as of 2009, the number of patients treated by Operación Milagro has grown exponentially.[2] McKinsey & Company suggested that insurance take a greater role in medical tourism, and Operación Milagro serves as a compelling example of how such insurance can provide for the needs of the poor—effectively tackling a debilitating disease while not undermining local health-care capacity in the country of service.

Specifically, Operación Milagro offers three key ways in which medical tourism can reduce harm and impact on local populations while offering much-needed services for foreigners. First, the capacity for foreign care is built upon Cuba's strength in domestic health-care services. Cuba did not have to invest in a second tier of health-care workers for a foreign market; instead, it utilized its domestically oriented strength in human resources for health for a foreign need. With well-established primary and tertiary care networks throughout the island and a proven ability to train community-oriented primary care doctors, Cuba did not have to bleed off domestic resources in order to fulfill this foreign request. Rather, it redirected parts of its domestic capabilities towards the needs of the poor from other countries, while ensuring continued care for domestic patients.

Notably, Operación Milagro has not compromised domestic capacity for ophthalmological treatment. However, with thirty-eight thousand of their own health-care workers stationed in sixty-six countries as of 2011, certain tensions have been felt in Cuba. Namely, primary care doctors serving in the country are taking on higher patient loads and they are not receiving equal remuneration to that of their colleagues working overseas. With this said, what makes Operación Milagro stand apart from this broader stress facing primary care doctors is that even though Cuban eye surgeons are working abroad, local ophthalmological centres across the country are equipped, staffed, and available for local needs to the same extent as they are for patients abroad.

The second lesson here is that nationals are not excluded from the foreign-directed care. With over 113,000 Cubans having received ophthalmological care as of 2007, citizens are not marginalized in preference for treating foreign patients. The resources and capacity available for foreigners is just as available for domestic needs.

The third lesson is that the existing and future physician labour pool for Operación Milagro is not massively redirected away from domestic needs in order to serve foreign patients. Operación Milagro does not offer a separate incentive structure to lure Cuban eye surgeons away from their domestic responsibilities, even though other Cuban medical internationalism programs do offer a pay bonus. For the workers of Operación Milagro no massive gains in salary or material incentives are offered within the program that would see surgeons purposefully avoid treating domestic patients. Certainly, the top-of-the-line equipment and a strong network of ophthalmological experts are professional incentives, but this is a far different form of incentive compared to that of a medical tourist surgeon in Thailand, whose main spur in treating foreign patients is to earn a generous salary.

Moreover, Operación Milagro creates space for the training of ophthalmology specialists and residents who will then have the chance to practise in Cuba's systems or within the health systems of other countries that have benefited from Operación Milagro. Unlike other brands of medical tourism that focus on elective boutique medicine, Operación Milagro is a program aimed at ophthalmology for the public, and economic, good rather than for a narrow, private market.

How the Global North Continues to Drain the Global South

Operación Milagro stands apart from other models of medical tourism as it aims to strengthen the poor through the public good. While medical tourism may grow in popularity and demand (depending on the role of insurance plans), many in the global North worry less about specialist care and more about simply having a family doctor. As a result of many factors, from higher pay to the culture of medical education, many Canadian-trained doctors pursue specialization over general or family practice. To cope with the lack of interest in family medicine, all provinces welcome and actively recruit health-care workers from abroad. In Alberta, Newfoundland, and British Columbia, there has been active recruitment of doctors from South Africa. In Nova Scotia, doctors from India, the Middle East, and Southeast Asia are given conditional licences with which they must serve under the supervision of a nationally licensed doctor. Ontario and Quebec do not have an active recruitment scheme, and in those provinces many foreign-trained physicians cannot find work in health-care services and some are driving taxis.

The supposed benefit of health-care worker migration is that a wealthy nation, such as Canada, is able to bring in skilled human resources for health for the needs of rural and underserved populations. Narrowly speaking, this is a positive move, but in a global sense, the problems are enormous. A doctor may leave South Africa to practise in Alberta, but there is no reciprocation or financial compensation. No Canadian doctor will head to the Eastern Cape to serve marginalized populations, and the donor country will receive not payment from the recipient country. Consider that Canada has about one doctor for every 450 people and South Africa has one physician for every 1,500 people. When a doctor leaves South Africa, the impact in the doctor-to-patient ratio is felt far more than, say, when a Canadian doctor moves to the United States. Consider the rigid divide in quality and service of care between South Africa's private and public systems, which the Health Minister of South Africa, Aaron Motsoaledi, has stated is like apartheid all over again (McLea, 2011).

Do physicians in the global South, who work in underpaid, undervalued, and at times collapsing public health-care systems, really have a choice to stay? Is migration on the same moral platform as is serving one's community? Or is it really a question of two different moral norms: choosing affluence or choosing martyrdom? Despite what some scholars have written about in discussions of the global migration of health-care workers, I propose that more than facing issues of money or prestige, doctors in the global South focus on the enormous frustration they feel about the conditions and systems in which they work. Having interviewed medical students in Uganda, Ecuador, and the Philippines, I can attest that many genuinely want to stay and help their communities, but when it comes down to practising in conditions where the wards are spilling over, the medicines are not available, and the physician can diagnose but cannot treat, the personal and professional frustration is so overwhelming that many give up, pack up, and head to the global North. Every single medical student I interviewed in western Uganda said that he or she would gladly stay in his or her own country to serve vulnerable populations, but not without appropriate working conditions in addition to proper remuneration.[3]

Some scholars suggest that physicians who migrate should take responsibility for their choice by repaying their home countries for loss of their skill (Snyder, 2009). In places such as western Uganda, there is almost no choice to stay that does not lead to massive personal and professional sacrifice on the part of the physician. However, just as Cuba has shown that the ethics of medical tourism can be turned around, so, too, can the ethics of health-care worker migration be turned so that those who want to serve the destitute might do so without such intense personal sacrifice. The ethics of health-care-worker migration in its current form is worthy of further discussion, and Cuba, yet again, provides a noteworthy example of what medical migration could be.

At a time when India, Peru, Southeast Asia, and the majority of countries in Africa are suffering from critical shortages of health-care workers, the indifference of the global North to assist in strengthening health-care systems in the global South is deeply disturbing. Snyder's (2009) recent piece in *The American Journal of Bioethics* argues for this indifference. Snyder argues that the migration process should not be labelled as poaching because the source countries and their health-care workers are active agents in the process. Snyder succeeds in proving that health care workers are not wild game. There are, of course, differences between shooting elephants for the ivory trade and fleecing poor countries of their health-care workers. While a change in language, as Harhay and Munera Mesa (2009) agree, is likely a useful gain, Snyder's opposition to the term "poaching" is simply because it does not adequately consider the decision-making of source countries or their health-care workers. As he puts it, "this language removes the agency of the individual worker—and his or her own potential wrongdoing—from the discussion of migration" (2011, p. W1).

For physicians working in resource-poor conditions and who face mounting discouragement and frustration on the job from poor salaries and watching patients die because they cannot afford the treatments recommended, heading to exodus is hardly a choice. Placing the burden of migration on the individuals themselves shows little regard for the constrained agency of health-care workers in resource-poor conditions, and is an argument that has little understanding of the broader socioeconomic structures that workers cope with. It also, less directly, suggests that the problem is with doctors who are fed up with the system in which they work, and, if anything, wealthy countries are offering them options. Such defences of health worker migration fail to acknowledge the enormous challenges faced by those working in tough situations.

Chronicle of South Africa

Fourteen percent of trained physicians in South Africa leave to practise in Canada and the United States, and an additional 4 percent migrate to the United Kingdom and Australia (Hagopian, Thompson, Fordyce, Johnson, & Hart, 2004). The migration of South African doctors to Canada, the United States, Australia, U.K., and New Zealand has been a long-standing trend. Governments (such as those in the Canadian provinces of Alberta, Saskatchewan, and Newfoundland) have directly recruited doctors from the country. Private companies, such as Kaplan (the corporation responsible for the preparation and administration of the United States medical board exams), have sought medical graduates from South Africa even before they enter domestic service.

While the exodus of physicians out of South Africa is disturbing, the growing flight of nurses is alarming. In 1998, 1,746 South African nurses applied for verification of their credentials, a necessary step in seeking overseas employment, while the following year over 3,000 nurses took this step (Xaba & Phillips, 2001). The Organization for Economic Co-operation and Development (OECD) estimates that South Africa has 23,400 of its trained health-care workers working overseas (Migration resources, n.d.).

South Africa has about thirty-five thousand vacancies for nurses despite the fact that an estimated thirty-two thousand nurses are unemployed in the country (WHO, 2006). The alarmingly high number of in-country vacancies combined with the high unemployment numbers suggest that in addition to migration opportunities abroad, the domestic service simply cannot attract and retain health-care workers. Health-care workers take flight, but also refuse to serve the public sector. Seventy-three percent of general practitioners work in South Africa's private sector—a system that is utilized by only 20 percent of the population (Padarath et al., 2006).

As several studies have shown, there is increasing fear of service in South Africa's public health sector (Buchan, Kingma, & Lorenzo, 2005; Dovlo, 2003; Padarath et al., 2006). HIV/AIDS populations, rising crime, and ethnic conflicts are all social struggles that disproportionately affect poorer South Africans. Physicians and nurses in the public sector are placed in work situations involving complex socioeconomic conditions that can undermine clinical confidence (Delobelle et al., 2009). Poorly resourced clinics in rural areas and in vulnerable communities, as well as a lack of resources and support staff, place health-care workers at risk of contracting HIV and being exposed to violence, and heighten stress. The majority of health-care workers surveyed were worried about contracting HIV through work-related duties and a lack of protective equipment (Dovlo, 2003).

The lack of accessibility to health-care workers has had detrimental impacts on health outcomes in the country. Two-thirds of all births take place without skilled personnel. The lack of specialists has led to a lack of specialized infrastructure for advanced and tertiary care. Further, the shortage of specialized health-care workers has led, in some cases, to the complete abandonment of specialized health-care centres, as was the case of a spinal injury clinic that shut down after its anesthetists migrated to Canada (Martineau, Decker, & Bundred, 2002). The country also lacks post-secondary medical teaching staff, which has detrimental impacts on the next generation of health-care workers for the country. Keeping doctors is tough, and finding teachers to train them is now even harder.

Although South Africa has a massive shortage of health-care workers and many leave to work abroad, health-care workers from Zimbabwe, Tanzania, Malawi, and Kenya are all seeking higher-paying positions in South Africa's public health-care system. Compared with the conditions and remuneration that is offered in their own systems, South Africa is a choice destination.

In response to the active recruitment by foreign governments and their third-party recruitment agencies, South Africa has implemented various policies that do little to bolster internal capacity or even overcome some of the obvious socioeconomic imbalances in health-care provision in the country. South Africa has become a destination country as much as a source country. Official policies prohibit the active recruitment of human resources for health from other countries; however, the migration of health workers from other

African nations to South Africa continues through informal channels (Bhorat, Meyer, & Mlatsheni, 2002; Department of Health [South Africa], 2006).

The policy on the recruitment, employment, and support of foreign health professionals is a strategy that places South Africa as a destination country, just as much as it is a source country. And like all destination countries, South Africa has taken specific steps to see that foreign health-care workers from other African nations work in the public service. While the South African government has started a dialogue with the Organization of African Unity countries about the ethical movement of health-care workers, their commitment to recruit health-care workers from other struggling nations without offering compensation is ethically troubling. Only eight nations in the African continent do not suffer from a critical lack of health-care workers. Constructing policy that worsens the number of health-care workers in other African nations without offering compensation at the local level is troubling, indeed. It also sends a message that the state is more concerned in supporting its public system with foreign doctors than providing South Africans with affluent opportunities to work in the public system. This sends a clear message to the poor: You do not count much.

The policy on community service by health professionals was adopted in 1999 and mandated that newly trained health-care workers serve in vulnerable populations or areas with critical health-care worker shortages (Department of Health [South Africa], 2006). All graduates of South African medical schools are required to put in service to a marginalized community as part of their licensing requirements. Only after serving in a vulnerable community for a set period would a medical graduate be considered qualified enough to migrate. While the goal of the program is to ensure a more even access to health-care workers in marginalized areas, policies of forced retention often cause tensions and conflicts in the communities they are meant to help. Health-care workers often approach the mandatory placement as a penance rather than as a rewarding opportunity (Huish, 2009). It is common for communities to feel a level of mistrust for inexperienced health-care workers who are not from those communities (Candib, 2004). In some cases, this can lead to the community building resentment against health-care workers and the services provided. Furthermore, the constant cycling of personnel in vulnerable communities can work against any sincere efforts to build trust and relationships in the community that might lead to public health strategies, education programs, and preparing community youth for medical education.

South Africa has introduced policies for financial compensation for overtime, continuing professional development, and supervised internships for new graduates. These strategies are certainly improvements. Still, with over 73 percent of general practitioners working in the private sector and migration holding at

18 percent (for physicians), these strategies need to be expanded and opened up further (Padarath et al., 2006). While these strategies seem to be aimed in the right direction, they must be accompanied by political and infrastructural support that will ensure that working conditions in vulnerable communities can be places that health-care workers could build prosperous careers. Here, the governments and recruiting agencies in the global North should play an active role in building this capacity for South Africa rather than depleting it.

The official policies in South Africa are not improving choices for workers. Rather, they surrender to a supposed inevitability of migration by creating service contracts in an almost punitive fashion. The country has not made noticeable gains to remedy poor public sector structural conditions as a result of migration and a lack of opportunities for health-care workers to flourish in that system. Because of this moral imbalance, it is hardly fair to judge the career path of a South African migrant doctor as having unbridled agency within a socio-economic vacuum as Snyder suggests; it is a career that is conditioned by these faulty structures. The policy responses echo this by furthering migration and creating forced-contract retention strategies. Such policy hardly opens choice for the health-care worker to build a long-term career as much as it is a desperate attempt to slow the bleeding of what is perceived to be an inevitable force.

Chronicle of the Philippines

The Philippines has an estimated 150,000 nurses and 18,000 physicians working in eighty countries, making it the country with the most overseas health-care workers. The country licensed 25,951 nurses in 2005; 31,275 in 2007; and 27,765 in 2008 (Lorenzo, Galvez-Tan, Icamina, & Javier, 2007). Of these licensed nurses, 46,507 have taken the National Council Licensure Examination (US NCLEX). In addition to the 80,000 Philippine-educated nurses in the United States, 2.1 percent of the United States physician workforce has come from the Philippines. With immigration opportunities for nurses being far more numerous and simplistic than for physicians, between 1,200 and 4,000 Filipino doctors are retraining as nurses in order to pursue migration in any given year ("Filipino doctors," 2007; Lorenzo et al., 2007). At this rate of attrition, it is estimated that by 2015 the Philippines will not be able to support a functioning primary care system due to a lack of trained physicians working in the country. Two hundred hospitals have closed in the last decade, and trained medical personnel do not attend to 60 percent of deaths.

Earning more money abroad in order to send home remittances is the principle reason for the mass exodus of health-care workers. A Filipino nurse earns about $2,400 or ₱120,000 (Philippine pesos) per year compared to a US nurse's average salary of $48,900. Considering that a Filipino physician earns about $40,000 per year, the switch in career paths to an overseas nurse for an additional $8,900 means that an additional ₱445,000 can be sent home. Indeed, one day's salary for a nurse working in the United States is equal to one month's salary for a nurse working in the Philippines. Were a Filipino nurse working in the United States to send home even one day's pay each month, the increase in familial earnings would be exceptional. Many families, and in some cases entire communities, pool their resources to send a member to one of the many costly private nursing programs in Manila (where tuition for a four-year program can total $80,000 or ₱4 million) in the hopes that he or she will migrate and provide much-needed remittances.

With the closing of two hundred understaffed hospitals in the last decade, and even as the domestic public health-care system stands ready to collapse, the Filipino government applauds the courage and dedication of the overseas foreign workers (OFWs). With 40 percent of the country's GDP going towards foreign debt repayment and less than 2 percent of the public budget spent on public health, the government has claimed that the road to well-being lies in remittances (Debuque-Gonzales & Gochoco-Bautista, 2007). It is hoped that through this boost in individual purchasing power, the domestic economy will sustain itself and citizens will be able to afford needed goods and services. At Manila's airport, the OFWs have special customs lines, and there are massive murals from the government welcoming them and/or wishing them good luck as national heroes. The hero status does not extend to the health-care workers who stay behind.

With such veneration from the state, it is not surprising that health-care workers who do not pass the foreign board exams or who choose not to migrate see their place as second-rate in the national psyche. In various first-person interviews with administrators at the University of Manila and the Philippine Nurses Association conducted in April 2009, there was a call for "managed migration strategies" where destination countries nations would compensate source countries for the receipt of qualified health-care workers. In the meantime, the training institutions have resorted to forced retention strategies and the under-qualification of degrees in order to curb the exodus. A nursing student is not able to graduate until he or she completes a term of service in a rural or vulnerable part of the country. Likewise, part of the degree qualification for doctors coming out of the University of the Philippines involves a one-year placement in the outlying islands. After students serve their time in these posts, they are free to seek migration opportunities abroad.

While this strategy may bring rural communities access to health-care workers where currently there are none, it sends a vicious political message to both health-care workers and vulnerable communities. The message reads that vulnerable communities in the Philippines are not worthy of qualified health-care workers. Indeed, it suggests that those professionals belong to other countries. Further, it says that the government values remittances more than it does the health and well-being of the vulnerable. To the health-care workers it suggests that qualified doctors are anywhere but in vulnerable communities. What is more, there is nothing to stop students from leaving the country before they graduate in the hopes that they could become a domestic service worker. Many nursing students already seek employment in South Korea and Hong Kong as domestic caregivers rather than as nurses. Although the salary of a domestic worker may be well below a nurse's wages in the host country, it is still more than a nurse's salary in the Philippines. If the goal is simply to send remittances, why wait an extra couple of years?

Sending the message that migration is both prestigious and inevitable, the Philippine policy leaves little desire in the next generation of health-care workers to serve rural and vulnerable communities. Clearly, the choice to stay falls on a different moral platform than the choice to remain in the country.

Chronicle of Cuba and Venezuela

In South Africa and the Philippines, there are few moral or economic options for health-care workers to enjoy affluent careers with appropriate remuneration, extended learning, stability, safety, and moral validation for their services to the poor and vulnerable. In these countries, lifelong service to the poor is an exception; it is not the norm. Hence, the choice to migrate is hardly a choice at all. Migration becomes a sort of inevitability, and service to the poor simply does not compete on the same moral grounds.

For this reason, the story of Cuba and Venezuela is tremendously important. Cooperation between the two countries has provided health-care workers with the choice to serve the vulnerable. The cooperation efforts may not offer opportunities for outrageous remuneration, but they do offer health workers political and social support to help the poor; something that few countries do. Since 2003, nineteen thousand Cuban health-care workers have left their country for Venezuela's vulnerable communities to provide health-care services to people who in some cases had never seen a doctor. Fifty-eight Cuban doctors signed up for the program, Barrio Adentro (into the neighbourhood), on April 16, 2003. By December 14 of that year, over ten thousand Cuban doctors were providing primary care services in the shantytowns of Caracas. The doctors live in the communities, providing twenty-four hour care. The program focuses on general health, and offers primary care and education in health promotion and disease prevention within the neighbourhood. Physicians come with and dispense their own medications, many of which could treat the majority of easily treatable diseases that run rampant in slum conditions (Sanchez, 2006).

The program attended to the needs of 17 million people by 2006 with four-teen thousand physicians participating. This ensured one physician for every 250 families. Five thousand additional nurses and technicians participated in the program. The program expanded to offer free dental care and to include Operación Milagro by mid-2004 ("Operación Milagro," 2006). By 2006, five thousand young Venezuelans were training for medical school alongside the Cuban brigades in the slums (Muntaner, Salazar, Benach, & Armada, 2006).

In 2004, Barrio Adentro recorded an average of 6.4 million consultations per month, which totals 76.8 million per year. From 1994 to 1998, there were not 70 million recorded consultations within the entire Venezuelan public health system. The free basic services have expanded to include six hundred diagnostic centres with twenty-four hour emergency care and 150 operating theatres. X-ray, ultrasound, endoscope, micro-analytic systems, electrocardio-graphic, and ophthalmology facilities are included in these sub-centres. There are also thirty-five designated hi-tech centres that offer CDIs, CAT scans, and MRI scans (Muntaner, Salazar, Rueda, & Armada, 2006; Sanchez, 2006).

For a country that lost 20 percent of its GDP in 2002, suffered through 25 percent unemployment, had growing hunger rates, and a steady out-migration of health-care workers, Venezuela's political cooperation with Cuba provided much-needed support to the impoverished.

This cooperation is grounded in amicable relations between the leaders of both countries, but it also provides mutual economic benefits. Their coop-eration worked to strengthen and legitimize the newly formed ALBA accord between Cuba, Venezuela, and other states in the Americas, and it helped to bol-ster Cuba's relations with members of the Caribbean Community (CARICOM) (Maingot, 2006). Indeed, these are notable political and economic benefits.

Barrio Adentro is also one of the only opportunities in the world today that allow health-care workers to build a sustainable career to the serve the poor. Certainly, the salaries are well below North American and European standards, but the Cuban and Venezuelan governments absorb many of the living costs for the health-care workers. Furthermore, the missions encourage health-care work-ers to develop innovative strategies aimed at public education and health promo-tion strategies. And indeed, for the physicians serving the program and the young trainees from the barrios, it offers an opportunity to serve the community where before there was no opportunity. Cuban health-care workers volunteer to serve in Barrio Adentro. The Cuban doctors maintain their monthly salary in Cuban pesos, which equates to about $30 per month. In addition, the Cuban govern-ment provides a $100 monthly bonus payable upon completion and return to Cuba at the end of their contract. This salary is held in a Cuban bank account and can be accessed by family members during the duration of the health worker's time abroad. Workers are also given $200 for living expenses above the provision of housing, supplies, and food by the Venezuelan government. Physicians in the program are able to train others and continue to build their careers as medical educators and specialists in community health. As a Cuban physician from Granma Province did in western Uganda, some even take to writing textbooks and education material for students and teachers in their overseas placements.

Often labelled "doctors for oil," Cuba offers to send doctors to any CARICOM nation if asked. Often the only requirement is that the host country cover the costs of airfare, housing, board, and stipends of the Cuban doctors, costs that would amount to less than $5,000 per year per physician (Macintyre & Hadad, 2002).[4] Venezuela, on the other hand, offers petroleum with reduced tariffs to any CARICOM country to reduce outlays of national revenue towards energy imports. Oil is sold to partner countries at market value, but only a fraction of its value is due upon receipt and the rest is paid through credit at about 1 percent interest. Indeed, these are two separate policies grounded in international forums that have done well to warm relations between the countries and the region.

Haiti has benefited from these pan-regional policies. Between 1995 and 2010, it received over six thousand Cuban doctors and even while paying for expensive food and industry imports from the United States (as directed by IMF-enforced policy), Haiti was able to save money by purchasing oil from Caracas. In a country with only one physician for every four thousand inhabitants, and with more than 7 percent of its GDP consumed by foreign imports, of which 0.5 percent is oil imports, these policies offer some financial relief and social benefit (Galeano, 2001).

Despite the impressive number of Cuban doctors and Venezuelan medical students who choose service to Barrio Adentro, some do leave to serve in the private sector or try for migration to the United States. As of 2007, 420 physicians have left the program. This number, based on both Cuban and US data, accounts for just 3 percent of all physicians involved in the program. This number is all the more impressive when one considers that the US State Department has a $10 million program aimed at recruiting Cuban and Cuban-trained doctors from poor areas. At a time when Cuba is making an enormous effort to offer support to serve the poor, the United States is doing all that it can to lure health-care workers away from the poor through the Cuban Medical Professional Parole Program (CMPP) (Millman, 2011). The US Department of Homeland Security created the CMPP to intentionally recruit Cuban and Cuban-trained doctors working in other countries. A total of 1,574 CMPP visas have been issued as of 2011 to Cubans and Cuban-trained doctors posted around the world.

The message here is clear that even a program like Barrio Adentro, one that offers service to the poor and solid career options for its participants, may be unable to quell completely the temptations of migration through CMPP initiatives. Be that as it may, the bigger message here is that 96 percent of Cuban health workers see it through. The overwhelming majority of *brigadistas* reject the temptation from the State Department. This sends a clear message to struggling health-care systems around the world: there is enormous moral will to overcome the global deficit of health-care workers in vulnerable communities. Instead of paying 40 percent of the GDP to foreign debt repayment or grooming students for health-care exodus, it is possible that systems can meet the needs of the vulnerable while building prosperous cooperation with other countries struggling to overcome the burdens of underdevelopment. And it is possible for health workers to choose service to the poor.

Barrio Adentro and the social missions between Cuba and Venezuela demonstrate that health care can flourish, not through massive remuneration but through promising good medical services that are politically valued, morally just, and financial rewarding. With a global deficit of 4.3 million health-care workers, how is it possible to address this deficit without offering choice for health-care workers to practise in vulnerable communities? Indeed, it is unlikely that the salaries in the barrios of Caracas could be compared to those found in Manhattan, but the immediate need for basic primary care is not the same between the two places either. If programs like Barrio Adentro can succeed in empowering people from poor communities to choose to work for poor communities (because, despite the modest salary, the costs of living are met, prestige is granted, upward learning can occur, and it is possible to balance the demands of career and family), the question becomes what is holding others back from flourishing in other poor communities?

If the health-care worker migration question continues to be approached with the sense that recipient countries are not, in fact, poaching and that individuals should be held to account for their own decisions, then the problem may never be completely solved. Indeed, the lucrative options in the global North will continue to exist, and the North will continue to encourage health-care workers from the global South to migrate. But if source countries could muster the political will to embrace programs such as Barrio Adentro, a real choice for health-care workers to serve the vulnerable would exist. It is possible that the choice to be a health-care worker does not come down to remuneration in all cases. Nor does the choice to migrate take place in a vacuum. And it is possible that people enter the profession because they feel compassion to care for the ill. And, perhaps, it is possible that some health-care workers get into the game in the first place because they are driven to serve the underserved.

A Moral Obligation for States to Cooperate, Not Compete

Before closing this chapter, there is more to discuss about the question of choice for would-be migrant health-care workers or would-be employees of medical tourism, and why Cuba's examples of Operación Milagro and Barrio Adentro hold potential for a new understanding of global health ethics. If a health-care worker enters medicine with the idea of performing plastic surgery in order to retire rich, or if he or she believes in the power of remittances, then that is a personal choice for which globalization will assist greatly. But what if that health-care worker chooses to get into medicine because he or she is unsatisfied with the current inequity in care and are passionate for the needs of the poor but find that there is no structural support to serve the vulnerable? Or what if they cannot make ends meet in the public system? Or what if they place themselves at risk or are not professionally valued at home? What if they then migrate or specialize in radiology so they can land a job in a medical tourist post because there are no structures to support their service ethic to the public good?

If this is the case, then the ethical debate goes well beyond the level of the individual and their personal agency; it involves the role of public health-care systems, nation states that condition that agency, and international financial institutions that regulate it. Instead of working competitively to lure health-care workers away from places where they are most needed, programs such as Barrio Adentro and Operación Milagro are grounded in cooperation to allow health-care workers to bring care to those who currently have none. Such cooperation between states will not occur through mandatory retention strategies or by devaluing a health-care worker's degree until service to the state is completed. It will only occur through positive supportive infrastructure that gives health-care workers a choice to go to a vulnerable community. It will need to begin with national innovation, and it will require international cooperation. If it is possible to see such service programs flourish, not through aid or small missions but through massive capacity-building campaigns, then it will certainly be one of the greatest advancements in modern medicine and public health care in the twenty-first century.

Galeano (1997) writes that philosophies of pillage have been around for hundreds of years, be it for material or human resources. Regardless of our habits of the past, Cuba's programs demonstrate that trends can be broken. They show, also, that national interests can be fulfilled through this sort of outreach. Political support in the international arena combined with participation in supportive economic trade relations speak to this. No state constructs foreign policy to go against its national interests, and in this case, Cuba has made a means of fulfilling its own interests by supporting others.

By the thousands, they see it through, and they do it often with meagre pay (compared to wealthy countries), sparse living conditions, and long separations from family. If health-care workers from these two, relatively poor nations can demonstrate this sort of enthusiasm, imagine the possibilities if wealthy nations followed suit. Could tens of thousands of health-care workers serving the poor swell to hundreds of thousands? Could resources for the training of people from vulnerable communities for vulnerable communities take off? Could nations offer health-care workers as much moral incentive to serve in Bujumbura as to serve in Stockholm?

To achieve this, however, there would need to be genuine cooperation between nations to address the severity of the global human resources for health crisis. Only then would it be possible to create apertures for dialogue and exchange. Here, the relationship between Cuba and Venezuela has much to offer the world. Together, they have demonstrated one of the greatest advancements in medicine: universal access through cooperation, not competition.

The global need for human resources for health is enormous. Cuba, the Philippines, and South Africa have positioned their health care workforce to respond to international needs. For the Philippines, the focus is on acquiring cash by having nurses serve the affluent. South Africa has made some attempts to confine the movement of workers, but the inequities continue to persist as the remuneration potential involved with working overseas outweighs government attempts to keep health workers at home. Cuba's approach is to garner monetary and political support through bilateral trade relations. As this chapter has shown, the Filipino model has devastated the domestic health-care system, but the Cuban approach has been able to meet the needs of vulnerable populations abroad without jeopardizing health care integrity at home. Even though Cuba suffers from material resource shortfalls, the state's ability to manage and regulate its medical internationalism is ultimately to the benefit of national needs than is a system that encourages massive outmigration in the hopes of remittance payments.

The message from this comparison is that regulation of some form is needed in both managing the training of human resources for health and for placing health workers into international geographies of care. If it is possible for poor countries like The Gambia to contribute peanuts (quite literally, peanuts) back to Cuba for the receipt of health-scare services, then it should be possible for resource-flush nations that drive the brain drain to contribute assistance to countries such as the Philippines that have given enormous contributions to the migration pipeline. Both Cuba and the Philippines demonstrate that it is possible to muster the political will to train a global health workforce. The challenge that remains is in finding a way to regulate the system so that it wants to offer health-care workers the opportunity to serve the marginalized as much as it currently wants to export caregivers for the receipt of wealth.

CHAPTER 4

THE NEW DOCTOR BLOOMS:

THE ETHICS OF MEDICAL

EDUCATION

As a form of development and security assistance to Latin America, the United States trained more than sixty-one thousand soldiers and police at the School of the Americas (Gill, 2004). It was a military training base funded by the US government but located in Panama. Many of the graduates went to work for dictatorships in Chile, Argentina, Guatemala, Nicaragua, and Bolivia. Officially established as a strategic initiative to quell leftist uprisings in the hemisphere, the program's curriculum also trained students in advanced interrogation and torture techniques. It was a curriculum for governments who wanted to see unions broken, activists intimidated, writers silenced, and artists disappeared.

When El Salvador and Honduras went to war with each other in 1970, both dictators had graduated from the School of the Americas. Other star graduates from the School of the Americas included Leopoldo Galtieri, who was a chief architect of Argentina's Dirty War, which saw thousands of leftist activists, union leaders, and students disappeared. Many were tossed out of planes or helicopters into the ocean. Roberto Viola was another graduate who became president of Argentina during the Dirty War; he was later convicted to seventeen years in prison for human rights violations. Guatemala's former dictator Efraín Ríos Montt, "The Death Angel," was also an alumnus of the School of the Americas. He ruled Guatemala with an iron fist beginning in 1982 and famously said that a true Christian carries the bible in one hand and the machine gun in the other (Roeser, 2007). Guatemala's civil war led to the deaths of 200,000 Guatemalans, the majority of whom were Indian. Ríos Montt's military regime committed atrocious crimes against humanity, including massacres, rape as a weapon, torture, and genocide against Guatemala's Indians. Two truth commissions have illuminated the crimes of Guatemala's civil war, and from these commissions, the rule of Ríos Montt stands out as the most alarming and gruesome of the entire thirty-six-year war (Lovell, 2000).

Blakeley (2006) points out that accusations of human rights violations have been made against less than 1.5 percent of the graduates of the School of the Americas. The human rights violations that occurred against the indigenous and poor of the Americas is known to be widespread, but not all of the criminals have been brought to justice and many likely never will. But Blakeley argues that looking at the impact of the School of the Americas on a case-by-case basis is not necessarily the best approach to critiquing this program. Rather, it should be viewed as a project of regimented protocols for torture, the forceful extraction of information, and as a product of broader tolerance for human rights violations. The tens of thousands of graduates from the School of the Americas were not monsters as Galeano (1992) argues, but merely technocrats.

Since the closing of the School of the Americas, there has been a broader consciousness to move towards capacity building that invests resources into policies that work to heal bones rather than in institutions that aim only to break them. Fortunately, in what can be taken as the complete antithesis to the school of the Americas, Cuba is doing exactly that: training health-care workers to go where few have had the chance to go in the past.

Why Human Resources for Health Matters

Building capacity for human resources for health is Cuba's national strength. They have done it well in the twentieth century, and for the twenty-first century, the country is working to train more health-care workers for the global South than the world has ever seen. At the rate that Cuba is going, in the next decade the country will outstrip the School of the Americas for the number of graduates that have gone into the field. While the US government's human resource outreach programs came through the military, Cuba's approach comes through medicine. And as this chapter will show, investing in people through humanitarianism, rather than militarism, can make a world of difference.

Despite the numerous global efforts to scale up the global health workforce, there continues to be too many patients without doctors and too many doctors without patients. Indeed, many countries have tried for decades to increase the supply of their health-care workers. Often, economic demand for health workers in the global North brings physicians to wealthy centres, while a lack of economic and moral incentives leaves poor communities behind. Such areas often have the highest health risks and rarely enjoy adequate services. It is a dynamic problem beyond the mere lack of trained physicians and public health-care workers. The outflow of health workers from the global South to the global North is the result of a global imbalance of wealth and economic opportunism. Cuba's efforts to bolster the number of health workers in poor areas are ambitious, as they directly compete against broader processes of globalization in order to present an innovative ethics of capacity building as humanitarianism.

Currently, the world's 1,691 medical schools and 5,492 nursing schools simply cannot fill the global deficit of 4.3 million health-care workers (Giraldo, 2007). Beyond the numbers, a more complicated problem emerges: How well equipped and confident are health professionals at meeting the needs of vulnerable populations? A health worker is someone who has a primary responsibility to improve health (WHO, 2006). But do the training processes equip graduates with the confidence to work in the field? For the WHO, the working actions of an individual that are directed at building health qualifies someone as a health worker, so a doctor employed by a mining company could be classified as a health worker despite working for an unhealthy industry, while an interior decorator at a hospital would not be considered a health worker even though his or her actions may contribute to health (WHO, 2006, p. 2).

How much attention is put into core health sciences curricula to prepare health-care workers for resource-poor conditions? The answer is not much. Recent efforts to assist in the 2010 Haiti earthquake speak to this. Archer, Moschovis, Le, and Farmer (2011) claim that many of the short-term aid workers arrived with very little preparation for the sort of conditions they would face let alone the historical and cultural factors that led to the endemic poverty in Haiti. Often, health-care workers who serve the destitute are accomplishing goals through trial and error, improvisation, some supervision, and, at times, lots of luck. Can medical education work to put essential competencies for disaster medicine or service in the global South at the heart of curriculum?

Any direct connections between health and the role of health-care professionals are also subject to debate. Much has been written from the point of view that health is the result of conditions beyond the product of a trained professional's craft. At times, this argument has been used as a way to avoid investment in human resources for health. However, health is the product of one's lived environment: both environmental and social. There are famous studies, such as Wilkinson's (1996), on how social inequalities worsen health outcomes for societies as a whole, and thousands of studies from epidemiology and environmental science connect health to our natural world. Nevertheless, when medical emergencies arise, a clean environment is not enough. The balance lies in ensuring that people enjoy a health landscape that is conducive to good environmental and social health determinants, but also has available resources, such as health-care workers, to treat illness and help to maintain health.

This understanding of health in place echoes concerns that we should de-medicalize health and move beyond concerns just about disease (Kearns, 1994). In new efforts to scale up human resources for health, there is room to work to overcome the characterization of health-care workers as concerned only with diseases and not people, so as to see health-care workers as stewards of health who are able to provide care through clinical competency and through knowledge of social and environmental determinants of health. It is this sort of broad understanding of health that Cuban-trained health workers bring to the world.

The WHO's (1946) understanding of health as "a state of complete physical, mental and social well-being, and not merely the absence of disease or infirmity" (p. 2), leads to notions of health stewardship as a broad and complex relationship where the health-care professional can have a leadership role in ensuring the healthy state of individuals and the development of healthy communities. The WHO approach recognizes health as a process of relationships; its constitution makes two important claims that merge health with considerations of rights and human security. It reads: "The enjoyment of the highest attainable standard of health is one of the fundamental rights of every human being without distinction of race, religion, and political belief, economic or social condition. The health of all peoples is fundamental to the attainment of peace and security" (WHO, 1946). In order to achieve these goals, the development of trained health-care professionals is fundamental in encouraging and maintaining health for individuals and their communities.

The WHO (2006) estimates that 59 million persons constitute the paid global health workforce. However, these people are unequally distributed across the globe. Often countries "with the lowest relative needs have the highest numbers of health workers" (p. 8). While Africa endures 24 percent of the global burden of disease, it only has 3 percent of the global health workforce at its disposal. Cuba is not alone as a Southern nation that possesses great potential to build capacity for human resources for health. Pakistan, for example, has the facilities to train 5,400 physicians, but is unable to recruit qualified students let alone retain many of its graduates. Almost 35 percent migrate or do not go into any form of practice (Talati & Pappas, 2006). Moreover, the overwhelming majority of these graduates would likely dedicate their skills to the private sector and to urban care centres (Thaver, Harpham, McPake, & Garner, 1998), which limits access for rural and indigent populations. Although one doctor exists for every 2,100 inhabitants in that country, Talati and Pappas (2006) admit that Pakistan cannot meet its health-care needs due to outmigration and service inequities within the national system. On a global scale, human resources for health vary wildly. Cuba has a doctor-to-patient ratio of 1:159; Switzerland has 1:277; the United States has 1:390; Canada has 1:467; Ecuador has 1:675; South Africa has

1:1,290; Haiti has 1:4,000; Nepal has 1:4,761; and Malawi has 1:50,000. These ratios do not adequately represent the quality of health-care or the state of health within and between nations, but they do provide a telling glimpse as to the inequality of health care capacity on a global scale. Seventy percent of the world's physicians and sixty percent of the world's nurses work in urban areas (WHO, 2006). Fifty-seven countries are unable to meet a minimal threshold for human resources for health; Southeast Asia suffers from the greatest shortage in absolute terms, and sub-Saharan Africa requires an increase in human resource of almost 140 percent to meet its threshold (WHO, 2006, pp. 11–12).

The WHO claims that millions of dollars are needed for training and development in order to relieve this situation. It is unlikely that money alone will be enough to overcome current inequities. Simply training a health professional does not guarantee an improvement in health-care accessibility or health promotion at the community level. It is important to consider the institutional ethics of medical training to assess whether health-care professionals have the commitment and the confidence necessary to meet community needs. Neoliberal health-care reforms to lower and middle-income countries (LMICs) increasingly distribute health-care resources based on an ability to pay, and physicians are often trained so that they will be successful in delivering pay-for-service care that rarely considers principles of disease prevention and health promotion.

Health workers face challenging structures that have furthered inequity. Neoliberalism, Harvey (2005) argues, is best understood as an intentional political-economic agenda of increasing the wealth and power of global elites at the expense of further marginalizing and impoverishing the poor. Often this is achieved through the systematic dismantling of social services that are then replaced with private, pay-for-use services. The state services become weaker or non-existent and the private sector gains market share. Broadly labelled as structural adjustments, poverty reduction strategies, or austerity measures, such reforms have had devastating effects on the public sector of LMICs (Bloom & Standing, 2001; Bundred & Levitt, 2000). Internally- and externally-driven reforms have weakened public health-care sectors in particular. In many health systems, austerity measures hamper much-needed capacity for long-term sustainability, and for expanding critical service provisions to the marginalized (Shah, 2006). Investing in public infrastructure is neglected by neoliberal policy that elides the overutilization and exploitation of public services. Material and human resources, all too often, find their way into the private sector, and the extremely marginalized are not able to purchase health-care services (Aluwihare, 2005), or will be forced to make difficult economic decisions, such as foregoing health care in order to pay veterinary bills for their livestock.

The prescriptions for better health care from the IMF all too often view public expenditure as a social malady, while investing in national resources towards external debt repayment is a means to wellness for the national economy. Human needs become secondary to economic needs.

When economic measures result in poor salaries, a lack of public resources, and deplorable working conditions, health workers tend to leave. The draw of physicians out of LMICs has significant consequences, especially for the most vulnerable (Cooper, 2005; Hallock, Seeling, & Norcini, 2003). Workers often face poor management, heavy workloads, lack of facilities, and challenging living conditions (Astor et al., 2005). As Aluwihare (2005) points out, the impacts of physician migration range from the loss of an education pool to service shortcomings, and these can hinder clinical and public health research within donor countries. He notes that systems must have a patient focus, but they must also ensure that there is continuing medical education (CME) (Aluwihare, 2005, p. 16). Physician renewal is very important to the well-being of public health services. Replenishing knowledge through CME at the national level is vital, especially in poorer countries (Chikanda, 2006).

Poor working conditions at home and lucrative opportunities abroad are macro-factors in encouraging migration, but as Astor et al. (2005) show, many medical schools in the global South furnish their graduates with highly specialized skills that are aimed at meeting market demand and earning prestige in the global North. This compounds problems of access to health-care professionals, as many graduates ultimately seek out prestigious and lucrative options in the global North because that is where their skills can be best utilized. To say that a simple increase in personnel will solve the problem is naïve. It overlooks the unequal geographical development of human resources for health. Specialists, who are trained to work in clinical conditions that have access to technology and resources, are unlikely to engage in public practices where clinics do not have even basic diagnostic equipment such as X-rays. In Zimbabwe, where public clinics are dangerously short of supplies and infrastructure, the national medical school graduates about one hundred physicians per year, but between 1995 and 1998, the number of practising physicians increased by only fifty-one from 1,575 to 1,626 (Chikanda, 2006). Brain drain is a major cause of this decline, but retirement and replacement also play their roles. Kirigia, Gbary, Muthuri, Nyoni, and Seddoh (2006) have calculated the cost of this brain drain in Kenya to be a loss of almost $518,000 to the national economy for each nationally trained physician that migrates out of the country.

Economic demand in the global North and the push for specialization of medical schools in the global South drives the migration pipeline (Garrett, 2007). As more and more health-care professionals seek placements in the global

North, the demand for physicians among vulnerable populations continues to grow in the global South (Talati & Pappas, 2006). Fewer skilled health professionals practising disease prevention and health promotion at the community level in the global South creates a culture of health care that is reactive rather than proactive, institutional rather than communal, and costly rather than affordable.

Cuba's ELAM works against this trend. Based on Martí's teachings of international solidarity, the school aims to send physicians exactly to the regions where other medical schools, directly or indirectly, are discouraging their graduates from practising. Encouraging physicians to practise in underserved areas not through a written contract or forced obligation but through a moral commitment to service is a phenomenon that deserves further exploration by medical schools around the world in order to understand how ethics can ultimately shape geographies of health care.

With many domestic health-care systems becoming increasingly inequitable, the future of global health equity looks grim. Even the hope of emboldening biomedical health-care provision in the global South can be just as problematic as it can be helpful. Western medical practice has a tradition of imposing ideals, methods, and technologies inappropriate to local conditions (Tong, 2001). Many critiques of Western medicine in the global South have taken exception to its tendency to be culturally invasive, dependent on extensive material support, and strictly inequitable (Waitzkin & Iriart, 2001).

Even humanitarian outreach programs run into challenges. An MSF brigade may work in an outlying area of the global South to provide vaccinations or HIV treatment, but basic elements of primary care may not be offered to the community by the brigade or by local health-care workers on a sustainable long-term basis. Such aid programs are the norm when it comes to providing health-care to the vulnerable through aid rather than through local-level capacity building. No doubt, the services provided do make a difference, but they do not necessarily enable individuals within the community to have control over their own promotion of health and well-being. There is a clear need to evaluate alternatives that aim to give control back to the community. MSF and Partners in Health realize the importance of local-level capacity building, and they are always expanding programs for local training. Indeed, one of the best examples of capacity building for human resources for health comes from Cuba.

The Origins of ELAM

Before it became home to the largest medical school in the world, the ELAM campus was a naval academy. Unlike the architects of the school of the Americas who believed the world needed more soldiers, Cuba believed the world could make do with fewer. Between 1998 and 2009, it has received over 16,500 foreign students from across the Americas, Africa, and Asia. ELAM students come to Cuba to receive a free medical education over a six-year period, with all services, books, accommodation, food, and necessities covered by MINSAP. It is a medical school exclusively for foreign students, and Cuba asks for no tuition. Their only debt upon graduation is a moral commitment to offer their services in their home country, preferably in the communities that are desperately underserviced. The goal of this program is to reverse the global brain drain by building capacity in under-resourced settings.

It is an innovative program developed in response to the aftermath of Hurricane Mitch in Central America in 1998. Cuban medical brigades working in the affected region realized that droves of doctors would be required in order to improve the region's human resources for health in primary care (Cockburn, St. Clair, & Silverstein, 1999; Giraldo, 2007, January 15; Sims & Vogelmann, 2002). Instead of offering its own doctors on an ongoing basis, Cuba decided to train students from those communities so that they would eventually serve them. Soon after, they expanded the school's enrolment from victims of a single hurricane to include victims of structural violence[1] from across the Americas and Africa. By 1999, ELAM had received 1,929 students from eighteen different countries (Castro, 1999).

While Cuba offered thousands of medical scholarships in the past, ELAM's student intake is on a scale never seen before. Although it was initially a regional response to a Central American disaster, ELAM expanded to include students from fifty-four countries. The course of study runs for a total of six years, not including pre-med training. The first two years are spent on the former naval academy campus where students enjoy a small teacher-to-student ratio. In the final four years, they train alongside Cuban medical students in thirteen of the country's twenty-six medical schools. ELAM represents a medical school for the Americas, an element of Cuban foreign policy based in solidarity, a multi-national student body dedicated to serving the international community, and a large-scale capacity-building project to give students the practical and ethical tools to serve those most in need.

Some students hail from the most remote and far-reaching places in the global South and others come from wealthy centres, but they all come to Cuba to participate in a unique, ethical approach to building popular health provision. ELAM builds capacity among its students with the hope that they may eventually create broader organizational and community-wide structural changes to health care in the locales in which they practise. Organizational changes are attempts to change the operation of current health-care institutions in terms of accessibility and the level of service provided. Socioeconomic structural changes refer to broader systems that govern the operations of health care. Rigour and discipline in medical sciences are important components to the program, but the institutional ethics of service to one's community is upheld with just as much thoroughness.

It is hoped that when the graduates return to the field, they will be able to practise in clinics and treat preventable health problems in cooperation with existing public health systems. Increasing public accessibility to health care, especially in marginal communities of the global South, is counter-hegemonic to the neoliberal emphasis on market-led health care. The receipt of health-care through a costly and limited private sector is impossible for the poor and limits their ability to access care. In defiance of such hegemony, ELAM's mission is to strengthen quality public health-care services by training a workforce eager to serve the vulnerable regardless of their ability to pay for that service.

Many documentaries, newspaper articles, essays, student testimonies, and even official ELAM documentation have given Fidel Castro sole credit for this capacity-building project that affects thousands (Castañeda, 2005; Woodford, 2006). Much publicity around ELAM is embedded in an overall discourse about Cuban altruism. Themes of solidarity, pan-Americanism, and health care as a human right all abound in most reviews of the school. Other narratives are less favourable, as they take exception with material resource problems, shoddy food, and close living quarters (Johnson, 2006). As argued in the previous chapter, a genuine commitment to achieving global health equity drives Cuban medical internationalism, and it is grounded in a sense of nationalism and pan-American solidarity closely related to Martí's thinking. However, without further discussion of the actual outcomes and potential benefits of the program, this discourse would be lacking, as it would overlook the challenges and rigidities of the program and of the professional experiences of its students.

In the March 25, 2007, edition of *Granma*, ELAM's rector, Dr. Juan Carrizo, discussed the challenges of reintegrating ELAM graduates into their home communities. The journalist diminished these concerns by saying, "in any event, there is no doubt that the Latin American School of Medicine is a Cuban achievement in terms of health" (Suzarte, 2007). It is certainly true that ELAM is a tremendous capacity-building achievement, but praise alone does not easily translate into needed dialogue about how to overcome the many challenges of meeting the program's stated goals of fostering solidarity and cooperation. A general concern is that ELAM is easily glorified by academics and the media alike as being outstanding against a global backdrop of feeble capacity building. Affection for ELAM may avoid important critical dialogue concerning its outcomes, impacts, and ability to create counter-hegemony to health inequity in the global South.

Critical dialogues of ELAM's curriculum, practice, and performance do take place regularly. In fact, MINSAP, The National School of Public Health (ENSAP), and ELAM itself have many articles and position papers in a publicly accessible on-line intranet called INFOMED that examine modifications and challenges to curriculum and pedagogy. This literature demonstrates that the school's community is aware of the limits to current operations and the challenges to future developments. After reviewing the program's internal discourse on INFOMED, it is clear that ELAM is seen as a work-in-progress rather than as an unchanging success story that will solve the health-care crisis in the Americas.

ELAM's mission is to train "general doctors who are oriented toward delivering primary care in an ethical and humane manner to regions that are in need in order to facilitate human development" (Matrícula, n.d.). Yet part of its mission relies on making changes at larger scales. The program builds ethics for service at the individual level, but it is quite limited when it comes to influencing broader organizational and structural levels of health-care systems in other countries. Change at these levels is out of the school's hands, and there is little that the directors or staff can do to influence policy in a student's home country other than continue to train thousands of dedicated physicians for the vulnerable. Still, the example of a medical school offering full scholarships for foreign students is a rarity in the global health landscape. Some foundations in the United States, the United Kingdom, and Australia will cover the medical expenses of students from resource-poor countries to study medicine in the global North, but the number remains small. Notably, universities in the global North, such as Dalhousie University in Canada, sell medical seats to countries such as Saudi Arabia at enormous prices—Cdn $75,000 per student per year. ELAM has removed the barriers of finance and geographical discrimination from medical education, which in itself is one of the most radical advancements in medicine in the twenty-first century.

The Colombian novelist Gabriel García Márquez (2003) wrote, "the scalpel is the greatest proof of the failure of Western medicine" (p. 10). It is a critique of how all too often health care is seen as an investment in radical repair rather than preventative measures. ELAM's evolving pedagogy of community health and clinical practice puts greater emphasis on building health through basic means rather than radical surgery. The principles of this medical ethics, according to MINSAP, include the "preservation and maintenance of health for the people … and to work constantly where society requires it and to always be ready to bring necessary medical attention in an internationalist spirit" (Castro, 1982, p. 11).

ELAM's Role in Training a Global Health Workforce

The WHO claims that embracing human resources for health can advance the equity of care for desperately underserviced regions. Cuba attempts this by taking action to increase the quantity of health-care professionals, mostly doctors and nurses, to work in underserved regions around the world. All too often, the demand for their services is overwhelming. In East Timor, for example, violent clashes in August 1999 displaced 75 percent of the population and left only thirty-five physicians in a country of about 1 million people. That made for a doctor-to-patient ratio of one physician for every 28,571 people (*Gapminder*, n.d.). By 2004, the number of physicians had increased to seventy-nine, according to WHO (2007) data, thanks to Cuba sending an additional 182 physicians and technicians to the country to train locals. Since then, the number of health workers in the country have increased somewhat but difficult conditions persist, and based on first-person information collected from interviews in Cuba, MINSAP has offered eight hundred ELAM scholarships for East Timor youth. If all scholarships were filled, and if all graduates returned home, the doctor-to-patient ratio is estimated to become one physician for every 1,250 people.

Perhaps one of the greatest benefits of Cuba's approach is that the national medical education curriculum focuses on primary care first rather than lining students up for specialization. ELAM builds capacity in the broad sense through clinical practicum and community-based educational experiences aimed at embracing overall primary care and broad local needs (Gorry, 2005). The idea is to train doctors to treat patients not just to cure diseases. Even Walter Sisulu University in South Africa, a university aimed at providing low-cost higher education for students committed to rural development, employs Cuban doctors as professors and leaders in clinical practicum education. Cuban physician Mayra Garí spoke to MEDICC about the effectiveness of regional-specific courses saying that it "puts emphasis on the diseases that are important for that particular country and community ... the students learn based on real cases [and] in that way are learning to apply knowledge in the medical context ... then, when they go to the community or the hospital they know what to do, they become a lot more effective" (Gorry, 2005, p. 15).

I, and other researchers, met with Manuel Torigo, Director of Cooperation at the Ministry of Foreign Affairs (MINREX). He reinforced the position Cuban-trained physicians employ an ethic that is about meeting the needs of the patient rather than the disease. Cuban-trained physicians aim to serve marginalized communities over many years and even decades rather than through intermittent campaigns. Moreover, Cuban doctors are qualified to mentor up to three students from the local community as assistants while working on an international brigade. In Cuba or in other countries, Cuban medical instructors train students in the clinic so that they can develop skills through experience and not only through memorized lecture notes.

This approach of training students in the clinic and in the community is called *morfofisiologia* or morphophysiology, and it is at the heart of the Cuban approach. In addition to the ELAM students in Cuba, students receiving medical training from Cuban physicians abroad spend 70 percent of their instructional time in the clinic and only thirty percent in the classroom. In a 2007 first-person interview, Torigo noted, "A lot of students would try to improve their own material situation in which they were raised. But if we prepare them there with the doctor in the community, first of all, we have not removed the student from his environment, and the people around him begin to identify him through the rounds of the physician. It builds better trust." Torigo contends that developing institutional ethics based on practice gives students clinical confidence so that they can have the self-assurance to make real impacts in their own communities.

Long-term primary care is the goal of Cuba's foreign cooperation, but MINREX admits that it does not regard its presence abroad as something permanent. Ten years of medical internationalism in Haiti and Central America may seem like a permanent fixture, as does the lengthy thirteen-month presence of the Henry Reeve Emergency Response Medical Brigade in Pakistan and East Timor, but the end goal of these campaigns is for locals to take over.[2] In order to facilitate this goal, Cuba looks beyond traditional medical training because the in-class model does not graduate students at the rate and speed that is truly needed.

Clinical and community-centred approaches are emphasized by the WHO in order to establish a workforce for equitable primary care (WHO, 2006). The Cuban approach is aimed at improving general health and well-being rather than simply offering disease-specific diagnosis and treatment. A careful examination of the ELAM pedagogy will better explain this point.

What Is ELAM?

It is difficult to know the exact number of ELAM students as the school is in a constant state of flux with students leaving the program early and others registering late. As of November 2007, there were 8,705 registered students. MINSAP and MINREX continually expand their scholarship offers to countries: Pakistan has had one thousand ELAM scholarships offered and East Timor has had eight hundred offers extended. Students who have already received some medical training in their home countries may fast-track into Years 3 or 4. These fluxes are relatively minor. Pre-med can entail one or two years of study, depending on the student, and it may include time for intensive language training as well.

It is a time to offer assistance to students to ensure that they have the appropriate toolkits to engage in a six-year program. Some students complete ELAM's pre-med requirements within six weeks and others may take two years. The program is designed this way to afford students the greatest opportunity to succeed over the long term. With 1,477 students registered in pre-med in 2005, and 1,016 registered in 2006, it makes for a sizeable portion of the student body that have yet to fix an exact graduation date.

The school's population peaked in 2005 at eleven thousand students. Until 2005, ELAM was only absorbing students and had yet to produce graduates. By 2007, 4,465 students had graduated and 11,500 were still participating in the program; others had left the program without graduating because they were unwilling to remain in the program or unable to pass the curriculum. Still, based on data from MEDICC and from MINSAP, it is possible to give an accurate impression of ELAM's demographics for the year 2005–6 in this chapter.

By August 2011, the school had received a total of twenty-four thousand students from fifty-four countries. Typically, ELAM brings in over two thousand students each year but with the creation of a new medical education program in Matanzas, where students practise in the clinic in their first year, the international enrolment has dramatically increased. From my time working in Cuba between 2005 and 2007, I can provide a detailed breakdown of students as of July 2006. That year, ELAM had 9,970 students from twenty-eight different countries. The ELAM campus housed 3,891 students in pre-med, Year 1, and Year 2. The Facultad Caribeña de Santiago de Cuba, ELAM's campus in Santiago, receives francophone students, and in 2006 it housed 348 students from Haiti, Mali, Djibouti, and Guinea Conakry in pre-med, Year 1, and Year 2. Facultad Caribeña received 663 students from these countries studying in Years 3 to 6 for a total francophone student population of 1,011. The 5,038 ELAM students in Years 3 through 6 are trained alongside Cuban medical students in thirteen separate faculties of medicine across the country and eight facilities in Havana. ELAM students constituted roughly 90 percent of Cuba's total of thirteen thousand international medical students. Medical students not affiliated with ELAM come from around the world, including Europe and Asia. In total, foreign students from 108 different countries are in Cuba studying to become health professionals (Marimón Torres & Martínez Cruz, 2010). Not every international medical student in Cuba is studying through ELAM. For example, special bursaries for four hundred Jamaican students, 138 of whom are studying medicine, are not a part of the ELAM project.

About half of the ELAM student body studied in Havana province in 2006. The largest concentration outside Havana was in Villa Clara, with 764 students from various countries including Mexico and Nigeria. Camaguey also housed 681 students, while Cienfuegos and Sancti Spíritus, two faculties that received students from Ecuador, received 242 and 155, respectively. The smallest concentration was in Guantanamo, with only 43 students. In 2006, 150 students from Guatemala, 80 from Honduras, and 70 from Haiti completed their sixth year of training in their home communities working alongside pre-existing Cuban medical brigades.

In the initial graduating class of 1,610 students from twenty countries, the average age was twenty-six. Women constituted 45.9 percent of the class, and thirty-three different indigenous cultures could be identified. Seventy-two percent of students were identified as being from rural or economically marginalized families.

ELAM accredited 74 percent of the 2005 class (1,143 students) as having *un alto rendimiento académico,* meaning that two-thirds of the class performed well above passing standards, and 12 percent of the class received the Título de Oro, Cuba's highest award for students in medicine, given to those who maintain an average of at least 84.7 percent from inception to graduation. According to two students from the United States, ELAM is not set on creating bell curves. "We could all pass, we could all fail. We're not compared to each other here," said a student from Oakland, California.

In 2006, for all of the medical faculties, including the Facultad Caribeña de Santiago, the ELAM population by year was as follows: 1,697 in Year 1; 1,526 in Year 2; 1,316 in Year 3; 1,539 in Year 4; 1,564 in Year 5; and 1,424 in Year 6. In 2006, ELAM also had about 644 students from eighteen different communities in Ecuador. These numbers are not static and are essentially a snapshot of the program in 2006, but they still tell a particular story of who is attending the school and how many students are involved in the project. While this book focuses on the fifty-four students from Ecuador who graduated in 2005, it is worth noting that in 2006, ELAM's Ecuadorian population had about 97 in pre-med; 91 in Year 1; 98 in Year 2; 123 in Year 3; 113 in Year 4; 64 in Year 5; and 58 in Year 6. The student population, once heavily concentrated in Central America, the regions devastated by Hurricane Mitch, is now experiencing a higher intake from South America, including Ecuador. In 2006, 699 students from the region affected by Mitch graduated ELAM, while only 284 were in first year and another 291 were in pre-med. In 1999, Argentina, Bolivia, Brazil, Uruguay, Paraguay, Ecuador, and Panama boasted about fifty graduates each. In 2006, the intake from these countries had doubled with about one hundred students in first year from each of these seven countries encompassing about half of the first-year student population.

The reason for the 2006 decrease in enrolments among Central American countries is, in part, due to Cuba increasing the number of scholarship offers for students from South America. In Ecuador alone, the number of ELAM scholarships offered has doubled from five hundred in 2005 to one thousand in 2007. At the same time, the total number of students from all countries has gone down from about 11,000 in 2005 to 8,637 in 2007. The initial post-Mitch intake has decreased and now other countries are participating in the program. This is likely due to two factors. First is the difficulty in recruiting students from marginalized corners of Central America. High school (*colegio*), let alone post-secondary education, is a rarity in countries such as Honduras, and there are not enough students from modest means who meet the minimum educational level for ELAM. Second, intake increases in South America can be attributed to the warming of political relations between Cuba and some countries and active recruiting by grassroots Cuban solidarity organizations. In Ecuador, the initial recruitment in 1999 saw only a few dozen applicants. Today, due to greatly increased demand, only one in three applicants is accepted to ELAM. The increase of scholarships and the dissemination of information about the program to young students through solidarity organizations, such as the Cuban solidarity group Eloy Alfaro Brigade in Ecuador, have radically changed the recruitment process in countries such as Ecuador.

Another noticeable phenomenon is the increased Venezuelan student population, which had only fifty students arrive at ELAM in 1999, but saw its enrolment more than double in 2002. The increase in enrolment is the result of close political relations between the Cuban and Venezuelan governments since 2002. In 2007, no Venezuelans were enrolled in ELAM's pre-med program. The disappearance of Venezuelans from pre-med is a direct result of the Barrio Adentro program, which not only has received over nineteen thousand Cuban health professionals to work in the slums of Caracas and in some rural areas of Venezuela, but also trains young Venezuelans in pre-med and the primary years of medical school. Venezuelans destined for ELAM begin their medical education working alongside Cuban doctors in their communities and, in later years, have the option of transferring to ELAM. The Barrio Adentro program affords Venezuelans the chance to begin their medical education through clinical practicum education within their own communities.

By no means is ELAM meant to exclude those from the global North. With five hundred scholarships offered to American students since 2001, just over one hundred students have come to ELAM so far. The first group arrived in 2001 and comprised eighty-nine students from fifteen different locations. US students are required to have at least a college-level diploma. The directors found that the pre-med curriculum was too advanced for American high-school graduates, and, as a result, the program requires candidates from the United States to have some advanced education (Latin American School of Medicine—How to apply, 2007). While this can be seen as an additional barrier for American students, it can help to fast track some, such as Cedric Edwards, who came to ELAM in 2001 and graduated in 2005.

Recruitment

It is no easy task to seek out and recruit thousands of students from over two dozen countries. During my attendance with the MEDICC delegation in 2007, one doctor asked Rector Juan Carrizo how ELAM is able to recruit individuals who want to return to their home communities rather than seek out lucrative gains. The rector replied that the students come with convictions to serve the poor; they have come from humble means, and when they arrive at the school, ELAM reinforces their ethical foundation of service and humanism so that upon graduation they will focus on their community's health-care problems before advancing their own monetary interests. Among countries, the recruitment process of ELAM students differs and continues to evolve. Applications to the program are ultimately handled by the Cuban embassy in each country, and qualified applicants are then sent on to ENSAP for final approval. In Ecuador, during the first years of recruitment, students applied through the Colegio Medico de Pichincha in Quito, which then forwarded their files to the Cuban embassy, who then made the final decision to send on the applications to ENSAP. ELAM graduate Jacqueline Rios Mateus was one of the initial recruits from Ecuador. She, along with her colleague, Dania Suarez, had been in medical school in Quito, but because of the costs of living in the city, they were uncertain as to whether they would complete their program. As with most of the Ecuadorian ELAM students in 1999, they had heard about the program through friends or various radio programs. "There was not a lot of public advertisement about this program," Jacqueline said. They told me they had an interview with a member from the Ecuadorian Ministry of Public Health and a representative from the Cuban embassy. They presented a portfolio of their credentials and then received the call to go to Cuba a few weeks later.

Of the ELAM graduates with whom I came into contact in Ecuador, all could be identified as coming from humble to modest means. The students I interviewed came from across the country—Dania from Ambato; Fany from Loja; Arlena from Zamora; Jacqueline from Santo Domingo; and Maria, Ricardo, and Elizabeth from Quito. All of these graduates except for Fany had some medical training at the public universities in Ecuador before moving to Cuba. Unlike the others, Fany came to ELAM immediately from a *colegio*. Maria and Fany told me that their parents were active members of left-wing political parties, and in fact Maria's father ran in the 2006 national election as a delegate for President Rafael Correa. None of the students came from indigenous communities; however, in later years, indigenous people from Ecuador became an increasingly large percentage of the ELAM intake. Alicia, a Quichua woman from Bolivar, told me that her sister was at ELAM, as well as many of her other Quichua friends.

Currently, the embassy handles applications directly and rapidly. While waiting in the lobby for an audience with Cuban diplomatic staff, I met Saskia Núñez Valverde. She was nervously awaiting a meeting with the embassy staff to determine if she would be accepted to ELAM. She said that she had sent in her application earlier, and the embassy had requested a meeting. She had heard about the program through a student organization at Quito's Universidad Central. I asked her if I could contact her again about the application process. She agreed to a more formal meeting, but before we could get together she was on a plane for Havana. She left within three days. The ELAM semester was already in progress, so she joined the program slightly late. On that Tuesday, she was unsure whether or not she would be heading to Havana, and by Friday she was on a plane. Saskia's departure is an example of ELAM's rapid acceptance process. Another student, Albania Gabrielo Tamayo, said that her interview took place on April 23, 1999, and on May 8 she was in Havana. This quick turnaround time not only demonstrates the students' eagerness and readiness to depart to Cuba on a moment's notice for a six-year commitment, but also the capacity for ELAM to receive and accommodate the students quickly.

Cuban solidarity organizations, as well as labour movements and leftist political parties in the student's countries, assist in the application process by disseminating knowledge, recruiting students, and helping them with their applications. The involvement of these organizations can have a filtering effect on the applications that are received by the embassy, as applicants from more humble backgrounds, indigenous communities, and rural areas may have better access to such groups. In countries such as Guatemala, Honduras, and Nicaragua, existing Cuban medical brigades help to coordinate applications to the embassy. This is a highly effective recruitment process, as the Cuban medical brigades are already in contact with some of the most humble and needy communities.

In the United States, the application process is handled through the religious organization The Interreligious Foundation for Community Organization (IFCO), more commonly referred to as Pastors for Peace. This organization, founded by Rev. Lucius Walker, volunteered to help with the selection process of all US applicants to ELAM. Moreover, the IFCO, in cooperation with MEDICC, conducts follow-ups and offers support for US students at ELAM.

The process by which applications arrive at Cuban embassies is far from standardized, and there is no consistent gatekeeping strategy in place. However, most applicants are from modest means, between the ages of 18 and 26 (30 for US applicants), physically and mentally fit, free of any criminal record, and willing to practise medicine in underserved communities in their home country. Students who are financially incapable of obtaining a medical education in their home country are favoured. So, too, are students who represent indigenous or minority communities. While a high-school education is required, many ELAM students have received some post-secondary training in their home country. Some students hail from the most isolated regions of their country; others come from the cities.

The definition of humble and needy is loose. In the first stages of the application process in Ecuador, when few knew about the initial five hundred scholarships, many applicants could be considered to be struggling financially, but they were by no means destitute. According to Ecuador's embassy in Havana and Cuba's embassy in Quito, since Cuba has offered an additional one thousand scholarships to Ecuador, and the total number of applicants has tripled, the Cuban embassy has given much more consideration to applicants from indigenous communities and of very humble means.

Students who can demonstrate a willingness and ability to return to humble communities stand a good chance of receiving an ELAM scholarship. A student from a humble background who is set on furthering his or her personal wealth through a medical education would stand less chance of receiving a scholarship than a student from Quito, dedicated to serving indigenous communities in the Amazon.

While embassies are ultimately responsible for sending the *carpeta* (file) on to Havana for final consideration, groups (such as the IFCO in the US), solidarity brigades (such as the Eloy Alfaro Brigade), socialist political parties, and universities all have the task of disseminating knowledge about ELAM. They are not gatekeepers; nevertheless, these organizations are more likely to come into contact with applicants sympathetic to Cuba who identify with the social and economic conditions of the marginalized. Spreading the news of ELAM through solidarity groups, political parties, and left-wing media narrows the application pool, and the majority of would-be applicants set on using a free six-year degree as a platform for personal gain and fortune are largely filtered out.

On the Other Side of the Desk

In 2006, the school's faculty had 466 doctors who had extensive teaching experience; most had practised overseas on medical brigades and through cooperation efforts. Teaching at ELAM is considered a prestigious posting for Cuban faculty. Rector Juan Carrizo claimed that elite faculty come to ELAM: "The best professor of anatomy will teach to a thousand students." The school boasts some of the most highly decorated researchers in medicine and science in Cuba. Dra. Estrella Rubio Bernal, for example, is a professor in biochemistry at ELAM and was awarded in 2000 the Premio Anual de la Salud, one of Cuba's top honours for health research (Professores, n.d.). Another recipient of the same prize was Dra. Lidia Cardellá Rosales, a professor in biochemistry and biological sciences. She has published various books and articles on biochemistry and general medicine (Cardellá Rosales & Hernández Fernández, 1999; Valdés Moreno, Cardellá Rosales, Rojas Palacios, & Gómez Álvarez, 2002), and she is an active researcher with the Cuban Association of Physiological Scientists. She is one of Cuba's most renowned biochemists. Indeed, many ELAM professors are active in research and publication alongside teaching.

ELAM student interviewees expressed a great deal of satisfaction not only with the thoroughness of the pedagogy, but also with how available faculty were to them outside of class. The students that I interviewed in Cuba and in Ecuador expressed much satisfaction with their relationships with faculty. Many said that it was normal to consult professors outside of class or office hours in order to seek additional help. "They want to see you pass and do the best that you can," a student from the United States commented. "I mean you'll have the top researcher in biochemistry, or someone with experience in other countries, as your teacher," a student from the United States told me. "The professors teach us in a way that emphasizes achievement … if you have an exam coming up, the professors may stay late conducting a review, or even come on a Saturday or Sunday if you need extra help," said Eugenia Amaralle from Argentina (Giraldo, 2007, January 15). Moreover, students felt that they could form personal relationships with the faculty, as class sizes at ELAM and in its partner universities are very small and intimate. Class sizes in Years 3 through 6 range between four and fifteen students per group. Sizes reflect the heavy emphasis on students working in clinical settings rather than just sitting in lecture halls to gain their clinical competency.

Students did not give the impression that classes were informal or contact with faculty was lax; rather, they expressed how comfortable they felt interacting in a professional relationship with their teachers. "The Cubans are no jokers," noted Abba Hydara, a Gambian student working alongside doctors in that country. She told MEDICC, "They taught us never to take anything for granted; to study and be disciplined; and their system was very good for us since it includes almost weekly evaluations. That kept us on our toes" (Gorry, 2005). Back in Cuba, two Costa Rican students told me that their professors were friendly but strict. They were thorough, they said. They said that if they needed help the professors would provide it. But, as they mentioned, the professors would not lower their standards to see a student pass. "You have to know your material," they said.

Preparing doctors in science, humanism, ethics, and solidarity begins in the classroom. For ELAM to produce a new kind of doctor, a special kind of professor is required. Specifically, ELAM's faculty are evaluated on their ability to involve students in the learning process. ELAM's vice-director, Midalys Castilla Martínez, emphasized that the instructors have an ethical commitment to involve students as members of the medical team throughout the learning process (Sariol, 2005). Participatory teaching shows students that they are more than able to successfully use their acquired skills. It is an important part of the pedagogy, as many students have come from poor conditions and are expected to return to them to not merely cope but to create improvements. For Castilla Martínez, an inadequate professor would throw too much information at a class all at once. Such methods "lose the motivation of the class" (Sariol, 2005). ELAM professors need to connect with students who have travelled from afar, who have remarkable differences in cultural and educational backgrounds, and who may feel daunted by their perceived personal shortcomings.

Besides the mandate to inspire students, professors who have an ongoing experience practising in other research, education, or assistance centres are sought by ELAM. "Many of our professors are adjunct with other institutions," says Castilla Martínez. "The ideal professor will be excellent in scientific and professional aspects, but also it is vital that s/he will be an ambitious educator. If s/he does not have a spirit of service then s/he will not be able to connect with the students" (Sariol, 2005). This type of connection—leading by example and bestowing confidence in the student—creates doctors dedicated to serving communities, which is the ultimate goal of Cuban health care (Alemañy Pérez, Otero Jacinta, Borroto Cruz, & Fernández, 2002). This is a crucial role in building institutional ethics and good sense.

In Cuba, medicine is meant to treat the patient before the disease. This is a professional ethic that ensures scientific rigour in medicine is used to meet the needs of the patient rather than just the disease. Medical schools around the world often encourage professional protectionism through specialization, advanced training in research, and elite networks for physicians to join (Boulet, Norcini, Whelan, Hallock, & Seeling, 2006; Hallock et al., 2003). The Cuban approach values scientific integrity, as the best researchers are highly commemorated with honours and titles, but they are not divorced from service to the community. Abba Hydara commented to MEDICC, "What I've found is that practising in a developing country is not easy. It has its limitations. The facilities for sophisticated diagnostic equipment often don't exist, for example. But if we can make a diagnosis based on a detailed clinical history and a thorough physical examination—which is true for 85 percent of cases—then we even have an edge over students trained in Western Europe or the States. And that's what our training concentrates on" (Gorry, 2005).

Hands-On, Intensive Diagnostics and Treatment Is at the Heart of the Cuban Approach

In 2007, I toured the hospital Dr. Gustavo Aldereguía Lima in Cienfuegos, Cuba, to catch up with Ecuadorians who were studying in their third and fourth year of the ELAM program. One physician commented that "for medical students, daily patient visits are an essential activity to build knowledge of the clinical setting," and daily contact is also important for a patient in secondary care. To underline this point, the physician invited me to the Cienfuegos hospital to witness the interactions of students with their professors and with their patients. The hospital has 120 residents in more than thirty specialties, and offers seventy-one postgraduate courses. It is responsible for a population of about 400,000 people. In 2006, the hospital received 242 ELAM students for upper-year training, along with an additional fifty foreigners on other scholarships.

After a brief interview in his office, the physician showed me around the hospital. Lecture theatres were modern, well lit, and equipped with digital projectors and other audio-visual devices. Notably, many of the classrooms could hold no more than fifteen students. They were purposefully designed for small class sizes and small student-to-teacher ratios. The students were consulting patients on the upper floors. A group of fifteen Cuban and ELAM students accompanied one professor and an assistant to various beds to diagnose patients, discuss their ailments, and confer over their treatment. Some critics have argued that Cuban hospitals are grim places with patients close to death's door (Golden, 2003). "Hospitals are not for the healthy," one doctor said during my visit. Given that patients are encouraged to remain their own living environments unless absolutely necessary, this would make sense. As depressing as the patient wards could be—many of the patients were terminal—the infrastructure was in no way deplorable. There were four beds to a ward, plumbing, some air conditioning, and good lighting. A nurse, student, doctor, or relative was by almost every bed doing something for someone. Seeing the seriously infirmed, the debilitated, and the terminal in this ward was sad, but it is a scene found in a hospital anywhere. What I found heartening was the sense that no one was alone—no patient was ignored or forgotten—and the ward was active with students and interims.

We journeyed up to the maternity ward on the sixth floor. In that ward, there were not as many medical students as there were nurses and nursing students. Clean and bright, the maternity ward had recently received about a dozen new and expecting mothers.

Leaving the maternity ward, we returned to the main ward and managed to have a brief conversation with a third-year student from Quito, who said that the teaching environment in the hospital was inclusive. Andrea was twenty-two years old and had experience working with indigenous communities in Ecuador. She came to ELAM with the intention of eventually working in Ecuador's Amazon. I asked her if she had ever been to La Joya de los Sachas. "That's where I want to go," she replied. Commenting on the diversity of students from Argentina, Chile, Paraguay, Uruguay, Colombia, Brazil, Venezuela, Peru, Ecuador, South Africa, and the Caribbean, she said she did not feel out of place. The small class sizes, but especially the small working groups gave her ample attention from her teachers. She commented on how there was a chance to consult with faculty and other doctors and that a strong network among the students made for a positive learning environment. She dwelled on how much time could be taken with faculty. Indeed, close contact with faculty seemed to be the norm in Cienfuegos as during that morning, students and residents seeking advice twice sidetracked my guide. Close contact with instructors and learning in the clinics seem to play an important role of building confidence and ethics in this empowerment process.

ENSAP purposefully encourages in all of its campuses close contact between student and faculty. As Rojas Ochoa (2003) argues, since 1962, Cuban universities have continually reformed their curricula, making higher education a participatory space rather than just a space to receive knowledge. Medical courses are divided into lectures, seminars, practical classes, and "education through work" that focus on in-clinic training. For lectures, ENSAP permits class sizes of ten to sixty-four students. A course on the philosophy of health has the highest number of students, while courses in society and health and hygiene and epidemiology have the smallest (Rojas Ochoa, 2003). The smallest seminar is on health administration, with a set limit of nine students. The largest seminar, psychology, has twenty-five. Practical classes do not have more than twenty-five students, and the class on society and health has only two students per instructor. "Education through work" is conducted with only one or two students and covers themes in integral medicine, hygiene and epidemiology, and the administration of health. Class sizes are small throughout the Cuban curriculum; however, a class size of one or two students for topics such as society and health, demonstrates the heightened importance of this subject material for ELAM. Society and health covers topics that deal with health promotion and disease prevention in the community. It encourages building up the health of communities and patients beyond just treating diseases. Rojas Ochoa (2003) claims that it is still a work-in-progress and that even further attention could be paid to public health in such classes. Certainly, further time and attention to public health would be beneficial, but the one-on-one class setting lends itself well to instruction on community-oriented health care.

Curriculum

While small class sizes provide an appropriate space for participatory learning and dedicated instruction, what is taught within the classroom is equally important in developing community-oriented ethics. The cornerstone for the Cuban curriculum is the two-volume set by Álvarez Sintes (2001), *Themes in Integral General Medicine* (*Temas de Medicina General Integral*). Every ELAM student receives a copy of this text, and it is meant to be kept nearby during his or her studies and into his or her practice. In the textbook, the emphasis is on the social and environmental determinants of health, as well as epidemiology. The value of disease prevention and health promotion is clear throughout the text; many chapters inform students as to what constitutes health risks in the community. Chapters consider community health, epidemiology in primary care, demographics, communication, and research methods, and the textbook as a whole has a dedicated focus on how to recognize and measure health determinants at the community level.

The first two chapters of the text explain how public health operates in Cuba. As Cuba employs an extremely integrated and intersectoral health network, it is important for students to understand how primary care requires the exchange of information and broader support from other sectors and actors. Of the fourteen chapters in Volume I, only five could be regarded as dealing specifically with core clinical competency: health, integral attention to health, family attention, primary care in health, and information on the health sciences (Álvarez Sintes, 2001). The majority of the text is either dedicated to or influenced by community-oriented care. "You study the health of the community, before the health of the individual," commented a former Mexican student who spent two semesters at ELAM.

The second volume focuses on epidemiology. Indeed, this is a departure from most medical schools that dedicate only a few hours of attention to community health and epidemiology. The Cuban approach focuses on the community level before addressing disease at the individual level. The second volume covers various health determinants ranging from accidents to infections, cardiovascular disease to nutrition. The focus of the second volume is to train students to be able to identify high-risk or at-risk patients in the community. Identifying working conditions, living conditions, and lifestyle choices are all part of approaching health through the lens of disease prevention and health promotion.

The core curriculum also dedicates time and attention to traditional and natural medicine (TNM or sometimes called, *medicina verde*). The Cuban approach encourages the adoption of alternative therapies and healing. For example, many Cuban doctors take some acupuncture training during their medical degree. It is understood that many ELAM students will return to indigenous communities where shamans are often the most trusted community health providers. Rather than reject alternative medicines, Cuban medical education embraces them. Alternative medicines are a means of understanding natural forces that influence the health of individuals. This philosophy does well to develop appreciative routines of disease prevention, health promotion, and rehabilitation in modern health-care systems (Bosch Valdés, 1999). MINSAP actively encourages continued the research into and the professional development of alternative medicines. They propose to "increase the knowledge, and existing uses, among medical technicians and professionals, about TNM" (Medicina natural y tradicional, n.d.). The adoption of TNM into the curriculum has two benefits. First, it gives greater attention to holistic disease prevention and health promotion using available and low-cost resources. Second, it affords physicians the chance to develop a sensitively towards, an appreciation of, and an acceptance of non-Western approaches to health. This is an important aspect of building community-oriented primary care in indigenous communities in South America, as more often than not tensions exist between Western and alternative models of health-care provision.

While Álvarez Sintes' (2001) *Themes in Integral General Medicine* is the foundation of ELAM's curriculum, the classroom builds on this foundation to deliver a multifaceted approach to medicine. In the classroom, students are exposed to population health principles, disease prevention, and clinical medicine (Frank & Reed, 2005). Roughly, 17 percent of all in-class hours in the six-year ELAM degree are dedicated to public health, while only 14 percent of class time is dedicated to primary care. Clinical skills are acquired mainly in the field and clinic rather than in the class. Of the total of 9,521 hours of class time that goes into a Cuban medical degree, 1,584 hours are dedicated to in-class instruction on public health and 1,388 hours are set aside for in-class training in primary care (Horas asignadas a las disciplinas, n.d.). In Years 1 and 2, the number of in-class hours devoted to public health issues is more than double the class time spent on core clinical skills. In Year 1, students spend 274 hours on public health and only 154 hours on primary care, and in the second year, students dedicate 108 hours to public health compared to 76 hours of primary care (Horas asignadas a las disciplinas, n.d.). Certainly, these themes can blend, but throughout the process, community-based care is strongly valued.

Working in the clinic, students are supposed to develop their clinical competency through experience. In the lecture hall, instruction deals with public health themes alongside traditional scientific curriculum. MINSAP claims that primary care pedagogy is not equal across the country, as some centres, such as those in Havana, are better equipped to train students in the clinic, while others, such as those in Guantanamo, require further materials and human resources. MINSAP also suggests that more time should be given for primary care instruction in *policlinicos*, as they combine spaces for practicum-based and class-based learning (Proceso docente educativo, n.d.).

While the amount of time dedicated to public health is impressive, and clinic-based learning in primary care continues to advance, it should be noted that training in essential medical sciences commands the curriculum. The conditional two years of pre-med training is almost entirely dedicated towards building competency in basic sciences and language skills. Meticulous instruction in biomedical sciences continues throughout the program. In Year 1, students cover anatomy, histology, embryology, metabolism, cellular and molecular biology, and medical informatics. Other courses, such as the history of medicine, English, and physical education (that includes physical fitness and organized sport) are integrated into the curriculum alongside medical science courses. In the first year, 26 percent of class time is dedicated to public health themes and about the same amount of time is allotted for courses such as English and physical education. The other half of class time in Year 1 is dedicated to medical science. Notably, English is taught throughout the program so that students can build competency in English medical terms, which will allow them to read the vast majority of medical literature. However, most of the ELAM students I encountered, except for those from Belize and the United States, did not command a strong oral competency of English.

In Year 2, the hours dedicated to public health are cut by more than half, and while there is a reduction in overall class time, about 80 percent is dedicated to medical science (Frank & Reed, 2005). In Year 2, students spend a greater amount of time in the clinics and in small seminars than in Year 1.

In Year 3, when ELAM students join Cuban students in the thirteen participating medical schools, almost all class time is dedicated to medical sciences such as pharmacology and internal medicine. Two courses in English are also offered in Year 3. In their third year, ELAM students go out into communities across Cuba. They assist physicians and nurses with house calls and participate alongside community health teams and family doctor–nurse teams. At this point, students are given the opportunity to use their multidisciplinary training to develop community health maps. Through in-house and worksite visitations, the ELAM graduates map out health information about the community. This includes core demographic data, vaccination records, common accident patterns, common communicable diseases, common chronic and degenerative disease, and various risk indicators. It is a skill that builds community-based learning and participation, and provides a rich understanding of health at the community level. Community health maps are an important part of Cuban health care as they provide physicians and nurses with a sound knowledge base to implement effective disease prevention and health promotion routines based on the data they collect.

Year 4 sees a return to in-class instruction in public health, with 234 hours dedicated to it, mostly through comprehensive general medicine and disaster medicine. Exactly the same amount of time, 234 hours, is dedicated to in-class instruction on primary care. During this time, students also work in hospital clinics and attend practical classes and seminars.

The first semester of Year 5 (Semester 9) is almost entirely dedicated to public health, health promotion, and disease prevention. In fact, 548 hours are dedicated to covering the topics of comprehensive general medicine, public health, psychiatry, disaster medicine, and English. Semester 10 offers a much heavier biomedical focus, with courses in otorhinolaryngology,[3] urology, orthopaedics and traumatology, ophthalmology, dermatology, forensic medicine, ethics, alternative medicine, and English.

Year 6 is almost entirely dedicated to working internships. The year breaks down into a rotating pre-professional practice with ten weeks for internal medicine, ten weeks for pediatrics, seven weeks for obstetrics and gynecology, seven weeks for surgery, seven weeks for comprehensive general medicine, and four weeks for licensing exams. Many Haitian, Honduran, and Guatemalan students return to their home countries to intern alongside Cuban medical brigades. Knowing that the realities of practice in Villa Clara are different from those of the Guatemalan highlands, ELAM encourages students to join the medical brigades for two reasons. First, it is a chance for the student to connect with the community and to foster relations so that they can eventually return after graduation. Second, it prepares students to work under conditions of poor infrastructure, hostile politics, and non-existent information networks. Cuban physicians enjoy a tremendous amount of institutional support, and even on international medical brigades, they are afforded some level of resource support from the recipient country. However, most ELAM graduates will have to find ways to reintegrate into poorly resourced clinics in local health systems alongside nationally trained physicians.

Reintegrating graduates is a concern for ELAM. The program of study is designed to give graduates a level of professional competency in clinical practice so that they can pass any qualifying exam in any country. However, this does not guarantee that all ELAM graduates will be employed after graduation. In interviews in 2007, Rector Juan Carrizo recognized the challenges and admitted that Cuba was hardly in a position to remedy the politics of licensing foreign health-care systems (Frank & Reed, 2005). ELAM's role is to build good sense at the individual level, not at the administration level within foreign systems. Political and infrastructural hurdles are in large part out of their hands.

Despite the looming challenges of reintegration, ELAM is steadfast in training doctors with the appropriate skill sets to meet the needs of the indigent. A review of articles and policy papers on curriculum reform and development published between 2001 and 2007 on INFOMED, called for greater attention to community health and modifications to curriculum to emphasize connections between individuals and their lived societies. Even papers written from the perspective of the more "pure" medical sciences, such as histology and physiology, called for greater understanding of the place of the individual in society.

Cuban medical education rejects siloed learning and embraces interdisciplinary routines. The connection between science and nature is not a radical innovation; it is a continuation of the nineteenth-century discoveries of energy transformation, cellular theory, and evolution theory. According to Rosell Puig, Dovale Borjas, and Gonzáles Fajo (2005), morphology is based on these three theories that are connected to nature and society. As Rosell Puig and Paneque Ramos (2007) argue, changes in society have significantly influenced the teaching of medicine. They regard pedagogy as socially constructed, and during the twentieth century, teaching habits typically became increasingly technical and moved from a colonial to a neocolonial form of instruction.[4] They consider post-1959 Cuban medical education as conforming to an alternative revolutionary framework that broke from the traditional paradigms. Under this agenda, scientific technology reached out towards humanity rather than humanity serving technology (Rosell Puig & Paneque Ramos, 2007).

The approach to physiology that the *Journal of Higher Medical Education* (*Revista Cubana de Educación Médica Superior*) shows a clear appreciation for the connection between the individual and society: while physiology in the nineteenth century focused on the biological characteristics of the individual, today there is more than enough evidence to show that the individual is intimately related to society and that the health of the individual depends greatly on the health of the collective society (Barber Fox & Barber Gutiérrez, 2000).

On the other hand, if it is recognized that physical and chemical elements in nature exist, biological beings have a greater level of complexity. For example, individuals eat to be social but there are biological processes involved as well. Therefore, the health professional and in particular the physiologist will have to understand this interrelation of the social and the biological not only to intervene on certain social factors that are causing some diseases, but also to understand that all disease has a social repercussion within the individual (Barber Fox & Barber Gutiérrez, 2000).

The Cuban approach to physiology, which is the study of mechanical, physical, and biochemical functions, requires professional training in these core relations, but also requires attention to individuals in their environments. The eating metaphor is helpful: while the food can cause disease or improve health, the social settings within which the meal occurs is also important. If a person consumes pork, it is important to understand both the metabolic chemistry of the process and the modes of consumption—where, when, and how often. The health of a person who eats high-fat bacon only rarely and in a sanitary environment would likely be different from that of a person who eats multiple servings of lean ham every day in a dirty environment. Understanding a person's health, beyond just elements of biochemistry, is an important epistemology for Cuban health-care professionals.

In Cuba, there is a reform movement within the curriculum to show more evidence-based relations between individuals and society.[5] As Barber Fox and Barber Gutiérrez (2000) see it, the lack of evidence-based relations between individuals and nature prevents a more social approach to physiology. The idea is to show how physiology should pay attention to social and environmental determinants that may impact mechanical, physical, and biochemical functions of individuals.

Approaching the health of individuals as part of broader society, even in a core medical science like physiology, indicates how the Cuban system is community oriented in its understanding and treatment of health. Within this approach, scientific instruction is rigorous, and students are expected to develop a profound understanding of the medical sciences. The students told me that they are rigorously examined on their knowledge of the biomedical sciences. Sound knowledge of the biomedical sciences is the cornerstone of medical education at ELAM. The scientific instruction offered at the school should not be seen as a radical departure from any other medical school found in the medical school directory of the WHO (2007). ELAM encourages students to appreciate how physical, chemical, and biological relations exist between individuals and society. For ELAM, science is not divorced from public health or from social determinants of health. Rather, science is approached as an essential part of those broader themes.

Within Cuba, the result of this mixed-method training is especially evident through doctor–nurse teams. These doctor–nurse duos offer in-house services to all Cubans. They visit worksites and houses to identify potential health risks from poor environmental and living conditions to social determinants of health. This allows doctors to build a better understanding of community-level health patterns in order to develop strategies of disease prevention and health promotion. As well, the doctor–nurse teams provide basic diagnostic and checkup services. It is a mixture between a clinical checkup routine and active epidemiology. Patients have close contact with a health professional, and these professionals can develop appreciative diagnoses based on clinical diagnostics and by witnessing broader social and environmental determinants. In order to identify risks and maintain health, the family doctor–nurse teams embrace social and biological determinants equally. But the question remains as to whether ELAM graduates, working outside Cuba can find ways to bring such inter-disciplinary community-based methods to vulnerable populations lacking basic infrastructure.

The Student Response

In 1994 and 1995, prior to the establishment of ELAM, MINSAP conducted a survey among students regarding certain disciplines taught in medical school. It focused on the community approach in the philosophy and practice of health care. Students were asked if they enjoyed classes, found the information important, and if they felt that it prepared them for practice. The survey covered the philosophy of health, biostatistics, psychology, hygiene and epidemiology, and comprehensive general medicine. On a scale of 1 (very negative) to 5 (very positive), the responses averaged between 3.2 and 3.8 for most of the classes. The exception was for comprehensive general medicine, a program of study that focuses on community-oriented primary care. For this class, the average student ranking exceeded 4, and 83 percent of students had a favourable impression of the course (Rojas Ochoa, 2003). This program was based on Álvarez Sintes' (2001) textbooks, upon which ELAM students continue to rely.

Indeed, most interviewees for this study and other publications from MEDICC show a sense of appreciation for the general medicine (*medicina general integral*) approach of Álvarez Sintes (2001). Dr. Cedric Edwards, ELAM's first graduate from the United States, said to MEDICC that, "I received training here in disciplines like acupuncture, homeopathy and herbal medicine, which I didn't receive in the States, nor was I ever aware of it being an integral part of any medical school curriculum in the United States. Also, in Cuba, there's more emphasis on community-based systems of care, preparation for international service, and disaster medicine—all of which seem to be lacking in US training programs" (Frank, 2005).

When asked about some of the limitations of Cuban medical technology, Edwards replied by saying that it made him a better doctor: "You don't want to be dependent on technology … you want to be able to do something to help people, to provide medical assistance without having to rely on something that isn't available" (Frank, 2005). Edwards reiterated the point that technological dependency is a problem for health care in the global South and even in some parts of the United States. He later told me in Havana "you are trained to know your patients." Edwards said, "when a physician has physical contact with the patient, knows their history, hears their stories and understands what puts them at risk, it is possible to make an accurate diagnosis." Speaking with MEDICC, Edwards said that he was confident that he would be able to adapt to a more technologically driven work environment in the United States, "I should mention that even though Cuba doesn't have … a lot of modern equipment, the training still covers [its] use or application. It's just that we don't get the same level of practice [with such equipment] as we might in another place" (Frank, 2005).

Sarpoma Sefa-Boakye, a 2007 ELAM graduate, also spoke with MEDICC about how an important part of *medicina general integral* is building relationships with patients, and that the Cuban approach trains doctors to listen to their patients' needs and take the time to do so. She added that "[Cuban doctors] integrate everything, and so they are physicians, but also psychologists … and they really know how to talk, to understand, and to listen. And so, we're really taught how to listen to the patient, to really get to what they want to say" (MEDICC Review Staff, 2005).

Nontembeko Sweetness Kunene, an ELAM graduate from South Africa, commented on how Cuba's approach to prevention differs from practices in his home country. "[Cubans put] emphasis on primary health care in all areas … [it] actually attack[s] the problem before it becomes bigger for them to handle. [In] the South African health system, we tend to attend more to sick patients … [rather than] … at the base of the problem before it gets to be a problem" (MEDICC Review Staff, 2005).

Wendy Pérez, a 2006 ELAM graduate and a Garifuna person from Honduras, perhaps best described the value of *medicina general integral*, "More than anything, we have learned to be students of science and conscience, to become doctors that are both scientists and conscientious. We are learning to serve people, as it should be, to treat people because of who they are—not because of what they have. We are being trained in the principles of solidarity (MEDICC Review Staff, 2005). Part of this, she told MEDICC, came from being able to learn in the clinic, as well as the classroom. Clinic-based learning, according to Pérez, endows students with a sense of confidence to handle difficult and complicated health conditions as they happen: "You go to operating rooms, to the wards, there you receive your lessons, and you get to know the illnesses. Your knowledge is deeper because you're in touch with reality, not only with theory. And we feel satisfied because the professors give us the attention we need, they know us well, if we have any difficulties they come and ask what's happening, if we have academic problems, they solve our doubts so that we can do better" (MEDICC Review Staff, 2005).

Indeed, according to Luther Castillo, the rewards of a hands-on approach to care and diagnosis come from the empowerment of the patients themselves.

He told MEDICC, "When I went back on vacation, someone told me, 'I'm 75 years old, and I had never been treated by a doctor without showing disgust for me.' They use this term 'disgust' to refer to a kind of rejection, you understand? And he said, 'No one had ever examined me with such delicacy, sitting by my side, holding my hand'" (MEDICC Review Staff, 2005).

Dania Suarez told me that the best part of the Cuban training was realizing the place of solidarity in medicine. Being "a humanist doctor," as she put it, is about practising medicine for those who need it, regardless of the ability to pay and regardless from where they hail. Fany Esperanza also praised her ELAM education, again referring to it is a "humanist experience." But some students did find the adjustment to Cuba to be difficult. Albania Gobrielo, who went to Cuba when she was seventeen years old and was the youngest member of the Ecuadorian ELAM delegation, said that some of her colleagues complained about the lack of Internet and the poor restaurants in Sancti Spíritus, but she said, "we were there to study medicine." Despite tough conditions, they were willing to take on the training. Ricardo Carrión also appreciated the quality education he received at ELAM and Sancti Spíritus, but when I asked him if he would ever go back to Cuba, he replied, "Never." In Quito's Jardin Shopping Centre, Ricardo gave me the impression that Cuba's humble material resources were not something he desired to be a part of any longer. Elizabeth Gallo extolled ELAM's medical education as well, but she noted, "When you graduate medicine in Cuba you are perfect for practising medicine in Cuba. In Ecuador it is different; they do not practise disease prevention and health promotion. They practise basic medicine."

Student Life

Becker notes that student life during medical school is an important component in understanding collegial culture (Becker, 1977; Sinclair, 1997). Becker's point is especially pertinent to ways in which the values of education play out through students' social networks, as medicine itself is highly dependent upon socializing and networking. Student life at ELAM reveals two key attributes in this area. The first is a sense of pan-American solidarity, as envisioned by José Martí (Martí, 1963). The second is an emphasis on cooperation over competition. These two qualities are invaluable attributes for making new doctors for the global South, and they warrant further discussion.

In July 2005, Dania Suarez was just weeks away from her final set of exams, but still she wanted to go to an ELAM party. She picked me up at 8:30 on a breezeless July evening, and, piling into the back of a Moskvich, we went out to Barrio Playa to take part in the events. We arrived to find a crowd of soon-to-be ELAM graduates. After six years of intensive training, this would be one of the few remaining moments where the students would all be together. Twenty countries were represented that night, and from group to group, Dania kept introducing me to new friends from various countries: "This is Mayra from Venezuela, Carmen from Argentine, Raul from Mexico, Mary from Uruguay, and Anita from Guatemala."

The white coats were kept in the closets that night, and the dance floor was a collage of traditional and modern dress. Somewhere between a round of rum punch and another offering of pork sandwiches, I tried to imagine another place on Earth where such a collection of students could be put together. The accents did not match; the faces from Punta del Este in Uruguay were not those from the Cuchamatanes in Guatemala. Belizeans were speaking Spanish with Brazilians, and the Paraguayans were not speaking Guaraní to anyone.

Rector Juan Carrizo says that solidarity is among the goals of the school, and on the ELAM entrance there is a famous quotation by José Martí: "It is not the intelligence received that gives man his honour, but the way and the spirit in which it is used." But the party begged the question of whether solidarity is formed through ideological affinity or through personal relationships. Or perhaps it is formed through a combination of both? Like any education, it forms characters and builds skills, but it also unites those who come from different backgrounds to hold common dreams. While some would say that solidarity is built through "exporting doctors" (Crutcher, 2006), I would say that solidarity comes from establishing close relations across cultures and between places and people that at first glance would seem to be too different to ever come together. The party was a small monument to Martí's *Nuestra América*, and a living testimony to how ELAM forms incredibly rich relationships across languages, time, and space.

While José Martí's vision lives with ELAM, the philosophy of cooperation over competition is just as important in understanding the school. The school has a goal to ensure that poor and forgotten communities receive quality health care through skilled personnel, and this means that ELAM has no incentive to limit the number of graduates for this cause. The attrition rate comes not from a natural rate of decline, but from students who are unable to cope with the intensive curriculum or the way of life. "You have to work hard here ... the teachers will help you as much as you need, but if you are unable to pass, you have to go," one student from the United States said. Another student from the United States said, "There is nothing wrong with having the whole class receive eighty percent on an exam ... but that would only happen if the whole class earned it; they don't give you a free ride here." While many universities set hierarchies among their students, the Cuban approach is to give every student as much time and attention as possible. In the class, this acts to remove competitive pressure, and socially, it tends to remove incentives for struggle and conflict. Most medical students throughout the Americas come to realize that competition for residency can be fierce, and they or some of their peers may not be able to land a place after graduation. No doubt, this fear exists among ELAM students; however, the competition is not among themselves but with the systems to which they will one day return. There is no incentive at ELAM for students to want to see their peers perform poorly. Rather, as students attested, the emphasis is on supporting each other through their studies and socializing at parties or at the Coppelia.[6]

Some accounts of ELAM student life have focused on the challenging living conditions of eleven students to a room or the food being subpar, but such accounts miss the story that I gathered from the students of how they support each other. I realized this after meeting with Cedric Edwards at Salvador Allende Hospital in Havana in July 2005. Hundreds of ELAM students study and take their residencies at this hospital. A multi-compound, single-storey hospital, its green spaces and colonial architecture resemble a retreat more than a hospital.

Cedric and I started the tour of the hospital in the triage ward. It was a busy place with many patients waiting to be seen. Nurses, secretaries, and physicians were coming and going from the waiting room, just as one would expect in any other hospital. We then went to a ward that had only one or two beds per room. The patients were elderly and bedridden or in wheelchairs. They were in the hospital for a variety of reasons, with no one specific cause. In each room, French doors opened onto a tiled balcony. The hospital was spotless. Unlike Cienfuegos, this wing of Salvador Allende Hospital was quiet. Nevertheless, each patient had someone close by him or her. Another ELAM student, in her sixth year, stopped us as we were walking out of the building. "Where are you off to?" asked Cedric.

"My patient wants sweets," she replied. "Yesterday, I made the mistake of telling her that I had some cake, so I had to share some with her."

"Medical students have time to bring patients sweets and cakes?" I asked.

"It's no big deal," replied Cedric. "At most, we might be responsible for two or three beds at a time."

Such a ratio not only affords the soon-to-be doctor time to get sweets, but it encourages relationships with patients. There is ample opportunity to get to know patients' histories, their families' histories, and many other attributes of their lives. This certainly rests on the willingness of the doctor and patients to communicate to each other. Fortunately, the Cuban system affords the time to create such dialogue.

After leaving the ward, we walked back to the student dormitory. Most of the students were in Years 3 to 6. Some were four to a room and some were six to a room—cramped conditions indeed, but slightly more spacious than the ELAM dorms for first-year students. This environment, however, seemed to foster collective participation rather than tension. In one room, students were huddled around a laptop that was acting as a DVD player. A girl from Venezuela had received the machine when her mother had visited a few months earlier. We went up to the top floor of the residence, walking past the lines of laundry in the halls. Another group of girls was cooking a giant pot of macaroni with cheese in their room. Across the hall, someone was playing a guitar. The place could have used a coat of paint, but the dorm was open, collective, and welcoming with spaces to socialize and spaces to study.

We met up with some students from Costa Rica and Ecuador and went down to the *Dítu pollo* for a soda and some croquettes, a habitual routine for many students seeking a mid-afternoon snack. We stayed for about forty minutes; I went through my questionnaire and then we made our way back to the dorm so the students could study a bit before dinner.

There is nothing atypical about the student dorm at Salvador Allende Hospital. People were studying, socializing, napping, and making calls home. It was a scene that could be found in any residence, but what was noticeable was the open and communal atmosphere. We could hardly walk more than a few steps without being stopped by someone asking if we were going to the upcoming party or asking Cedric something to do with the upcoming exam. Cedric mentioned that he felt there were people here he could count on for support and that he would be there for his friends as well. As I remember it, ELAM is an institution and social space that builds a way of life that exudes cooperation and solidarity rather than competition and prestige.

ELAM Evolves

As of 2007, the social setting for international medical students training in Cuba has evolved. Under the ALBA agreement, Cuba and Venezuela have proposed to train 100,000 physicians from the Americas. Saskia Núñez wrote to me about her experiences as a student in the new ALBA medical education program. She was studying in a small school in Matanzas in her first year. Over four hundred other Ecuadorians were in the program as well. Her first-year class had almost as many students as the entire Ecuadorian ELAM population. In 2006, MINSAP set up small, country-specific schools across the country. In their first year, students study theory and basic practices of medicine. However, unlike ELAM where student–patient contact begins in the third year, the new program brings first-year students into the clinic to work and train alongside their Cuban mentors. It is a program that is much more in line with the training methods employed by Cuban doctors working abroad, who also train medical students along the way. The impacts of the new ALBA program are a long way off; however, changes in the social and pedagogical practices are already noticeable. ELAM will continue to offer scholarships and carry on its program, but clearly, the ALBA program is designed to increase training capacity exponentially.

ELAM is a work-in-progress, and no doubt there will be continuing evolutions to its content and methods of instruction as similar capacity-building projects unfold. As the program evolves, the program's strength of having students obtain clinical knowledge through closely mentored clinic-based learning and dedicated assistance from faculty will be maintained. ELAM's programs endow students with confidence and experience that allows them to practise in regions where there are few people from which to seek advice and little time to review lecture notes. Most are recruited from the areas to which they are meant to return. Not all will leave with white coats on their backs and not all came with any shoes on their feet, but all have undergone a selection process, as unstructured as it is, that determines that they are able and willing to serve the underserved. The curriculum, even in the most basic of sciences, reinforces the idea that individuals are a part of the society in which they live, and their health relies on relationships with their communities and that society.

A Bold Act of Diplomacy

In 2001, ELAM scholarships were extended to students from the United States as well. A year earlier, Fidel Castro had travelled to the United States for the Millennium Summit at the United Nations. While there, he had travelled to Harlem to give a public speech at the church where he had stayed during another United Nations meeting in the 1960s. At that time, the United States had imposed a hotel embargo on the Cuban delegation, and they were forced to hole up in a church basement in Harlem. Castro never forgot the hospitality, and in 2000 he returned to the church to give thanks. The public speech attracted a massive audience, including members of the US Congressional Black Caucus, who met Castro personally. Members commented to Castro that they had heard much about the strength of Cuba's health-care system. They also mentioned that certain states, such as Mississippi and Louisiana, suffered an endemic physician shortage in rural areas. Others told Castro that health-care inequities in the United States disproportionately target the African-American population. Upon hearing the stories of massive health inequity within the United States, Castro offered five hundred scholarships for US students to come to ELAM (Castro, 2000). It was an offer that came from an economically hobbled country that had faced over forty years of aggression from the very country that was now seeking its help. The symbolic capital of a resource-poor country training physicians for the largest economy in the world was enormous.

The IFCO volunteered to handle the receipt of applications from US candidates before sending the portfolios on to ENSAP. The IFCO sought, but did not limit selection to, African-American and Hispanic students, women, and individuals coming from modest means. In addition to the application, candidates were invited to New York or California to participate in a three-day selection process involving an in-depth orientation on what to expect in Cuba. The first group was comprised of eighty-nine students from fifteen different locations. Enrolment to the programs has fluctuated year-to-year; in 2006, only about twenty US students went to Cuba.

From the onset, the US students faced political challenges from their own government. Regrettably, the Bush administration, as part of a broader policy to restrict movement to and collaboration with Cuba, took harsh action against the ELAM students in 2002. The US Department of State and the US Treasury Department sent warnings to students stating that they could face jail sentences and fines upwards of $40,000 for pursuing a medical education that contravened the Trading with the Enemy Act. In response to this threat, ELAM fast tracked the US students through their first year and encouraged them to return home until the political hostility subsided.

The IFCO and individual members of the Congressional Black Caucus lobbied Secretary of State Colin Powell, who then convinced the Bush administration to permit the US students to complete their medical degrees. Powell agreed that it was unconscionable to threaten medical students, ones dedicated to serving the underserved, with prison terms and stiff fines. By 2003, travel licences were permitted for US citizens to enter and complete their degrees at ELAM. Twenty-four students from the original eighty-nine did not return to Cuba after the exemption was made. Today, enrolment continues on with 115 US students registered at the school. Nevertheless, the US embargo against Cuba persists, and the US students endure prolonged separation from their families, which is compounded by poor access to communication and few chances to return home during their studies.

ELAM graduates are trained specifically to treat the poor and underserved, which includes the millions of US citizens who are underinsured, unemployed, and unable to keep up with the costly means of clinical care. These graduates should be seen as specialized practitioners who can provide a skill set aimed at serving populations through primary care, health promotion, and disease prevention. Instead, the US federal government has treated ELAM students as renegades, which demonstrates enormous hypocrisy considering that the Department of Homeland Security continues to recruit Cuban health professionals through the CMPP. The message is clear: The US government is willing to spend money on attempts to weaken Cuba's health-care system and the health systems of countries that cooperate with Cuba, but it is unwilling to help its own citizens become physicians in order to improve care for the poor. It is a distorted sense of values for a government to actively seek the destruction of other health systems at the same time as showing contempt for the health needs of its own citizens.

As of 2012, sixty-six US ELAM graduates have returned home in order to fulfill their promise of service to the vulnerable. In themselves, they are not enough to overcome the dilemmas of health equity in the United States, but they are a group willing to make a start because they are willing to serve the vulnerable. While some graduates have been successful in finding internships for residency, US graduates from ELAM have faced several challenges in finding suitable placements that will allow them to exhibit their skills and commitments to serving underserviced populations. On one hand, ELAM grads face similar obstacles to integration that other international medical graduates (IMGs) face, such as the US Medical Licensing Exam (USMLE) and the General Medical Exam (GME) for residency (Boulet et al., 2006; Schenarts, Love, Agle, & Haisch, 2008), but ELAM grads face additional challenges to fulfill their moral commitment to serving underserved communities. Few spaces exist to match the graduates with community-oriented residency placements. The Residency Program in Social Medicine (RPSM) of Montefiore Medical Center, in the Bronx, New York, is one program that has a dedicated community-oriented focus (Stelnick et al., 2008). The program has received ELAM graduates, but in order to ensure that ELAM graduates can best serve the vulnerable on a national scale, immediate policy action and coordination is required at multiple levels to develop suitable placements.

Based on continuing research with faculty, administration, graduates, and students of ELAM, the grand challenge that ELAM graduates face in finding internship options in the United States comes down to a lack of structural capacity in placing community-oriented doctors into service. I offer three policy actions for which local, state, and federal authorities could pursue in order to place these dedicated graduates within communities that desperately require their services. It is in the best interest of US policy makers to design strategies for ELAM graduates to match with communities that are crying out for care (Ebrahim, Anderson, Correa-de-Araujo, Posner, & Atrash, 2008; Kirby, 2008; Pathman, Fowler-Brown, & Corbie-Smith, 2006). Because of the pedagogy, clinical experience, and community-oriented care within Cuban curriculum, ELAM graduates have a heightened ability to offer care as well as health promotion and disease prevention schemes in resource-poor and vulnerable communities.

Government-backed cooperation for ELAM graduates could be invaluable for two reasons. If the federal or state governments were to support ELAM graduates through dedicated residency programs, it would offer up a much-needed pathway for care to vulnerable communities, and this could be an important bridge for dialogue and exchange between the two governments (Bloch, 2009).

In addition to being lumped into the IMG pool of graduates, ELAM students have a lack of externship opportunities during their program. Because they are not insured for malpractice in the United States and because their six-week summer break does not coincide with the standard eight-week break at US schools, the students have struggled to secure clinical externships at home. This is a major disadvantage, as residency programs look for and value students who have had practical experience in the United States (Cowley, 2006). Considering that the ELAM students begin physical contact with patients in their second year, and they are by the bedside in their first year, they do not lack in-clinic experience. But without clinical experience in United States, few residency programs are open to accepting ELAM graduates. There is little reason to justify this. This is entirely a political decision that can be overcome when the public and political leaders embrace programs towards health-care equity.

Politics aside, bringing this skill set to vulnerable communities will not be without structural challenges. ELAM graduates will have to face similar challenges to any other IMG, which is that domestic medical graduates are often preferred for residency than foreign-trained. Because there is a dominant culture within US medical schools of not wanting to practise "where there is no opera," there is a general assumption that no medical graduate would actually want to work in marginalized settings. Many residency programs in the United States focus on urban specializations rather than service to the marginalized. While some residency placements do focus on the needs of the vulnerable, such as Charles Drew University in California and the Montefiore Medical Centre in New York, these programs remain the exception rather than norm (Edelstein, Reid, Usatine, & Wilkes, 2000; Stelnick et al., 2008).

Furthermore, the ELAM students are not able to receive adequate financial support to prepare for the US board examinations. The Cuban state exams are not attuned to the US board exam system, and the students struggle to receive sufficient mentorship and preparation for the exams back home. Board preparation courses are currently unavailable in Cuba, and their cost can be well out of the reach of many of the students at ELAM.

A final challenge is that students and graduates do not have direct access to advertising for residency spots, as they rely on support from the IFCO and MEDICC to help seek out and coordinate residency positions and mentorships. These two groups have made fantastic gains in partnering ELAM graduates with US schools; however, other universities need to recognize, if not offer preferential status, to ELAM graduates. Given that there is no formal political relationship between Cuba and the United States, it is not surprising that coordination efforts remain small.

Without bilateral cooperation and cultural acceptance of Cuban-trained physicians, the ability for ELAM to facilitate structural change in the United States remains limited. Since 2001, over 500 scholarships have been offered to students from the United States. Only 66 US students have graduated as of 2012, and 124 students remain in the program. Not even half of the scholarships earmarked for US students were accepted. The structural challenges mentioned above, combined with growing economic constraints in Cuba have led to the cancellation of the ELAM scholarship for US students as of 2012. The current 124 students will be able to complete their program of study by 2018, but there will be no incoming students from the United States in 2013 or beyond. The IFCO announced the news in May 2012 on their website stating that economic pressures from the US embargo led to the cancellation of the scholarship for US students. Blaming the embargo for this decision is perhaps too simplistic. The scholarship remains open and available to other students across the world. In some cases where countries have rising economies but frail health training facilities, ELAM requests direct remuneration from the student's home government to offset the scholarship costs. For example, Ghana now pays ELAM directly to train its medical students. While economics certainly play a factor in this decision, the lack of official bilateral cooperation between the two countries continues to be poor. It is likely the lack of cooperation and openness for collaboration at the bilateral level that has led to the cancellation of the scholarship for US citizens. ELAM has facilitated greater cooperation and improved political relations with many other countries from its internationalism, but the United States remains unwavering on its embargo despite the generosity of the scholarship. Furthermore, the numerous challenges that ELAM graduates face in going back to the United States presents challenges in their ability to meet the needs of marginalized populations in the United States. ELAM has fostered incredible person-to-person diplomacy between Cubans and Americans, and the work by NGOs like MEDICC has facilitated cooperation, exchange, and collaboration. Their efforts have led to assisting US ELAM students and raising funds for hurricane relief within Cuba. The decision to cancel the scholarship does not reflect on the nature of this person-to-person solidarity. Rather, the cancellation of the program is an expression of frustration by the Cuban government towards the US government in its unwillingness to forge bilateral relations after eleven years of scholarship, and its inability to facilitate assistance to ELAM graduates so that they could help build health care capacity in marginalized communities.

The Value of ELAM

On one hand, the training of thousands of students as doctors is aimed at fulfilling a demand for human resources that neoliberal hegemony has created. On the other hand, ELAM's education is much more than a process of just meeting demands. It focuses on building a culture of physicians committed to service. The lessons learned from Cuban medical internationalism are brought to students in the classroom. Their texts are based on proven methods of primary care that emphasize disease prevention and health promotion, and their instructors are leaders in their fields, with many having served in medical brigades overseas. The counter-hegemony of medical internationalism along with core clinical competency permeates throughout ELAM's culture. At this stage, building confidence in students to practise medicine against the grain of neoliberal norms can be seen as a tremendous success.

The students come from 54 different countries, 101 different ethnic minorities (including 33 indigenous cultures), and speak a variety of languages, but they have come together to build a culture of cooperation and solidarity aimed at making health care accessible for all. All of these ingredients make ELAM an exceptional capacity-building project for the needs of the marginalized. The question that remains is whether the program can bring about structural change in the health-care systems for which they will serve. To see if empowered individuals with the right skills, knowledge, ethics, and compassion will be able to make an impact within their communities, it is important to consider the health-care landscapes within which they will work—the places where public health care has been ravaged and the socioeconomic division broadened thanks to decades of neoliberal policy in the global South.

CHAPTER 5

THE BLOSSOM OF COOPERATION:

CUBAN MEDICAL INTERNATIONALISM

THROUGH ELAM IN ECUADOR

Advancements in medical technology are truly amazing. Research continues to evolve understanding of the human body, and diagnostic and treatment capacities continue to progress at an amazing rate. Consider that a diagnosis of HIV/AIDS or some cancers in the 1980s was a death sentence. Today, with access to a proper pharmaceutical regime, HIV positive patients can live a full life and many more cancers can be survived. Our ability to detect and screen various forms of cancer has greatly improved, and late-stage interventions have come a long way. A team of Spanish surgeons successfully completed a face transplant (Siemionow & Gordon, 2010), and robotics have come into the picture. Today, in place of trained health workers, physicians can use robots to diagnose remotely and even operate with the help of a skilled surgeon linked up somewhere else in the world (Mendez, Hill, Clarke, Kolyvas, & Walling, 2005).

As these biomedical advancements continue, the ability to prevent suffering from the most basic ailments wanes. Health systems in West Africa, for example, have little capacity to ensure that no child dies of diarrhoea. The medical challenges that most people face in the twenty-first century are a result of dirty water, mosquitoes, and a lack of skilled attendants during childbirth. Over 18.5 million lives are lost each year due to preventable reasons (WHO, 2006). Medical advancements are widely celebrated, but in both academic literature and popular media, inaccessibility to these advancements is rarely discussed. How is it possible to celebrate costly technological advancements while overlooking the structures that prevent access to even the most basic levels of health care? The answer lies firmly in a normative belief that the production of well-being through health care resources is a costly social burden, and high-technology innovations, let alone quality care, can come only to the affluent. This belief, however, is a luxury of the financially secure and the adequately insured global minority for whom basic health care is assumed. The problematic assumption with this argument is that advanced and innovative technologies are the only means by which to provide health care. The idea that health care is a costly economic burden that can only be granted to the affluent completely overlooks the importance of low-cost interventions in low-resourced areas.

Attempts to improve health-care accessibility in poor areas have been going on since biblical times. Philanthropy and outreach have long been part of medical practice. Rarely, however, has this outreach involved demystifying medical knowledge so that individuals and communities could better take health care into their own hands. In 1973, David Werner published *Donde No Hay Doctor* (*Where There Is No Doctor: A Village Health Care Handbook* [1st English edition, 1978]) with the Hesperian Foundation. The book was initially crafted as a basic health-care guide for *campesinos* (farmers) in Central and South America. Knowing that most peasants do not have regular access to health-care professionals, Werner used basic language and detailed images to guide individuals through various health calamities. The book was meant for community leaders, and many of the treatments called for group-based participation. The guide instructs community health workers on the basics. It explains how to make stretchers and crutches from the materials found in the jungle. It offers lessons on identifying the severity of dehydration in infants, and it shows the basic steps of assisting with childbirth, including dealing with the all-too-common occurrence of counselling a mother when her child dies during delivery.

Donde No Hay Doctor makes two major assumptions about the general state of health-care services in the global South. First, as the title implies, it accepts that doctors and health-care professionals will not be there. Second, it assumes that material resources will be absent. These assumptions are based on the lack of health professionals in rural landscapes due to a lack of economic demand (i.e., ability to pay) for their services. Using basic tools, crafting crutches from tree branches, and using basic materials to monitor expecting mothers speaks to the reality of poor communities using whatever resources they have at hand in order to provide some level of care. It assumes that communities will not be able to purchase what they need and that philanthropy will not always get there in time. The poor of this world are forced on a daily basis to make hard choices about accessing professional health care or handling health calamities on their own.

Accessing health care is not politically, culturally, or economically neutral. Patients, especially economically and socially marginalized ones, often choose between health care and economic security at the family level. A visit to a private clinic in Ecuador's Amazon, followed by diagnostic services and medicine could cost local petroleum workers a week's wages. A visit to a private clinic starts at $30 and some petroleum workers make only $1,500 a year ($28 a week).[1] Even in the global North, the poor are faced with difficult decisions in purchasing health care. In the United States, it can be a question of buying medicine or paying for the heating bill (Heisler, Wagner, & Piette, 2005). Indeed, it is a global problem: in Haiti, purchasing a treatment can come at the cost of purchasing food or even the seeds for next year's harvest (Farmer, 2005). In India, many farmers forgo health for their families in order to pay the veterinary bills for their livestock.[2]

The populations most at risk have the worst chance of receiving sustainable, long-term quality care with a focus on prevention. There are two reasons for this. First, the natural resources of many countries in the global South— from Ecuador to the Congo—are extracted and exported without adequate compensation and/or without compensation remaining in the country to support public health systems. Energy and mining corporations take most profits to wealthier countries, and their investments in the local economy, let alone public infrastructure, remain paltry. Trade liberalization of natural resources often results in fewer gains staying in the country let alone going to support public services. On top of this, many nations in the global South sell off social services to the private sector as conditions of structural adjustment programs or internally driven austerity measures. These two actions work to deteriorate already frail public services. Countries such as the Philippines find themselves ordered to repay their foreign debt to the tune of 45 percent of their GDP and, thus, have little capacity to strengthen the capacity of their national health programs. Wait times in public hospitals in Manila are lengthy and the presence of a doctor on some of the country's smaller islands is unheard of.

The irony is that many countries in the global South are not naturally poor; they are, in fact, wealthy with natural and human resources. But under current liberalized trade conditions, the benefits of their natural wealth rarely filters down into improvements to the health and well-being of citizens. In Ecuador's highlands, export-oriented flower plantations are quite common, so, too, is malnutrition. Sustainable food networks, accessible health care, and land ownership for the majority poor are all in short supply. In Ecuador's Amazon, public health resources are minimal: oil is abundant and so is cancer. An ELAM graduate returning to rural Ecuador faces the challenges of coping with landscapes that have few human resources and even fewer material resources. In conditions where natural resources benefit foreigners more than locals, there is little social or political support for establishing disease prevention and health promotion for those who live on top of those resources.

If ELAM graduates return to serve in these areas, they may help to overcome Werner's (1978) first assumption that the global South lacks physicians. But even if the graduates return to where they are needed the most, Werner's second assumption—the lack of medical resources—will still be an issue in the absence of active political support. It is important to consider this reality in order to identify the challenges that ELAM graduates face. The previous chapter argued that Cuban training is appropriate for the needs of the poor. Even so, it can only go so far without appropriate social and political support from local governments. This chapter identifies some of the broader inequities and conditions that shape health, particularly in Ecuador.

Ecuador is a fitting place to understand how ELAM graduates fare in the global South. In recent years, the Correa government has significantly warmed up relations with Cuba, but between 2005 and 2007, the country had no special relationship with Cuba. Cuba has 184 foreign embassies in Havana and cooperation efforts with many of those countries. Venezuela stands out as a notable case, as political affinity has led to a level of deep integration. For many countries, however, cooperation with Cuba is done without a special relationship, and the lack of social and political support presents challenges for *brigadistas* and ELAM graduates who seek service in marginalized communities. Ecuador, then, is a fitting example of how Cuba usually deals with countries in the global South: cooperatively, but without special status.

In Ecuador, Cuban internationalism has facilitated widespread professional and medical cooperation between the two countries, but in the initial stages, the cooperation efforts were quite limited. It came down to the convictions of individual ELAM graduates to sustain their moral commitment to their work as they did not have opportunities to work in designed brigades and cooperation programs. Today, however, Cuban brigades service dozens of rural communities, many of which are on the impoverished coastal zone ("The Andes have Cuban doctors," 2012), and technical assistance and scholarships are exchanged between the two countries. The recent warming of relations warrants further discussion, but it is beyond the scope of this book. When this study took place, the political view towards Havana from Quito was neutral, if not apathetic. Moreover, Ecuador was by no means in a state of emergency for health-care workers (as Haiti was). As its name and geographical location suggest, the country rests in the middle. It is not at the top of the development index, nor is it at the bottom: it is right in the middle for most major health indicators. In many ways, Ecuador shows how Cuban medical internationalism can encourage cooperation with a politically neutral country that can then blossom into warmed relations. By focusing on Ecuador, this chapter contextualizes the social and economic disparity that ELAM graduates may experience in trying to develop sustainable community-level practice anywhere in the world.

Ecuador's Burden of Natural Wealth

Inequity and structural violence largely determine health care provision to Latin America's vulnerable communities, and Ecuador is no different. Cuba and Venezuela are providing proximal responses[3] to health risks through their public sectors rather than through distal interventions that rely on third-party donations.[4] Their collaborative initiatives to bring doctors to communities in order to offer universal primary care and to train health professionals for broader social and environmental determinants of health effectively address the sources of inequity that lead to structural violence and inequity in health outcomes. Ecuador, however, lacks this capacity. Along with many other states that subscribed to neoliberal structural adjustments in the 1990s that involved massive austerity reforms to the public sector, Ecuador had limited public resources to put towards a robust public health system. Ecuador responded to structural violence in a reactive sense. It attempted to repair calamities at the individual level as or after they occurred and often at a cost to patients. The country did not have the capacity to muster material or human resources towards health promotion and disease prevention that would get to the root of poverty.

Ecuador ranked 83 out of 175 in the 2006 United Nations Human Development Index (United Nations Human Development Program, 2006). The country's human poverty index, a marker to determine the proportion of the population living below a development threshold, was 8.9, just ahead of Thailand. Twelve percent of children up to the age of five are underweight, and 6 percent of the population has no access to clean water: "Social, regional and ethnic disparities, which have historically affected the country, remain pervasive" (Larrea & Kawachi, 2005, p. 166). Repeated economic disasters since the early 1980s also hobbled Ecuador's national wealth. A major economic crisis took place in 1998 that saw the sucre, the national currency at the time, plummet taking with it the purchasing power of most households: "In 1998, 63 percent of the population had a household consumption below the poverty line" (Larrea & Kawachi, 2005, p. 166). This depression would continue for many years, and even in 2005, per capita income was still below 1980 levels. Then, as now, the low individual purchasing power equated to low participation in the popular health sector.

Ecuador's transitional economy and fragile social services provide little security to marginalized populations. This is due to the country's management of foreign-capital investments, which influence the development of many sectors of its economy, from transportation to petroleum extraction. One of the country's most notable foreign developments is based on Texaco's discovery of massive oil fields in the Amazon in the 1960s. Sixteen companies, including the national enterprise Petroecuador, have been pulling oil out of the 4.6 billion barrel deposit since then. While Ecuador maintains national rights to minerals, international investors control the oil. In Oriente, the region where La Joya de los Sachas is located, three hundred wells were in production in 2005 (San Sebastián & Hurtig, 2004a). In order to attract foreign investment, Ecuador did not impose strict environmental management regulations. As a result, over 200 billion gallons of oil were extracted between 1967 and 1993, and 18.6 billion gallons of untreated waste, toxic gas, and raw crude were released into the ecosystem (Jochnick & Zaidi, 1994). The people of La Joya de los Sachas were thus exposed to excessive environmental pollution but had little public infrastructure to address its social and health effects.

The right for businesses to pollute, along with their right not to invest in infrastructure has long been positioned as a comparative advantage for the developing South. Lawrence Summers (1991), former Chief Economist of the World Bank, stated as much in a leaked memo from 1991:

> Shouldn't the World Bank be encouraging MORE migration of the dirty industries to the [LMICs]? ... The measurements of the costs of health impairing pollution depends on the foregone earnings from increased morbidity and mortality ... I think the economic logic behind dumping a load of toxic waste in the lowest wage country is impeccable and we should face up to that ... The demand for a clean environment for aesthetic and health reasons is likely to have very high income elasticity. The concern over an agent that causes a one in a million change in the odds of prostate cancer is obviously going to be much higher in a country where people survive to get prostate cancer than in a country where under 5 mortality is 200 per thousand.

Responses to Summers' (1991) memo were immediate but ineffective. José Lutzenburger (1991), Brazilian Secretary of the Environment, wrote, "Your reasoning is perfectly logical but totally insane.... Your thoughts [provide] a concrete example of the unbelievable alienation, reductionist thinking, social ruthlessness and the arrogant ignorance of many conventional 'economists' concerning the nature of the world we live in" (Puckett, 1997). Sadly, Lutzenburger was fired from his post while Summers went on to become Secretary of the US Treasury, President of Harvard University, and, recently, Director of the National Economic Council for the Obama administration.

While Summers' memo was not aimed specifically at Ecuador, it illustrates the impunity with which structural violence results from principles of comparative advantage. For Ecuador, the supposed gains of petroleum development come at the expense of brutal health and environmental impacts. Hurtig and San Sebastián (2004) show that each drilled well produces an average of four thousand cubic metres of waste, including drilling mud, petroleum, natural gas, and formation water: "These wastes are frequently deposited into open, unlined pits called separation ponds, from which they either are directly discharged into the environment or leach out as the pits degrade, or overflow from rainwater" (p. 207). Despite a thorough epidemiological study of the health and environmental effects of this development and protests by indigenous communities and activists, the pollution continued in the Amazon, and Summers' approach to development continued unabated (Brelih et al., 2005; San Sebastián, Hurtig, Breilh, & Peralta, 2005). Meanwhile, there has been no construction of a social safety net that deals with these and other health calamities.

Ecuador's oil development exacerbates an already dire situation. Foreign companies overseeing oil extraction, such as Halliburton, take an overwhelming share of their profits out of the country, leaving desperately few resources to develop social infrastructure. Because of the increased marginalization of communities across the country, oil development in the Amazon, and uneven landholdings in the Andes, the poor's coping strategies have become increasingly varied (Hentschel & Waters, 2002). This often involves "temporary migration, increased female and child labour, and decreased consumption" (Hentschel & Waters, 2002, p. 38). Moreover, the nature of oil extraction negatively impacts the health of poor communities that surround it (Heynen, 2007; Jochnick & Zaidi, 1994; Kimerling, 2001; Whitten, 2004). Cancer rates, birth defects, dead livestock, and adverse impacts on biodiversity are all part of the environmental and health fall out of petroleum development. At the same time, the state is left with minimal resources to devote to public health: "Even though most social expenditures are progressive, their budgets are a sufficiently small share of GDP and their incidence is … poorly targeted so as to yield only a small reduction in overall inequality" (Younger, 1999, p. 347). Indeed, Ecuador offers a low level of resources for public health care. Considering this, as well as regional variations of wealth, it is not surprising to see gross inequities across the country (Robertson et al., 1991).

Ecuador's Health Inequities as Structural Violence

A transitional economy, environmental degradation, and inadequate public resources have deepened negative health factors across Ecuador. Oriente is not alone in experiencing unnecessary degradation and environmental pollution while enduring underfunded public health-care services. Handal, Lozofil, Brelih, and Harlowl (2007) argue that children exposed to excessive pesticide spraying in flower-growing regions, such as Cuenca, are at increased risk of neurological development disorders. Contreras Díaz (2006) found that in one of Quito's poorest barrios, Dos Puentes, women employed for cleaning and domestic labour experienced adverse health complications linked to automobile pollution. Larrea and Kawachi (2005) explored the relationship between stunting and economic inequality. Stunting, a reduced growth rate in development that is caused by many factors including malnutrition, affects 26 percent of children under five in Ecuador. The authors argue that the financial disparities between urban centres and rural areas, especially in indigenous communities in the highlands, lead to a "statistically significant deleterious effect" (Larrea & Kawachi, 2005, p. 165).

Ecuador's Amazon is testimony to the health inequality that emerges from poorly regulated resource extraction development. In the Amazon in 1993, a group of community health workers conducted an epidemiological study comparing descriptive renderings of health conditions in communities with and without oil developments. "The study suggested that, compared to communities free from oil exploitation, communities in oil-producing areas had elevated morbidity rates, with a higher occurrence of miscarriage, dermatitis, skin mycosis, and malnutrition, as well as higher mortality rates" (San Sebastián & Hurtig, 2004a, p. 208). Indigenous groups and local communities claimed that the rivers once abundant with fish had little to no aquatic life and that cattle often died after drinking water from them. As San Sebastián and Hurtig (2004a) note, "These are typically the same waters that people use for drinking, cooking, and bathing" (p. 208). San Sebastián and Hurtig (2005) claim that the main value of this 1993 study was that it emerged via participatory processes at the community level, and while Texaco ran newspaper advertisements in 2005 trying to discredit the findings, they have been tested and recognized as valid by non-partisan experts: "Local organizations set the agenda of the research; they were involved in the hypothesis formulation, consulted in each step during the study and responsible of the dissemination of the findings. This process is known as popular epidemiology" (p. 799).

Research such as this contributes towards finding and mapping health consequences that arise from oil developments. The Manuel Amunárriz Institute of Epidemiology and Community Health has been involved in research to assess the potential health impacts of various physical symptoms. Jochnick, Nomand, and Zaidi (1994) found that women closer to petroleum developments suffered higher incidences of "skin mycosis, tiredness, itchy nose, sore throat, headache, red eyes, ear pain, diarrhoea, and gastritis" (San Sebastián & Hurtig, 2004a, p. 208). Texaco maintains that these conditions are the result of abject poverty and the lack of resources, and cannot be blamed on the oil developments (Breilh et al., 2005). But as San Sebastián and Hurtig (2004b) point out, diseases not typically related to poverty, such as cancer and various forms of leukemia, are also abundant in the region. San Sebastián and Hurtig's study (2004b) notes that the under-reporting of leukemia, thanks to minimal health-care access, likely means that incidence rates are actually much higher than thought.

Against such perilous environmental and social determinants of health, Ecuador has done little to care for the needs of its citizens. Rather than emphasizing greater attention to health promotion, disease prevention, and addressing policies that aim to diminish the structures that cause poor health, Ecuador has de-invested in health and health care. The result is that the most vulnerable have the worst access to health care resources. As Puertas and Schessler (2001) argue, the "goals of health sector reform include improving quality, correcting inefficiencies, and reducing inequities in current systems. The latter may be especially important [for] indigenous populations, which are thought to suffer from excess mortality and morbidity related to poverty" (p. 133). Health-care reforms for Ecuador should "develop a comprehensive plan for health improvement; conduct research on the appropriate mix between TNM, primary health care strategies, and high-technology medical services; train local health personnel and traditional healers in primary health care techniques; improve access to secondary and tertiary health services for indigenous populations; and advocate for intersectoral collaboration" (Puertas & Schlesser 2001, p. 133).

Focusing on the Cotopaxi region, a highland area south of Quito, Puertas and Schlesser (2001) assessed the accessibility of indigenous communities to public health services. They found that about 22 percent of residents in Cotopaxi have the means of transportation to reach medical attention in less than half an hour, while 43 percent need more than an hour to get to a health professional. Seventy percent of their respondents reported missing work due to illness at least once in the month prior, and 68 percent of this group missed up to five days. Sixty-seven percent stated that they received treatment in their homes. Treatment was provided from a range of sources, not all of which could be deemed professional under the WHO definition: family member (47 percent); self-care (21.3 percent); physician (20.8 percent); other (e.g. semi-skilled worker) (7.2 percent); and Ya´chag, *brujo*, or *colundreno* (traditional healers) (3.7 percent). Only eight percent of respondents received care in a clinic.

The results of the Cotopaxi study show that individuals rely most often on family networks in order to receive health care. The majority of this rural population does not regularly participate in the public health-care system and relies on more local coping strategies. Often this involves homemade remedies and shamanism as treatments. While Western medicine is retracting in its accessibility, Miles (1998) argues that TNMs have gained popularity in Ecuador's urban commercial circuits, especially among the poor, as a result of marketing meeting a growing ideology for TNM. It is a mix of people unable to afford primary care, others who have no trust in primary caregivers, and others who look to family and community knowledge networks for advice. Puertas and Schlesser (2001) identify a number of products that their respondents regularly relied on for treatment. The most common products were medicinal plants (34.4 percent); chamomile tea (9.2 percent) was used most often but borage infusions (3.8 percent) were also popular. (Borage infusions are made from a plant native to Ecuador and are used to treat fever.) Other common products included milk alone or with garlic or chamomile (2 percent), various compresses (1.3 percent), and cane sugar liquor (1.7 percent).

The Ecuadorian state does not value TNM, but Cuba's MINSAP calls for a greater integration of traditional remedies into core clinical care (Padron, 2003). Cuba does not see such remedies as alien to health care, but as complimentary to it. It takes the position that incorporating TNM into biomedical approaches builds knowledge, both scientifically and locally, of the potential uses, benefits, and risks of alternative treatments. ELAM doctors are encouraged to embrace TNM through their curriculum. Ecuador, however, has yet to demonstrate a similar initiative. Instead, TNM remains localized, outside of the public domain, and occasionally falls into a novelty discourse.

In Guaranda, a small town in the province of Bolívar, there is a clear division between the cultures of clinical practice and traditional healing. Visiting the community of Palta-Bomba, located on the outskirts of Guaranda on three separate occasions, I quickly realized that the mistrust of service is just as strong within indigenous communities towards the biomedical model as the Ecuadorian public health system is towards the TNM model. Building trust between these two communities would be a challenging feat for returning ELAM graduates.

I arrived in Palta-Bomba as a part of a group conducting research on local environmental health impacts. Members of the group weighed and measured some of the town's children to see if there were signs of stunting. Stepping off the bus, it did not take long to realize that many of the town's children were hobbled by poverty and poor nutrition. The children had mature faces on little bodies. The physicians in the group determined that many of the children were below the average body mass and height indices for their age group.

An elder told me that his son would be back from studying in Cuba in a month and that I should meet with him. A month and a half later, I returned to find Gonzalo, a recent Cuban graduate. Gonzalo's house was a typical house for Palta-Bomba—sparse with no sure plumbing. A few chickens and a couple of dogs milled around us while we talked. His mother came out with giant maize and cheese tortillas. With such a serving, it was hard to believe that hunger engulfed the town.

Gonzalo had gone to Cuba with the 1999 cohort of ELAM students, but his scholarship was for agricultural sciences not medicine. According to officials from first-person interviews at Cuba's MINREX, Medicine is only one of several scholarships that Cuba offers to students in Latin America. Other subjects include sport and physical education, natural sciences, social sciences and the humanities, economics, technical sciences, agricultural sciences, teaching, and drafting and fine arts (self-funded). In 2006, Gonzalo returned to his home community with a master's thesis in agricultural sciences. His degree was free, and he had made a moral commitment to return to his home to apply his skills and to transfer knowledge to his community. His master's thesis focused on a potato breed that is adaptable to the Andes and that can flourish with only organic inputs. He hoped that promoting knowledge about this type of potato would allow farmers to reduce or abandon conventional agriculture that requires costly fertilizer and pesticide inputs. If he were successful, there would be two significant advantages to his community: it would provide greater access to healthy food at the local level, and families would have more disposable income from money saved by not having to purchase pesticides. Ultimately, Gonzalo's thesis could aid in health promotion and disease prevention.

We shared stories about Cuba for a while and then we included his mother and sister in the conversation to talk about health-care services in the community. Quite simply, there is none. There is a first-aid station in the school and little else. The road to Guaranda takes about thirty minutes in a truck, as the road is in poor shape. It is washed out in parts, and it makes for a treacherous drive. His mother said she takes care of most of the family's maladies with traditional herbs, soups, and teas.

"What if someone has an intestinal infection with severe diarrhoea?" I asked.

"That can be treated here with what we have," she replied.

"But what if someone was pregnant and needed a doctor or, say, had a very high fever? Would you see the doctor at the free clinic in town?"

"They experiment on us," she replied. "They try to convince us to take all of sorts of drugs. They discriminate. Someone from the community will not be treated with the same respect as a person from Guaranda."

Turning to Gonzalo, I asked for his opinion. He said that sometimes it is necessary to take someone to the hospital, but most problems are dealt with in the community. This often involves consulting a shaman or *colundreno* to help with the healing process. Fany, a recent ELAM graduate, later told me in the town of Loja that the most vulnerable populations in Ecuador are often the ones that rely heavily on the *colundrenos*. She was critical of such dependence. While she praised the use of TNM and noted the value in exploring treatments outside of the biomedical model, she had serious concerns about the *colundrenos'* lack of scientific knowledge: "They do not know the basics, such as physiology or histology." For Fany, and several other ELAM graduates, the problem with TNM in Ecuador is that it has not been standardized and researched well enough to understand the biomedical processes, the benefits, and the consequences that come with the practice.

I asked Gonzalo if he knew any of the Ecuadorian ELAM students, and he said that he knew quite a few.

"Do you think that they would be able to help out communities such as yours, offering services and advice?" I asked him.

"They won't come to us. They will take their degrees and work in the private sector. There is more money for them there. That is where all doctors are going to go; none of them are working in the communities. There is no other place for them to go."

Pessimistic about the current situation as he was, Gonzalo talked highly about his time in Cuba. He reflected upon his interaction with the professors, the rigorous study, and the friends that he made. But back home, frustration engulfed him. Despite his master's degree and his pitch for a new type of potato, he was without work. He admitted that he might have to leave his community in order to find work, and he felt that many ELAM graduates would be in the same position. In Palta-Bomba, existing socioeconomic structures offered very few opportunities for young leaders such as Gonzalo to help meet the needs of communities.

When it comes to meeting the public's needs, Ecuador's health-care system provides free services only for pregnant women and newborn children. Ecuador's Ministry of Public Health provides a small set of services free of charge to children less than five years of age, as well as to expecting and recent mothers. The Maternity and Infant Free Services Act includes the following services, along with medication, vitamins, examinations, and all other necessary materials. For pregnant women, the act includes services for

- control of the pregnancy,
- complications of the pregnancy,
- normal or Caesarean birth,
- pap tests,
- blood donations, and
- dental care.

For the mother and her partner, the state provides sessions on

- family planning and
- education sessions on sexually transmitted diseases.

For the child, free services include

- attention to newborns with or without complications,
- regular checkups,
- treatment of typical infant diseases,
- treatment of complications during hospitalization,
- blood donations, and
- dental care.

And at the bottom of a flyer hanging in the Sachas clinic that listed these services, barely noticeable as it was faded from the sun, was a statement telling patients to "Exercise your rights! Visit a hospital or a health sub-centre."

Puertas and Schlesser's (2001) study confirms the increased participation in this sector compared to other sectors of the Ecuadorian health sector. Their findings show that services covered by the Maternity and Infancy Free Services Act are used widely by citizens. They found that 34.7 percent of recent mothers had prenatal checkups with a physician and 24 percent with a midwife, 19 percent consulted a family member and only 4 percent did not receive a checkup at all. However, when it came to the actual delivery itself, only 12 percent of recent mothers gave birth under a physician's supervision (Puertas & Schlesser, 2001). Family members were the principal attendants for 45.4 percent of the births, midwives oversaw 29 percent, and nurses attended only 4 percent.

Puertas and Schlesser (2001) show two clear trends. Under the Maternity and Infancy Free Services Act, individuals, especially women and children, are more likely to seek out health-care services from the public sector. The percentage of mothers who received prenatal examinations from a physician is higher than the percentage of people who received physician treatment for maladies not covered under the Act. However, even though prenatal services are widely used, there is an incredibly low level of physician attendance at birth. This is a free service, but it is not one that has high levels of use. Hospitals are quite inaccessible from rural and indigenous communities. Further, if Palta-Bomba is any indicator, there is a low level of trust towards the public system and novice physicians. This would contribute to mothers seeking out home-birth options in their community rather than entering into a clinical setting. Both trends demonstrate barriers based on a lack of infrastructure and sociopolitical support.

Ecuador's Public Health-Care Capacity

In Ecuador, some level of payment is required for all non-maternal services. At the public clinics, the fee may be as little as a dollar per visit. The country has five different health-care sectors. The Ministry of Public Health covers about thirty percent of the country's population; the private sector operating across the entire country offers care to those who can afford services (20 percent) the Instituto Ecuatoriano de Seguridad Social covers state employees (18 percent of the population); NGOs offer care to some of the poor (5 percent); and the military provides coverage to its personnel and their families (2 percent) (Cavender & Albán, 1998; Country Health Profiles: Ecuador, 2006). In 1998, the Pan American Health Organization (PAHO) determined that 30 percent of the country had no sustainable access to medical care, which was up from 10 percent in 1980 (Country Health Profiles: Ecuador, 1998). In 2002, PAHO figured that 25 percent of the population remained unattended, most of whom "are Amerindians, of rural areas located in the central provinces, the Amazon area and in urban shantytowns" (Country Health Profiles: Ecuador, 2006). PAHO suggested that 52 percent of the population has the financial capacity to access both private and public insurance, while 23 percent have no financial capacity at all (Country Health Profiles: Ecuador, 2006).

The Ministry of Public Health operates auxiliary health-care posts for small communities of less than two thousand people, medical sub-centres staffed with physicians and nurses for communities up to five thousand people, and provincial and national hospitals that operate in major urban centres. For Ecuador's poor, the sub-centre is usually the entrance point into the public health network. Typically, they are humble structures with a few consultation rooms, limited supplies, and some degree of dental facilities (Cavender & Albán, 1998). These facilities are meant to handle basic treatments and some more complex procedures that would require minimal diagnostic equipment. Physicians do refer patients to provincial or national hospitals for more complex conditions; however, the means of transport is left up to the patient.

Ecuador has one physician for every 675 people, one nurse for every 636 people; it is challenging, but by no means the worst global case (WHO, 2007). Still, where Ecuador's human resources are physically located and how accessible they are to vulnerable populations, hinders universal accessibility. PAHO estimates that up to 92 percent of the country's human resources for health are located in urban centres, with only 59.2 percent of the workforce employed in the public sector (Country Health Profiles: Ecuador, 2006).

The over-accumulation of resources in urban areas, the lack of access for indigenous and indigent communities, and the lack of human resources for health have produced an anti-model of health care (Candib, 2004). It is a model that is not equipped to maintain health, but only to deal with death and illness. Mechanistic and distal, both private and public health care are regulated by cost-benefit analysis. People are not given the greatest amount of care possible; rather, they are relegated services based on their capacity to pay or how much time and attention the public system can afford. Physicians, Candib argues, perpetuate this anti-health model because they are tied to "a system of power and knowledge dependent on the dominant ideology and by consumers [who] see health care as a ... good that should bring happiness once acquired" (Herrera Ramirez, & Garces, 2003 as cited in Candib, 2004, p. 280).

A reactive and poorly equipped health system emphasizes health as a product of the physician's skill to mend illness rather than a society's ability to practise health promotion. This leads to three cultural underpinnings: physicians gain prestige through an elevated knowledge of science; prestigious physicians should be able to practise medicine for lucrative rewards rather than for service to the indigent; and primary care does not require elevated scientific knowledge and does not merit large financial remuneration. Primary care is treated as a charitable obligation, and one that is not necessarily regarded as noble. A public sector family physician is not eulogized as highly as a private sector specialist in Ecuador.

This is an important cultural discourse as it affects the training and development of physicians. Ecuadorian medical schools focus almost entirely on science and encourage students to seek out for-profit specialization. Community service is mandatory and seen as a nothing more than a rite of passage. In this country of about 14 million people, there are only seventy residency-trained family medicine physicians practising (Herrera Ramirez & Garces, 2003, as cited in Candib, 2004). Of the 18,335 physicians, not even 1 percent of them have specialized in family medicine. The country's five public medical schools (Facultad de Ciencias Médicas—Universidad de Cuenca; Facultad de Ciencias Médicas—Universidad de Guayaquil; Facultad Ciencias Médicas—Universidad Nacional de Loja; Facultad Ciencias de la Salud—Universidad Técnica de Manabí; Facultad de Ciencias Médicas—Universidad Central del Ecuador) and three private institutions (Facultad de Medicina y Ciencias de la Salud—Universidad Católica de Cuenca; Facultad de Medicina—Universidad Católica de Santiago de Guayaquil; Colegio de Ciencias de la Salud—Universidad San Francisco de Quito) collectively graduate well over three hundred *médico general básicos* each year. Yet, due to lack of spaces, almost none of the grads enter family medicine residency.

With the exception of Cuenca's medical school, which offers innovative training geared towards social medicine, Ecuadorian medical education encourages students towards specialization. The training focuses on scientific rigour and the student's ability to test for diseases using high-tech medical resources. The curriculum is dedicated almost entirely to pathophysiology, and little time is dedicated towards disease prevention and community-based medicine.

I met with three medical students from Quito's Universidad Central. They were all from Quito, and they all hoped to work in the city. They do not pay tuition at the public institute, but they are responsible for every bit of course material throughout the program of study. Aside from purchasing textbooks, students must also pay for lab equipment and various other materials. They figure that they spent about $500 each semester on materials. The students felt that despite the free tuition, the costs of living combined with the incidental costs of the program were quite high, and they had to rely on the support of their families in order to pay for school expenses, rent, and subsistence.

They said that the classes were large, and they spent a great deal of time in the lecture hall until their third year. They also said that the first two years are difficult, with a great deal of time handling biomedical sciences in the lecture hall. In the Universidad Central, the number of the students in the first year is reduced to half by the second, and after six years only a small proportion of students graduate from the program.

Degrees can run between six and eight years for the title of *médico general básico*. These basic general doctors must spend one year of obligatory service, regardless of the graduating institution, working for the Ministry of Public Health in rural or indigent communities. After that, these doctors must receive a registration licence from the Colegio Médico de Pichincha, awarded for passing a competency exam and residency. The Ministry of Public Health then grants licences to practise. It is a fairly typical process to any medical licensing procedure anywhere in the world; unfortunately, the Colegio Médico de Pichincha has a limited number of residency vacancies available each year, leaving the majority of basic general doctors searching for placements in other countries. Recently, many have gone to Chile to find work. Chile's doctors are moving into the private sector while Ecuadorians migrate to that country's rural areas to work for lower wages than those found in the Chilean private sector, but better wages than are found within Ecuador. Colombia is another appealing destination to secure a specialization as it offers more abundant residency spaces.

Ritha, a post-doctoral fellow at Ecuador's Facultad Latinoamericana de Ciencias Sociales, told me that emigration to Chile is having a massive impact on Ecuador's human resources for health. Seventy-three percent of the medical technicians in Chile are Ecuadorian: "They are graduating from our public medical schools in order to serve another country."

The students from Quito's Universidad Central admitted that they would likely seek employment or specialization out of the country, at least for a while: "You can make a lot more money in Chile," one student commented. Another student added that in Chile your medical degree is accepted, and it is easy to get a residency placement: "The Chilean doctors work in their cities, and we go to work in the rural areas." Another student mentioned that she is seeking specialization at a medical school in Mexico City because "it is a prestigious institution." The students complained that Ecuador does not offer spaces for specialization. The private schools have spaces, but the tuition can be as high as $10,000 a year. Other countries such as Argentina often receive Ecuadorian students for specialization, but the tuition and cost of living are quite high as well.

Ritha and I discussed how physicians who are dedicated to serving the public sector manage to make ends meet. A monthly salary for a specialist working in the public health stream is no more than $350 a month, while a specialist working in the private sector can make ten times that amount. She said that public physicians work in the private sector as well because they have to. If a family doctor can put in eight hours a day, he or she can dedicate four hours to family practice in the public stream and the other four hours to his or her specialization in the private sector: "It is a broken system," she said. Of course, physicians cannot delegate their time that evenly. Physicians will be expected to attend to ten times as many patients during their public hours as their private billing time: "There is a great divorce between the two systems, and family doctors practicing in the public system are over-occupied with their commitments to private practice," said Ritha. Such a system fractures a physician's skills and time between the need for profit and a commitment to charity.

In the end, family physicians are left without prestige or worthy remuneration, and because the system has rigorously valued specialization and privatization, very little public understanding exists as to who family physicians are and what they do. In order for Ecuador to overcome this problem, the Correa government would not only have to guarantee more residency placements in family medicine, but also actively work to build a popular culture that values family physicians.

The Año Rural—Compulsion or Compassion?

Before succumbing to the lure of lucrative business and scientific recognition, every single *médico general básico* must serve a rural or indigent community in Ecuador. This obligation is called the *año rural*. It is a one-year contract with two, three-week holiday periods included. It amounts to sending the annual graduating class of doctors from Ecuador's medical schools to rural communities. Specialists are also expected to enter a year of rural service, but they practise in hospitals, rather than the smaller clinics. On the surface, it may seem in line with the ELAM goal. However, the *año rural* has numerous problems in terms of retaining physicians and building community trust. Cavender and Albán (1998) studied the program and concluded the success of the *año rural* depended a great deal on the physician's attitude towards health-care service in vulnerable communities.

Compulsory service programs have been implemented throughout the hemisphere with the general assumption that the presence of health-care professionals would improve health indicators in marginalized communities (Asturizaga Rodriguez, 1996; Ugalde, 1984). However, studies have shown that compulsory service is problematic and may have an adverse effect on developing quality, community-based care (Rubel, 1990). There are some readily identifiable problems in Ecuador's *año rural*. First, the curriculum from the country's medical schools, with some possible variation in Cuenca, is heavily focused on clinical care in urban centres that have reasonable material resources and information networks. In Bolivar and Oriente, resources are few, and networks non-existent. Basic general doctors are thrown into a system for which they were not trained and, more importantly, a system that their training did not value. Second, the physicians going into the *año rural* are young and inexperienced. Gonzalo's family, who believe that the physicians in the clinic were experimenting on the indigenous, may have good reason to believe so. Young doctors, lacking clinical experience and confidence, might suffer from a lack of confidence in dealing with new patients and seem to be hesitant or experimental in their treatments. Third, the *año rural* is only a year. For communities that rarely access health-care services to begin with, a perennial turnover of *médico general básicos* does not allow for the development of long-term patient–doctor relationships. For the physician, the year of service is an obligatory transition period, and from the point of view of the communities, these doctors are all fly-by-nighters. Unfortunately, these doctors are the only face of health care many of Ecuador's most vulnerable will ever know. The *año rural* is a program presented as altruistic, but it is an experience that many young physicians view as a form of penance, which does little to bolster services for the indigent. Sending in new physicians under compulsory contracts demonstrates a lack of moral commitment for prioritizing the needs of the marginalized.

Of course, there may be some dedicated souls who embrace a culture of service and try to foster long-term connections with the communities, but even if some young physicians manage to build trust with communities, the Ministry of Health does not often allow them to stay on in these communities. When their contracts terminate they are expected to seek out specialization and residency. Not that it matters, as, according to Ritha, physicians on the *año rural* "have their hearts in the cities." Certainly, the year in the field is an eye opener for many, and it likely does some good to bring doctors to face a reality that they have never experienced, but in the end, it is a government law, a compulsorily activity rather than an activity to further individual prestige. The students from the Universidad Central all expressed a degree of excitement about the *año rural*, but they all admitted to wanting to serve in Quito.

"Do you think that you will practise in the public or private sector?" I asked them.

"Both," they all replied. "We could not afford to remain just in the public sector, but our services will be needed there and we want to help."

One student suggested that if she were to be admitted to the specialization program in pediatrics in Mexico, she would not have to commit to the *año rural* upon her return to Ecuador.

Understandably, some young doctors would not want to participate in a year of rural service. In a study by Cavender and Albán (1998), 59 percent of physicians received no orientation training before the *año rural*, and many felt overwhelmed by the entire experience. Basic medical resources are often in short supply. Anything other than disinfectant and cotton can be hard to come by, and maintaining cleanliness of equipment and observation rooms is difficult. Aside from the minimal infrastructure and the overwhelming poverty in the communities, some physicians (35 percent) found the transition to basic living conditions quite difficult, and 38 percent said that they experienced problems of cultural differences while in the field. Nevertheless, over 90 percent of respondents felt that the *año rural* was a positive experience that furthered their awareness of the poverty and the need for improved services in outlying areas (Cavender & Albán, 1998).

The sub-centres in Oriente, Bolivar, and many other places are staffed with *médico general básicos* on the *año rural*. They are on the front line between the indigent and public health. Lacking equipment and proper skills, and loosely supervised, they are thrown into an unfamiliar context. Rural communities know that the state is sending young graduates whose skills and capacities are still green. This is a clear message to indigenous and poor communities that the specialists and the senior physicians are reserved for the sector of society that is willing to pay for their superior skills and celebrated merit.

On December 19, 2006, the Minister of Public Health, Guillermo Wagner, was quoted in a large newspaper, *El Expreso de Guayaquil,* as saying that there is an advance in the country's health indicators, but there is also a lack of resources for basic needs (Constante, 2006). The minister assured the reporter that advances were taking place in moving the country closer towards the millennium development goals. Malaria and some of the base indicators, such as infant and maternal mortality, were declining, in part thanks to the Maternity and Infancy Free Services Act. However, the minister mentioned nothing about improving primary care.

With a quarter of Ecuadorians lacking primary care and new medical graduates taking flight to other countries, any improved indicator could be deemed a shining success. Nonetheless, the broader issues that prohibit public health care from reaching out to indigent communities have yet to be overcome. Poor infrastructure, minimal support, transitional medical personnel, mistrust between communities and physicians, and an operating culture that values profit above compassion, are all factors that Ecuador's fifty-four 2005 ELAM graduates had to face. Ecaudor's health services represent a broader global trend of de-investing in health services for the poor. The system lacks the capacity to meet the needs of the vulnerable. How Cuban medical graduates fare in this landscape is important in understanding the challenges and opportunities to their moral commitment to rural service. The place of ELAM graduates working in Ecuador's public health landscape provides important insights into how the ethics of service go up against structures of inequity. In what ways do graduates find ways to cope with resource challenges and structural challenges that further inequities? ELAM graduates are entering a system greatly different from the one in which they were trained. Cuba's system embraces social cohesion, participation, and the public good. In July 2005, I spoke with many soon-to-be ELAM graduates, and they all expressed a mix of apprehension and excitement about their return home. They were delighted to return to their homes, but daunted by what would face them in the clinic; they would go back to skeletal public infrastructure and overwhelming health-care needs. Their stories would demonstrate the challenges of pursuing counter-hegemonic service in systems that reinforces marginalization.

In August 2005, the fifty-four Ecuadorian ELAM graduates knew that this would be the landscape that they would face. They had known it even when they made the decision to Cuba in 1999. Could these fifty-four Cuban-trained doctors make a difference in a country where one in four people are without medical care and where not even 1 percent of doctors are specialists in family medicine? They returned to Ecuador because they embraced Cuba's ethics of medicine as service and because they were trained in the broader determinants of health. Yet most of them felt that they, along with the three hundred nationally trained *médico general básicos* entering into the *año rural*, would not make the slightest bit of difference in the country's health landscape. That is why only eleven of the fifty-four went back to Ecuador from Cuba in 2005.

"There are only ten of you?" I asked her.

"Eleven, actually," Dania replied.

"Eleven? I thought that the first graduating class had fifty-four students from Ecuador."

"It did, and the other forty-three are still in Cuba. And one more, who is actually in Quito now, will be returning to Cuba in November."

"But that is only one-fifth of the graduating class! Why did everyone stay in Cuba? I thought the plan was to use your skills to serve the *campos*?"

Dania Suarez told me that only a handful of Ecuadorian ELAM graduates had come home. In fact, close to seven hundred students from the graduating class stayed in Cuba after convocation. They stayed to continue their studies in a specialization of their choice. Those who remained in Cuba took advantage of MINSAP's offer for free training in any specialization in addition to a specialization in integrated family medicine.

In 2005, reintegration strategies for ELAM graduates existed with Venezuela, Ecuador, and Paraguay. Other countries such as Guatemala, Nicaragua, El Salvador, and Honduras had less formal arrangements for the graduates to work alongside existing Cuban medical brigades in rural areas. Venezuela had a strategic reintegration plan put into place to see graduates return to vulnerable communities involving a set time of service. After this contract, students could pursue specialization opportunities (Muntaner, Salazar, Benach, & Armada, 2006). In Ecuador and Paraguay, students were integrated into one-year contracts for service in rural areas, which, in the case of Ecuador, meant participation in the *año rural*. After the one-year contract, no formal employment arrangements were established. Other countries— Peru, Antigua, Argentina, Guatemala (despite the presence of Cuban medical brigades), and Brazil—refused to acknowledge the ELAM degrees. However, in 2007, Argentina and Guatemala declared that the ELAM degrees would be accredited. Antigua recently restated its unwillingness to accept ELAM degrees, demanding that students pursue further training in their national system (Huish, 2009). The United States had a mixed reaction to ELAM graduates. It recognized the value of the degrees by attempting to impose fines of $40,000 for trading with the enemy on US ELAM graduates. Although it sought to punish its own citizens, it welcomed ELAM graduates from any other country if they applied for residency at a US medical school through CMPP (Carrillo de Albornoz, 2006).

Other than in Venezuela, no long-term reintegration program for ELAM graduates existed as of 2005, and instead of risking unemployment for graduates in their home countries, Cuba offered training for additional specialization.[5] The family medicine specialization would be over a course of two years, and the additional specialization could be anywhere from three to five additional years. The offer was a response to ensure that the ELAM students would not be driving taxis and seeking out private sector employment, as is the case of so many physicians in Latin America (Frenk, Knaul, Vázquez-Segovia, & Nigenda, 1999).

However, this raises two questions about the continued retention of ELAM graduates in Cuba. First, to what extent is Cuba leaning on ELAM graduates in order to offset the number of physicians that it sends to other countries through comprehensive medical brigades, the Henry Reeve Brigade, or other health collaborations? The specialization offer may help replenish Cuban physicians gone overseas, but additional retention of ELAM graduates working in rural Cuba for their family medicine specialization is a small contribution towards offsetting the absence of thirty-eight thousand health professionals committed to overseas service.

While it may seem that allowing ELAM graduates to remain in the country goes against the central premise of the entire ELAM program, this policy can be understood as a deeper investment to training human resources for rural care. Because many public health sectors in the global South are unable to receive new physicians, either because of a lack of funding in the public sector or because of a lack of infrastructure, the fate of many ELAM graduates would be either unemployment or service in the private sector. By allowing graduates to stay on, Cuba benefits by having skilled physicians working in areas outside of Havana, but it also allows these students to continue to develop their skills and capabilities. Their skills do not go to waste. The real tragedy would be for such a precious investment in human resources aimed at the poor to be lost to the private sector or outside of medicine altogether. By remaining in Cuba, ELAM graduates have the opportunity to participate with Henry Reeve Brigade or to work with Cuban brigades in other countries. The ultimate challenge for ELAM is to ensure that the investment in human capital is not lost due to infrastructure or budget deficiencies in other countries. Although still fraught with challenges, by continuing the mentorship there is a better chance that graduates of the program will apply their skills over the long term.

Another question that is raised, however, is how ELAM graduates, who are undergoing an additional five to eight years of education in Cuba, will manage to reintegrate into their home communities after such extended absences? Specialists are far more likely to work in hospitals and in urban areas where resources are more abundant. In Ecuador, specialists who are trained overseas must commit to the *año rural*, but they are sent to a large hospital, not a local clinic. Moreover, what cultural and social challenges would an ELAM graduate experience after being removed from the field for eleven to thirteen years? Most of the Ecuadorian ELAM graduates from 2005 to 2007 have fallen into this category. Their home country has not properly accommodated them, and many have stayed on in Cuba to further their knowledge of medicine and community health-care service. Dania Suarez reminded me of the value of specialization when she said that it is "incredibly important to continue studying and to become the best physician possible." Her commitment to community service and her desire to master her medical knowledge opens up a spatial dichotomy that health-care systems in the global South, or the global North for that matter, have not yet fully overcome. How can physicians further their professional education yet remain available for service to vulnerable communities? While the Cuban health-care system allows for specialists to work at the provincial level,

Ecuador has very little infrastructure to retain specialized human resources outside of the main centres of Quito, Guayaquil, and Cuenca.

"So why did you come back to Ecuador? To work in La Joya de los Sachas?" I asked Dania.

"We made a commitment to Cuba to serve our communities."

I asked her if perhaps the others are not as eager to work in the remote locations of this country, or is there something personal keeping them in Cuba?

Even Rector Juan Carrizo admits that the work environment awaiting ELAM graduates is not overly comfortable. He said that they face landscapes "without electricity, without other doctors, and with many, many mosquitoes." So perhaps from this point of view, extra time working in Cuba is not such a bad deal.

After six years in Cuba, Dania is one of the graduates who came back home. She returned because she felt compelled to serve, but after the *año rural,* Ecuador's ministry did not hire her or any of the other ELAM graduates working in La Joya de los Sachas. She was left without a job and had to seek out specialization options in other countries, including Cuba. Dania and Albania said that they felt a commitment to serve the marginalized. For other Ecuadorian graduates, being closer to their families was just as important as the commitment to serve. And for one graduate, a commitment to serve combined with a desire "never to return to Cuba" brought him home. Community service, pining for home, and wanting to get somewhere that had a wider variety of food and other consumption choices all played a part in the return of these ELAM graduates. These are personal choices, not contractual obligations, and they present a unique case against many of the tried and failed incentive plans that contractually bind doctors to serve in rural areas (Hutten-Czapski, 1998).[6]

It's a Private Affair

While the interviews with ELAM graduates took me into Ecuador's public health-care system, it was in late September 2006 when I stumbled upon Cuban involvement in the for-profit side. Walking along Avenida de Amazonas in Quito, I noticed a sign across the street: "Cuban–Ecuadorian Medical Specialists: International Centre for Medical Reference." Something did not seem right. Perhaps it was the neighbourhood. Amazonas is one of the wealthiest parts of Quito. The foreign automobile dealerships, the large mall, and the lack of sidewalks suggest that the poor are not invited to this part of town. The vehicles parked in front of the clinic were expensive Japanese SUVs. There was no Cuban flag, no national iconography, not even a bust of José Martí or Ecuadorian national hero, Eloy Alfaro. Then, from across the street, I saw the little logo that gave it all away: "We accept Visa." Was Gonzalo right? Had the Cuban-trained doctors gone into the private sector?

I entered the clinic, the International Centre for Medical Reference (CENIRMED). Inside I found a long queue of patients. They were waiting for triage. Two nurses were handling most of their requests, and slowly the line became shorter. Considering how many people were in the foyer, I figured the clinic was understaffed. I told the secretary who I was, and she invited me to wait upstairs and said someone would be along shortly. I sat in the waiting room between four doctors' offices, each with a physician inside. I waited for an hour. Every so often, the odd patient would come up to see a physician. Most came out with written prescriptions, and one family emerged from an office with their little child holding a lollipop but bursting with tears, having been freshly stung with a vaccination.

After an hour, I had enough of waiting. I knocked on one physician's door, but he told me that he was too busy to talk. Ten minutes later he left, hat on his head and umbrella under his arm. I knocked on another door and interrupted a doctor playing a video game. He invited me in to have a chat. I asked him about this clinic.

"This is a private clinic. We do not have any relations with the Ministry of Public Health or with Cuba."

"But your sign reads Cuban–Ecuadorian clinic."

"Yes, there were some physicians here who once took a couple of specialist courses in Cuba."

"So you have no Cuban doctors working here and no students from ELAM?"

"No, none."

"But the name of your clinic?"

"It was another group of physicians who came up with it, and, besides, patients respect Cuban medicine."

Later, I noticed a second clinic on Avienda de los Americas that advertised specialists in Cuban medicine. Ecuador's private sector advertises Cuban medicine as a competitive edge, one that can attract clients knowledgeable enough about the benefits of having a physician with a Cuban medical education. Ecuador's public health system may not show preference to Cuban medical education, but the private sector sees the competitive edge for marketing purposes. It is a bizarre affirmation of the ELAM program that public knowledge of the quality of Cuban care creates market incentives. Unfortunately, it does not overcome public sector indifference.

A Decision Not to Go

The Ecuadorian ELAM graduate Maria returned briefly to her home in Quito. She had had a baby in Cuba and after a visit to her family, she had decided to postpone her service in Ecuador's *año rural* and instead return to Cuba to practise with her husband. She told me that the greatest challenges in rural health in Ecuador were in educating people, but advancing her own education was her focus at that time. She was getting ready to return to a small Cuban village about forty minutes to the south of Havana where she would live with her family in a *consultorio*. The town has about five thousand people, she said, and her clinic would be responsible for 1,300 or so. The *consultorio* would be typical of any other family doctor practice in Cuba: nurses and doctors would work together receiving patients in the morning and doing house calls in the afternoon.

She praised Cuba's ability to allow doctors to meet with their patients in their homes, especially those too old or too infirm to come to the clinic: "There are many good social and family relations there," she said. She preferred the idea of patients knocking on her door at one in the morning over working in conditions where they would find it difficult to make it to the clinic, such as in La Joya de los Sachas. She said that in her opinion, "Life in Cuba is not necessarily better, but it is unique." Going back to Havana province to serve a community was, she felt, a way of repaying Cuba for her free medical education.

Postcards from the Field

The working conditions experienced by returning graduates are incredibly diverse. I spent time with five of the ELAM graduates in their work sites. I also spent time in other Ecuadorian medical facilities: private and public hospitals in Quito, private clinics in Cuenca and Quito, and a public clinic in Bolívar. The following three postcards from the field are sketches of my time spent with Fany in Loja, with Arlena in the public hospital in Zamora, and with Dania and Jacqueline in the clinic in La Joya de los Sachas. They are meant to show what a day in the life of an ELAM graduate in the field entails and the different experiences between graduates.

Loja

Fany met me at the bus station in Loja and we went to meet the other medical students. "You're having a meeting?" I asked.

"No, we're having a *manifestación*," she replied. "We are demonstrating because the medical society will not allow us rights to the hospitals, and we need more pay."

Ecuador's Ministry of Health would not allow a *médico general básico* hospital rights to visit patients, and the governing union for the doctors on the *año rural* felt that $300 a month was too low a wage for recent medical graduates. Considering that many of these doctors could receive higher wages and benefits in Chile, Ecuador's non-response was fuelling serious tensions. Fany was the only Cuban-trained physician in the group of about forty young doctors. They had been trained at various medical schools across the country and their posting just happened to be in Loja. Fany's family was from the city, and after the rally, we went to her parents' home for a meal.

"So, while you are on strike, who is attending to your clinics?"

"No one."

The collective bargaining had taken every *año rural* doctor off their post, leaving people to seek service in the centralized hospitals.

"There is a bigger problem here, though," Fany said. "I am a doctor. I can treat and diagnose the ill. I can deliver babies. But the hospitals will not let me in. Will not let us in. We need to ensure that our titles are recognized. We have many doctors in Ecuador, but they cannot be recognized and accredited by the national college in Pichincha. What a difference we could make if we had jobs and we had hospital rights."

Fany explained it well. The hospital rights issue was just one problem among many poorly organized health-care labour practices in Ecuador. By denying a doctor in the *año rural* hospital rights, the system transfers custody of the patient to another physician who does have rights, and this adds a layer of bureaucracy and disconnection. In any system, it is generally good advice to see a physician who has hospital rights so that they can do necessary follow-up work and dialogue with specialists about the patient's needs.

Fany's posting was at a hospital located more than an hour away from Loja. If she needed to refer a patient to a larger facility, her rights to the patient would end there. Already the *año rural* faces the difficulty of building doctor–patient relations with the mandatory 365-day turnover.

After five days, the doctors went back to work with a slight pay increase, but they continued to lack hospital rights and recognition of their degrees. Either trained at home, or, as in the case of Fany, trained abroad, *médico general básicos* are not afforded the opportunity to apply their skills in a manner that would work to further expand health-care accessibility in Ecuador.

Zamora

Zamora is a town where the mountains and jungle meet to produce a suffocating humidity in a lush and beautiful jungle landscape. It is legendary as having the longest life expectancy anywhere in Ecuador. The record has been held for more than one hundred years. Although a state-of-the art hospital exists in the city, the locals figure the water has some properties to fend off old age. Arlena Rodas met me at the bus station in the late evening. I had been on a bus for four hours, buried under a family of three who had snacked on a full chicken dinner during the cramped ride along narrow mountain pathways. Arlena made sure that I was fed, and she found me a decent place to stay. She said that she would come by the hotel at nine the next morning to show me around town.

"You don't have to work?"

"I don't have a job," she said.

Arlena had finished her *año rural* and had yet to be accepted into a specialization or residency. The other ELAM graduates were soon to be unemployed as well. After touring the city, we went to the hospital where she had been stationed. She had spent her *año rural* working in the hospital's emergency room.

"How many physicians are usually working in the ER?"

"Sometimes three, but usually just one."

The hospital seemed large enough to accommodate at least half a dozen ER doctors. It is a massive structure for a town so small.

"Do patients wait a long time for treatment, or do they ever go without?"

"Sure, they wait, but they never go without."

Already at eleven in the morning, there was a lengthy queue in the ER. About a dozen patients, all walking wounded, were waiting to see the one ER doctor on shift. Nurses were handling the triage, and some patients seemed to be carrying their complaints over to the pharmacist whose office was in the room across the hall.

Arlena took me up to visit the maternity ward. The ward had twelve beds, all with clean sheets, good lighting, and air conditioning. Three women were in the ward. One was tending to her little newborn with a doctor closely hovering over her bed. Family, gifts, and diaper bags surrounded the second. The third had her husband by her side. She lay on her back with an IV attached to her arm, looking straight at the ceiling. Something had gone or was going wrong.

The maternity ward did not give the impression that there was a lack of personnel or resources. Leaving it behind, we went further down the hall to the pediatric ward and to other wards. All were deserted. The pediatric ward did not have a single child in a single bed. "Is it usually this quiet?"

"Sometimes there are children in here, but yes, it is pretty calm."

In a country with so many endemic health problems, especially among children, here is a pediatric ward vacant because of economic and social barriers. On paper it looks good to have such resources available, and in the public sector no less, but something else is needed. Sure, the road to the hospital is no picnic, but it can be negotiated. What separates the maternity ward from the other wards is money. Only the services in the maternity ward are fully covered by the state. Every other service, from the $1 consultation fee to a night in a hospital bed, must be paid for by the patient. It is a basic-needs approach (Nussbaum, 2003) to essential services, but it does not experience active participation from Ecuadorians. The free services stop after the age of five, and it would seem that despite the obvious need across the country for health-care services, the poor stay away.

We continued to look around the hospital. We visited the dental clinic, the X-ray lab, the cardiovascular clinic, and the ophthalmology unit. The equipment seemed adequate. It was not the latest, but it was not outdated either. The odd bit of paint was missing, but then I noticed something else missing.

"Arlena, do you receive many indigenous patients?" Given that Zamora's indigenous population is substantial, I thought this a fair question.

"No, hardly any. They do not come to the hospital. There is discrimination in the system, and they do not come to us."

Gonzalo mentioned issues of mistrust, but Arlena blatantly labelled it as discrimination. After speaking with her about this, I understood her to mean that the system structurally discriminates against indigenous culture by not providing guaranteed access to their communities. She also suggested that health-care workers themselves bear prejudices against indigenous peoples.

"The hospital really seems quiet for its size."

She looked at me, shrugged, and said, "Those in need are very far away, and we do not have that many doctors working in the public system."

At the heart of Zamora's vacant hospital are themes of economic and social discrimination. While there may be infrastructure and human resources available in this town, ethnic tensions, poverty, and a lack of attention to the structural causes of inequity leave this hospital without sick people, while within the province there are many sick people without this hospital.

La Joya de los Sachas

The Canadian government advises its citizens to avoid this part of Ecuador. Discontent with foreign oil exploitation has led to foreigners being kidnapped. I had to fly in close to the Colombian border, find a taxi, and then find a bus to go an hour further into the jungle. The taxi driver was shocked to get a fare, and the bus driver told me, "Only mercenaries and missionaries come through here." The Amazon is a rolling boil of humidity and mosquitoes. The lushness creates an endless canopy. La Joya de los Sachas is hard to miss, as it is the first major town the bus passes through that has a giant oil pipeline sharing the main street. The sidewalk gives way to it. Teenagers sit on it at night drinking booze.

I met Dania and Jacqueline for lunch. I had not seen Dania in a year. "We would invite you stay with us in the clinic, but we have no space. Literally no space. It is so cramped."

We went to the La Joya de los Sachas public clinic. It was the only public health-care facility for eighty kilometres. There was another facility that operated as a public–private–NGO partnership, and, of course, there were private clinics in town. The public hospital in Coca could be reached with an hour of speedy driving. The La Joya de los Sachas clinic was two blocks in from the main pipeline.

Dirt roads, riddled with potholes, would just about guarantee a snapped ankle if one were to stumble. Standing pools of water, breeding grounds for mosquitoes, surrounded the clinic and the neighbourhood. The clinic was a hive of activity. Doctors (all on the *año rural*), nurses, and secretaries were handling the needs of about two dozen patients. Of the six *consultorios*, three were flooded and two were equipped with only the most basic examination equipment. The building advertised that at one time it had received handsome donations from the European Union, but those seem to have fallen short of supplying the clinics with necessary equipment, let alone a sump pump to handle flooded clinic rooms. A couple of rusted-out fans tried to keep us cool with little effect.

The next day I went to visit the clinic again, and again, the clinic was bustling with patients, most of whom were mothers and young children taking advantage of the free services and vaccinations. Dania invited me into her *consultorio*. A young mother was in there with her child, who was only a few weeks old. The mother handed Dania a government folder that keeps records of the free services.

"How many children do you have?"

"Four."

"Have any died?"

It is a common question in a country where the under-five mortality is 25 per 1,000.

The child had a respiratory condition and a sizeable rash around her midsection. The rash turned out to be a symptom of gastrointestinal trouble from the mother feeding the infant hot food. The mother, who Dania later told me suffered from a mental illness, started on a torrent of complaints about her house, her husband, and this child who was keeping her up all night. Dania filled out a prescription and a referral to have the infant looked at in the main hospital. All the time, she kept focused on the woman's conversation. In her ranting, the mother revealed all sorts of clues about her way of life. She had no education, lived by humble means, and it sounded as if her husband had trouble keeping a steady job. Once the mother calmed down, Dania approached her with the prescription and offered detailed instructions on how to give the medicine. She then repeated the details once more, along with strict instructions on how to feed the infant.

After the young mother left, Dania received a middle-aged man who brought in a slew of prescriptions to be renewed. Some were for his wife and others were for his children. He also had a fungus infection that Dania looked over before adding another prescription to his pile.

Then a prostitute came into the *consultorio*. She brought with her a standardized card that needed Dania's signature. The form needed a physician's signature to certify that she was free of sexually transmitted diseases. Prostitution is a way of life in La Joya de los Sachas; most of the petrol workers are from other parts of the country, and with migratory labour comes sex work. The police tolerate prostitution, but they may fine or jail the girls who cannot produce clean health records.

Then a woman came into the clinic with a large cyst growing over her eye. She had cut her inner eye socket, and it had become infected. The infection had created a large cyst that was now hindering her vision. It was not pleasant to look at, and the woman looked both to be in a great deal of discomfort from both pain and embarrassment. Dania got up from her desk and put on her white gloves. I asked if there was anything that I could do for her.

She said, "Yes. Put on some white gloves."

I dropped my pen and paper and put on the gloves. Dania took out a scalpel, one of the few instruments that was available in the clinic, and made an incision in the cyst. My role was to be quick and ready with clean cotton to keep the fluid out of the eye and to dab alcohol when needed. After about ten minutes of steady hands and concentration, we put gauze over the wound, and the woman went on her way with eyesight restored.

When the next man came into the *consultorio*, I still had the white gloves on. Before I could switch back to taking notes, Dania had me back at the examination table. The man was diabetic, and as a result of poor diet, he had developed open wounds on his body. He was complaining about the one on his buttocks, one that had been previously cleaned and dressed. With alcohol and cotton, I cleaned the open hole as Dania pulled out six inches of dressing, once soaked in iodine but now coated with various bodily fluids. The man howled in pain. Pulling out six inches of dressing must have felt like pulling out a python, and then, having removed the old dressing, we needed to replace it. I went to find more gauze while Dania cleaned his wound. I found very little, but we managed. I delivered the gauze to Dania inch by inch, and with the forceps, she pushed the clean gauze, drenched with iodine, back into the hole. The man yelped with pain. There was nothing that we could give him to take his mind off it. Inch by inch, he clenched his fists, bashed them on the bed, kicked, groaned, and sweated. After two minutes, it was over. Dania finished the dressing. The man got up, thanked us both, and hobbled out of the clinic with his teeth still clenched in pain.

By 4:30 p.m., it was almost time to call it a day and to take a break for some fruit salad. We met with Jacqueline. The patients in the waiting room had dispersed, and the clinic was quiet. Coming out of the back door, we met a man with his arm slung over another fellow. The hobbling man had his foot bandaged, and he could put no pressure on it.

"What happened?" Jacqueline asked.

"I just came from the hospital in Coca."

We were silent.

"I've been shot. I don't think that they got the bullet out. I can still feel it."

We took him back inside. His friend laid him out on the bed. Dania, Jacqueline, and I put on white gloves. Jacqueline undressed the foot, and Dania arranged the alcohol and dressing. She brought in a bright light and a magnifying glass as well. With Jacqueline now on the scene, my role was to hold the light and the magnifying glass, and pass the alcohol to the two doctors when they needed it. This man's foot was blown apart. The wound was open, and the bullet, at least most of it, must have gone through. Bones were torn apart, muscles and nerve endings were destroyed. He would never walk properly again. Still, Dania searched for debris, and with tweezers and a bulky magnifying glass, she found metal pieces in the man's foot. His friend held him down. Dania and Jacqueline meticulously searched the wound. After about fifteen minutes of picking, cleaning, and screaming, Jacqueline redressed the foot.

"There, it is all out," Dania said. The man, whose face was nearly blue from exhaustion and whose eyes were red from tears, thanked the doctors and hobbled out of the clinic.

The next morning we went with an NGO medical brigade out into the jungle. A makeshift clinic was set up in a small schoolhouse. Volunteer doctors, pharmacists, and dentists were offering free consultations. The school was bare bones, and running through the soccer pitch was an oil pipeline. The doctors offered brief consultations, and the medicines on hand were mostly generic antibiotics, donated from the European Union.

Jacqueline was *de guardia* (on call), and we needed to get back to the clinic. She had a young girl in labour—the same girl mentioned in the first chapter of this book. The 14-year-old had been raped at a New Year's party, and it would be the girl's first time giving birth. Dania reminded me that childbirth is risky business in Oriente (one mother dies for every 760 live births) (Country Health Profiles: Ecuador, 2006).

Dania and Jacqueline told me that they had cried almost every night in their shared room during the early part of their time in La Joya de los Sachas, but they managed to continue on for an entire year. It was a different reality than Cuba. The cyst in the eye, diabetic ulcers, the gunshot wound, and pregnancy are all easily prevented, treated, and/or supported with the right conditions and support, but in La Joya de los Sachas they are health calamities. The physicians are on a treadmill that keeps them too busy repairing the ill to maintain the healthy. The *año rural* may seem to be, on paper, a short amount of time, but working in the La Joya de los Sachas clinic the contract could seem interminable. Although the doctors know that without their presence, conditions for these patients would be considerably worse.

Informed Community Members

Effective disease prevention and health promotion requires willing participation at the community level as well as sound knowledge of imminent health risks. In La Joya de los Sachas, the environmental degradation from oil development is a major health determinant (Breilh et al., 2005). In Zamora and Loja, child hunger exists (Larrea & Kawachi, 2005), and in Imbabura hunger coupled with poor education and lack of sanitation are all key determinants (Angeles, Trujillo, & Lastra, 2007). Across all of these regions are major incidences of diseases due to poverty, poor nutrition, and non-potable water.

Interviews with ELAM graduates explored how well their community members knew about social and environmental determinants of health. We discussed whether initiatives were in place to further education and awareness on various health indicators, how such initiatives were organized, and what role they, as doctors, played in the process. Some of the graduates said that they could never see patients in their homes. Patients live too far away, and the long hours at the clinic did not give them time for outcalls. All of the graduates claimed that their patients were generally unaware of their health conditions, let alone broader environmental determinants: "It is not like Cuba," Elizabeth said, "where people are informed." Dania explained that people are generally aware that oil development has caused problems to the environment, but some villagers living in an area that has been impacted by hydrocarbons seeping into the ground water will continue to drink and bathe in the water. There are some educational campaigns organized by the provincial health authority, Jacqueline told me; one is against tuberculosis and another seeks to educate people about sexual health, "But very little about disease prevention and health promotion." They felt that the campaigns had some impact in building awareness about specific maladies, but they did little to improve the basic health risks that come with poverty. Occasionally, the ELAM graduates in La Joya de los Sachas had gone to a public health rally or hosted an information session in the clinic, but very little medicine in the community was occurring in this part of the Amazon.

In Loja, Fany told me that her patients knew very little about their own health challenges let alone the broader determinants: "They deal with the *colundreno*" (traditional healer). She said that she was able to visit some patients in their homes depending on the time and distance, but it was not the norm: "This is not Cuba."

Arlena told me that she had no time to visit patients and that most of her duties were in the hospital. Few people, she said, had a good idea of what their health conditions entailed, and she blamed it on a general lack of education in Zamora. She mentioned that having meetings with community leaders about disease prevention and health promotion was not possible on her work schedule, although she added that the Ministry of Health and various NGOs ran active public awareness campaigns on HIV/AIDS and tuberculosis.

Ricardo and Albania stood apart from the rest of the group when it came to this series of questions. They experienced the poorest levels of clinical support but had the greatest potential to educate patients in the community setting. Ricardo said that many people who visit his clinic were quite ignorant of their personal and community health needs. His biggest challenge was to build basic education with his patients, as many of the adults had not completed an elementary school education. In his clinic, he held information sessions on themes from proper nutrition to effective hygiene. He said that he was lucky because in his town there are a couple of primary schools and a high school that he could work with to organize information sessions. Meetings with community members took place regularly, according to Ricardo. The objective he told me was "disease prevention, because it is the most effective form of medicine." He felt that his case was unique, as other provinces had not put resources into disease prevention and health promotion strategies. I asked him if he felt that such routines were effective, and he responded, "Absolutely." But he admitted that the poor state of education and infrastructure in the province was a big hurdle to overcome. As much as people can be made aware of how to improve health, non-existent economic or social capacities ensure that they continue to live in conditions that hinder good health.

Albania admitted that the lack of education and lagging sanitation infrastructure in her community were two enormous challenges to providing quality care. She said that she was able to talk to community leaders and NGOs to organize information sessions, but even so, there is little infrastructure for comprehensive disease prevention and health promotion routines. Her primary concern was for infant health, and she tried to organize information sessions on neonatal health with community groups with the assistance of the NGOs working in the region. As neonatal care is a guaranteed service in Ecuador, Albania's desire to see people take part in this existing support network, minimal as it is, was a fitting move. The goal, she said, is to educate people on the value of the prevention of illness, especially for young children. She felt that her efforts were effective, but given that most of the community makes it only to the sixth grade and then work in the agricultural sector, they do not receive education and information on proper hygiene in the home. Albania did house calls and found that hygiene was the biggest culprit of poor health in the community. Sanitation and clean water were not reliable, and health problems could easily spread through the community.

In all of their accounts, the ELAM graduates acknowledged that they tried to educate their patients in the clinic, the classroom, or in the community about the importance of preventative routines. However, it becomes a battle of good advice going up against poor infrastructure. Albania and Ricardo, working in small clinics in Imbabura that afforded them the opportunity to work in their communities, managed to take the message of disease prevention and health promotion beyond the clinic, but the others, working in the larger public health infrastructure, felt helpless to do so. Ultimately, the ELAM graduates working across Ecuador were on their own. With little structural support from the Ecuadorian government, it came down to their own motivation to build health education in their communities.

Did these health information sessions impact lives? Certainly. Did they manage to overcome structures of inequity? Hardly. The place of the ELAM graduate working in their home country differs from Cuban doctors. With constant support from MINSAP, Cuban health workers operate in a normative structure to facilitate rural outreach and community-based primary care. The exceptional ELAM graduates returning home to face little to no support take on the role of humanitarians. Humanitarian doctors do what they can with what they have, and often, as Orbinski (2008) notes, can make only imperfect offerings. The humanitarian doctor gives beyond expectations, and they become exceptions to the normative behaviour of the system. The question then is how the system can make outreach and education less about humanitarian duties and more about the norm of public health care. Do the changes come from government? Can such changes be triggered by individual actions being repeated across a national health system? Perhaps it is both. And perhaps the acknowledgement of ELAM graduates willing to take on this moral obligation is a first step forward.

In my final days in Ecuador, I met with representatives from the Cuban embassy to talk about the reintegration of ELAM graduates.

"Cuba cannot rebuild a country's health-care sector; we can only train doctors and offer help when asked," said First Secretary Jorge Gómez Rodriguez at the Cuban embassy in Quito. Manuel Torigo, from MINREX, later told me the same.

I told the first secretary about my experiences at the various clinics and my thoughts on the ELAM program. The challenges lie with the constraints in the field, I said. He agreed, and he suggested that now with the Correa government in power there could be room to find solutions to these problems. While Cuba does not want to rearrange Ecuador's health-care sector formally, they continue to increase capacity by doubling the number of available scholarships to ELAM for Ecuadorians and by expanding the intake of students into the ALBA program. The embassy received only a few dozen applications for ELAM in 1999, and they had been pre-screened by Ecuador's Ministry of Health. At the time, all of the applicants who made it to the embassy were offered scholarships. In

2006, the embassy received thousands of applications for one thousand placements directly from applicants.

"When we take in the applications, there is a large crowd in the street," said
Gómez Rodriguez. The popularity and awareness of the program has grown so
much since 1999 that the embassy is accepting only one in three applications.
As of 2006, Cuba is furthering enrolment and expanding training through programs such as the ALBA program that work alongside ELAM. Already Cuba
has implemented a reintegration process for ALBA students where they will
spend their sixth year of training alongside existing Cuban medical brigades in
their home country. This could be advantageous; rather than working through
existing national infrastructure, students will have the chance to practise and
connect with their communities as part of their education.

Building upon strengths is important, no doubt, but the question of how to
build capacity within communities has yet to be answered. By increasing medical training capacity in Cuba, will more doctors like the eight that I followed
be able to apply their convictions and compassion in the rural clinics? Or will
the majority, like the forty-three who stayed in Cuba, remain far from the field?

I talked with the Brigada Eloy Alfaro, an Ecuadorian–Cuba solidarity
group, about this. They said that they keep in touch with Ecuadorian ELAM
students while they are in Cuba, and they help to find them suitable places for
the *año rural* when they return. They also play an active role in spreading the
word about ELAM (and now ALBA), and they arrange for solidarity exchanges
between members of their group and groups in Cuba. While they do maintain
contacts and relations with the ELAM graduates during and after the *año rural*,
they do not have the capacity to assist them in finding long-term work. Both the
brigade and the embassy are aware of the challenges of reintegration. Instead of
giving up, they are working to increase capacity on the recruitment end.

The experiences of the ELAM graduates in the field are diverse. It suggests
that there are regional variations in the organization and utilization of human
resources for health among the provinces. Some of the differences are a result of
variations in infrastructure between the central hospitals and the rural clinics,
but they are also products of decisions made at the provincial level, as access to
a hospital in Loja, for example, is far easier than it is in La Joya de los Sachas.
Then there are Albania and Ricardo in Imbabura who seemed to be making
changes that are aimed at building capacity from the bottom up. Imbabura is
testimony that despite a neoliberal hollowing of social resources, political and
social support can still be mustered through political leadership in order to
overcome the constraints against community-based care. With a new national
government in power, political change may be possible, but this will take years
to redress the deeply ingrained structures of inequity. In a place such as La Joya

de los Sachas, a naturally rich landscape where only a few cents of every barrel of oil pulled out of the ground comes back to the community, political support needs to be acquired to improve the restructuring of health-care services so that physicians and patients can go beyond the treadmills of repair and despair.

Having completed their service in the *año rural* and standing on the brink of an uncertain career path, none of the ELAM graduates seemed the least bit disenfranchised with the idea that medicine should be a service. Ricardo admitted that he might not stick with medicine, and Jacqueline will eventually seek a pediatrics specialization in Spain because her father is a citizen there, but none of them, not one single ELAM graduate, said that he or she would dedicate his or her medical skills to the private sector.

This is in stark contrast to the medical students from Quito's Universidad Central who all said that they wanted some hand in the private sector. Some ELAM graduates admitted that it is financial suicide to stay in the public system, and others noted that specialists working for the public system do receive higher wages, but they all detested the idea of opening a private for-profit clinic such as CENIRMED.

This brings back the question of whether individuals working as humanitarians in trying conditions can change a system or if that system will change them. In the end, very few of them managed to counter the hegemony of Ecuadorian health care within the time and resources that they had available. Gramsci (2006) wrote that counter-hegemony could not occur in one sweep. It takes time to position alternatives against the system (Cox 2005). The current challenges of mistrust in communities, of being overworked in the clinics, of lacking resources, of poor education and sanitation, and even institutional racism within the public sector are all working against them. The ethics of Cuban medical internationalism, which the ELAM graduates embrace, have yet to scale up through their interventions in Ecuador to overrule these hegemonic processes. Organizational and sociopolitical change will require broader social support in places such as La Joya de los Sachas. This does not mean that ELAM's good intentions should be dismissed. At the moment, dialectics between the ethics of the graduates and the norms of the system are under way. If support can be placed in the values of the ELAM graduates then the good sense of counter-hegemony against health inequity can be put into motion.

It is an important process that is unfolding. Cuba is continuing to build capacity for human resources for health without fully knowing how these health-care professionals will integrate into their home communities. The idea is to continue building capacity with the hope that increasing the number of graduates will tip the scales, and the system will have to accommodate their compassion.

CHAPTER 6

THE FRUIT OF SOLIDARITY:

HOW TO MAINTAIN HOPE FOR

GLOBAL HEALTH

Recently I was at a conference on medical education. I gave a brief presentation on Cuban medical internationalism. A senior medical specialist asked me, "Do you think that the Cubans would benefit from my knowledge?" He was a top surgeon in his field, and figuring that Cuba was defined by poverty and lacked resources in its health-care system, he felt that the Cuban people needed his skills and knowledge. Perhaps Cuban surgeons could benefit from his knowledge, and I am sure they would welcome the dialogue. But I wonder if this surgeon would not benefit more from their knowledge about the ethics of practice, the focus on accessibility, and the issues of long-term patient care. More broadly, one could ask whether the global North could benefit from Cuba's knowledge and experience. To this, I would say yes.

There are many specific lessons to take out of Cuban medical internationalism. There are notions of soft power diplomacy that come from placing health care and outreach into the heart of foreign policy. There are lessons about how medical education can play a role in ensuring that health workers are trained to treat the poor, rather than focusing on the needs of the affluent. There are other lessons about how medical tourism through neoliberal globalization is loaded with potential peril, but how it is possible to use the same tools of globalization to meet the needs of the poor. There are lessons that come from the experiences of Cuban graduates who choose to work in underserviced areas and the struggles that they face in delivering health care. And there are lessons about the migration of health-care workers in the global South who have no viable option to stay and serve their communities.

But of all the lessons that come from Cuba's place in the global health landscape, the one that stands out the most is the moral commitment to refuse to accept health inequalities that result from rampant socioeconomic inequality. The commitment and effort of Cuban-trained health-care workers and the political leadership that allows them to serve the underserved is a needed example of global health ethics for which health-care workers in many nations, rich and poor, currently lack. This is not to say that the Cuban experience should or even could be copied everywhere. Rather, Cuba's place in the global health landscape is as an example of an alternative to the dominant sociopolitical structures that abhor humanitarianism, solidarity, and cooperation. The Cuban case shows that such traits can be part of a normative process and not just as products of altruism and exceptionalism. The Cuban case shows that the desire to help the marginalized should be normative and not exceptional to a health system. Certainly, there is room to embrace such values in the sociopolitical fabric that governs the practice of medicine and the practice of foreign policy—values that embrace the desire to address the needs of others on this planet no matter how desperate, or distant, their situations might be.

For broad social change to occur, there must be change to the dominant political discourse, and as history has shown, this may come slowly and with struggles between ideological opponents. But the lofty goals of ensuring global health equity where the receipt of health care is seen as a human right will require a broad, multinational movement that embraces service to the poor as an ethical value. For this, Cuba offers five clear lessons:

- Invest in people, not always in physical things. Survival from massive economic hardships need not be found through austerity protocols. It can occur by scaling up education and reinforcing the public sector.
- Building strong human resources for health capacity and intersectoral partnerships allows health to flourish even in resource-poor settings.
- Building capacity does not have to stop after the management of a national crisis. Capacity building can, and should, address broader global health challenges. Doing so can still act within a nation's own best interest.
- The decision to not close a single university or hospital during an economic disaster requires the popular acceptance of narratives that view health as an intrinsic human value, not as a social burden.
- With appropriate political leadership that values health, and with popular support to deal with health through frameworks of disease prevention and health promotion that value community-level education, immediate and long-term global health goals can be achieved.

As much as Cuba is in a position to offer lessons to the world, it is also in a position of struggle, particularly when it comes to warming relations with the United States. With relations frozen between the two countries, it is likely that tensions over Cuba's access to material resources and the United States' determination to draw out human resources for health will continue. But if the two countries could move towards dialogue aimed at official cooperation, it is possible that the immediate and long-term needs of both countries could be addressed. Beyond medical and material resources, both countries have a tremendous amount to gain by working together rather than against one another. Could multilateral cooperation through projects to deliver needed aid and outreach in countries such as Haiti be the way to open a dialogue?

Many tourists who come to Cuba often come away thinking, "What will happen when Cuba opens up to the United States?" This question suggests that US franchises will pop up all over the place and Cuban doctors will leave the country in droves. However, this speaks more about the assumptions foreigners make about Cuban society than about how Cuban nationalism and the popular support for safety and security of the nation state truly operate. Most Cuban doctors are not waiting to leave for Miami, even though northern news outlets might see it this way (Millman, 2011). From my own research and from numerous personal communications with Cuban health workers, I can see that there is a strong desire to see the health-care system maintained and strengthened with good internal management and supportive foreign cooperation.

Although most Cuban health-care workers are proud nationalists that have a secure place within their own country to practise, many desire to serve others who desperately need their services, be it in the global South or the global North. With the United States ninety miles away and in desperate need of human resources for health, Cuban doctors should be able to help meet the needs of underserviced Americans, and yet they should also have equal remunerative and social comforts available to them if they choose to remain in their home country. The choice to work in the United States should not be one that comes down to gaining windfall salary over dismal wages at home. This choice should come from a value system based on cooperation and solidarity and helping your neighbour, as it is for the Cuban health-care workers working around the world. Until this sentiment of solidarity is embraced between Cuba and the United States, tensions will continue to run high, and there will continue to be a gnawing temptation for Cuban doctors that the offer of larger salaries is worth giving up the way of life at home.

The role of nationalism, pride, and ties to one's history and family cannot be overlooked in this. All around the world, individuals and corporations are offered lucrative gains to take their businesses offshore. Tens of thousands of

Filipino health-care workers are one such example. But money is not always the temptation one thinks it might be. IKEA, SAAB, and Erikson, successful companies based in Sweden, pay substantial corporate taxes to their government, but they have all rejected offers from Amsterdam to come and set up their main headquarters in The Netherlands at a lower tax rate. Even in the corporate world, nationalism counts. Similarly, Cuban physicians do not easily give up their nation for higher profits. The United States continues to recruit Cuban doctors through the CMPP, but it has seen only minor gains. If this program were withdrawn and replaced with bilateral cooperation with the Cuban government, then perhaps new relations of solidarity could emerge.

Beyond the current tensions with the United States, Cuba has shown the world that it is important to train health-care workers with an imperative to serve those who are in desperate need, even in countries that are politically cool or outright hostile. Currently, 18.5 million people are lost each year from preventable reasons. What is the end goal of continuing to train doctors who know how to score high on exams, but who know nothing about serving in under-resourced settings? Perhaps some will say that until it is possible to ensure the proper infrastructure to meet the needs of the poor there is little point in training doctors with the ethics of service to the poor. Others might think that the challenges are just too great and ethical doctors will just burn out and abandon their posts for better paycheques.

Certainly, the challenges are enormous. Few rural clinics in India have a phone or running water. Throughout South America, the public clinics are under-resourced or closed altogether for a lack of staff. In many parts of Africa, clinics simply do not exist. Governments tied to the IMF and World Bank operations are often caught up in cost cutting and have little room to widen access to health-care services to the poor. Such sociopolitical structures are enormous, this is true, but politics created them and that means that politics can change them.

Cuba's large-scale formation of doctors trained in humanism and cooperation rather than self-interest and competition demonstrates that the ethics of health-care service is dynamic and that current systems are not interminably doomed to cope with physicians who do not wish to serve in economically hobbled regions. It also suggests that if the structural ethics of inequality are not static then they must be dynamic processes that are held together by collective sentiments of acquiescence to suffering and poverty. This is why alternatives matter. They show that committed individuals with brave ideas can work to change that global system.

ELAM doctors are the living example that a paradigm shift is possible starting with individuals. These physicians possess the conviction to help others regardless of the challenges in the field and despite the fact that they endured personal sacrifices and hardships. Considering their experiences, and keeping in mind that Cuban medical internationalism, as soft power, is building respect among countries in the global South, the question is how to build the appropriate social and political conditions for institutional ethics and soft power to come together at the community level to overcome the hegemony of health inequality.

The Ecuadorian graduates spoke up to say that ELAM should not be changed to adhere to the Ecuadorian reality; they felt that Ecuador should be changed to adhere to the ELAM reality. In May 2007, Ecuadorian alumni from various Cuban institutions, ELAM included, created the Front of Multidisciplinary Professional Graduates from Cuba with a goal to lobby the Ecuadorian government to find ways to accept their skills within the public sector. Within this group is a select group of ELAM graduates who call themselves the Internationalist Federation of Health (FIS) and who seek state support in implementing programs to administer socialist and humanist medicine alongside primary care. Their goal is to help create, on a broad scale, the necessary political and social support to facilitate widespread programs of disease prevention and health promotion.

The FIS manifesto states that they will return to Ecuador as doctors, but also as leaders in popular health provision. They asked President Correa's government to lead structural changes to the health-care system that will better allow them to practise medicine in their communities. By engaging their political leaders, they sought opportunities for much-needed organization and environmental change. Since 2009, Correa's government has warmed relations with Cuba in commerce and medical cooperation. As a result, hundreds of Cuban doctors are now working in the country to provide medical services and training for marginalized communities.

The ELAM graduates accept the difficulties and the challenges that await them. Instead of giving in, however, and instead of finding lucrative positions in the private sector, they have organized, vocalized, and encouraged the government to change its normative behaviour. These medical doctors have refused to say that poverty and unnecessary inequities in health care are inevitable. What they have said is the problem with health-care inequity is not with them. It is with the system. They do not need to change to meet the system's expectations. Rather, that system needs to change to meet their expectations.

US ELAM graduates are saying the very same thing. Many US ELAM students and graduates have returned their country to participate in community outreach programs in places such as New Orleans. They have organized themselves through social media, and found dedicated mentors, and current students and recent graduates are gaining invaluable experience by going out into some of America's poorest communities to offer treatment and to learn about rampant health inequality within their own country. Other students and graduates have formed their own medical brigades to organize missions to West Africa where they focus on the challenges of maternal health in that region.

There is also the story of Luther Castillo who, upon graduating from ELAM, returned to Honduras to establish the first comprehensive medical clinic in the Garifuna region of Honduras. Until the 2009 coup, in which his life was threatened by the military dictatorship, his clinic offered services in the region that had never been provided locally. The clinic had received donations and assistance from both Cuba and US NGOs, and youth from the community were being mentored for future medical education. After the coup, the government sacked his clinic and ordered the nursing staff fired. Castillo left the country for a brief time to gain political support in the United States and Canada, but he returned to Honduras to continue his commitment to bring health care to those who needed it most. Surely, Luther's story shows that it is possible to build multilateral partnerships and open dialogue across politically hostile borders.

Across the border in El Salvador, the ELAM graduates there have organized into a supportive nation-wide network aimed at sharing ideas and strategies for disease prevention and health promotion. They work closely with Cuban physicians in the nation and participate in the growing number of comprehensive health brigades that are offering basic services to rural and underserved populations across the country. They, too, show that it is the current system that needs mending, and by organizing and working together, they can create structural changes for their country.

And what about the global North? It comes back to the key lesson that Cuba offers: There should be a refusal to acquiesce to the massive inequities in health care in an era of scientific and social advancements in medicine. Often health care is positioned as an instrumental privilege that can be measured and partitioned according to wealth. It is up to the citizens of those nations in the global North to refuse to accept global health inequity.

Beyond moral refusal by individuals, it is time for communities and societies to organize to pressure the regulators of health-care inequality, the IMF, the World Bank, and national governments and say that tolerance for unnecessary mortality and suffering in the name of progress is not acceptable.

Looking at the state of global health and global health education it is hard to say if such idealism makes a difference. With all of the conferences, articles, and book chapters written on the subject, and with statistic after statistic showing that health inequalities are worsening, it is hard to say that a difference has been made over the years. There are still clinics with flooded treatment rooms, and there are still too many children who will die from preventable diseases. Too many mothers will not live through childbirth because they could not afford a health-care worker or, worse still, there was simply not one available. There is still not enough political energy to address global health inequality, even if new leaders speak boldly about the need for change when it comes to HIV/AIDS and tuberculosis. Preventable diseases on the whole continue to outstrip the mortality count of these two highly illuminated diseases.

With such challenges ahead, it is worthwhile to take a moment to consider what F. Scott Fitzgerald (1937) wrote in "The Crack-Up," that the "test of a first-rate intelligence is the ability to hold two opposed ideas in the mind at the same time. One should, for example, be able to see that things are hopeless and yet be determined to make them otherwise" (p. 139). In the midst of increasing global health inequity, is it possible to build on the examples of Cuban medical internationalism in order to realize that things are utterly hopeless for many of the world's poor and yet be determined to make them otherwise?

I come back to what one of the doctors working in that clinic in Ecuador told me. After being laid off after a year of working in overwhelming conditions, she started to lobby the government for change, and she said, "This inequitable system didn't turn us into it." And it did not. The ELAM graduates resist the pressure, and they continue to pursue their commitment to global health equity and global health ethics. The resistance of ELAM graduates is the best example of the moral values of Cuban medical internationalism. And they are, in themselves, a tremendous triumph.

Cuban medical internationalism can be understood in multiple ways: as an aperture of altruism, as a clever foreign policy tactic, as an example of systematically valuing the poor, or as a work-in-progress. No matter how one chooses to see Cuban medical internationalism, one thing remains certain. Cuba has not changed the global health landscape but neither has the global system of inequity changed Cuba. If anything, Cuba has made deep impacts into that system while maintaining its ethics and values.

That system Cuba rejects is the one in which a global health workforce offers quality health care to those who can pay for it while the poor are left to die; the one in which governments continue to make policies that break bones instead of healing bones; and the one in which doctors are trained to value profit more than caring for the destitute. There have been tens of thousands of Cuban health-care workers who reject this system, and millions of other health workers who share Cuba's commitment to global health equity, and although they may not have changed that system yet, that system has not changed them either.

NOTES

Notes to Preface

1 All dollar currencies are US dollars unless otherwise noted.

Notes to Chapter 1

1 Translated literally as "The Jewel of the Weeds." This is a town in Ecuador's Amazon, located 80 km from the city of Coca.

2 Cuba's provision of medical services has been labelled as "medical diplomacy," "medical export," and "trading doctors for oil." There are, however, flaws with these, and other, definitions. This book employs the term "Cuban medical internationalism" as defined by Huish and Kirk (2007). The idea is that Cuba's medical efforts around the world are a convergence of two evolutionary trends in public health and foreign policy. This definition emphasizes that the reasons for, and impacts of, medical internationalism are not just limited to public health or foreign policy. Rather, there are impacts and benefits within both sectors, and they cannot be divorced from each other.

3 "Forward innovation" refers to the development of pharmaceutical products that currently do not exist for treatment therapies. "Backward innovation" refers to the process of researching existing products and reproducing their recipes for low-cost use.

4 The Declaration of Alma-Alta is the 1978 international agreement that declares health to be a human right and that universal health care would be a reality by the twenty-first century.

5 The word "tokenism" refers to highly symbolic, media-ready, short-term interventions that do little to create transformative health benefits on the ground.

6 The breakdown of Canadian government aid to Haiti following the earthquake was as follows: $43 million to the World Food Program for food assistance, air transportation, emergency telecommunications, and logistics; $33 million to match Canadian citizens private donations to the Red Cross for foreign debt relief programs; $30 million to Canadian organizations for short-term recovery and reconstruction projects; $16.5 million to a police training program; $10 million towards Haitian justice and security institutions; $5.8 million in support of the November 2010 elections; $4.5 million to support an agricultural credit financing program; and $500,000 to CANADEM (an association of Canadian technical experts) for deployment of Canadian experts to United Nations organizations (Aid Facts on Haiti, 2011).

7 It is currently illegal for a Canadian physician to provide both private and public health-care services (although many travel clinics get away with it). The idea that a second tier of health-care services could increase efficiency is madness: such a system would certainly retain more physicians for the needs of those who could afford

to pay a higher price than it would retain doctors in the public system. It is not as if Canada, or any nation, can increase public efficiency through a reserve army of doctors waiting to be unleashed to off-load patient demand by market liberalization. For more explanation on the politics and history of the Canada Health Act and medicare in Canada, see Steven Lewis et al. (2001) and Greg Marchildon (2005).

8   By 1965, Cuban physicians largely went on salary (though some stayed on the fee-for-service model). Cuban medical students in the 1960s took a pledge upon graduation that they would not bill for services.

Notes to Chapter 2

1   Martí's work on "Nature" is tremendously important to understanding his later, more radical, understandings of society. The use of the word "Nature" is not taken to mean natural flora and fauna, but meant as a broader understanding of the connections between humans and their lived worlds.

2   The 1992 Torricelli Act prohibits the sale of medicine and food to Cuba directly from the United States. The 1997 Helms–Burton law goes a step further to allow US corporations to sue foreign corporations that maintain business relations with the United States while also exporting goods to Cuba. It is a loose law, as many exports do make it to Cuba, but the export of medical resources and pharmaceuticals remains under attack. In one case, a Canadian exporter served four years in federal prison in the United States for selling water purifiers to Cuban hospitals.

Notes to Chapter 3

1   MEDICC is Medical Education and Cooperation with Cuba, an NGO out of Oakland, California. They offer both news and scholastic publications on Cuban health care.

2   These clinics are staffed by both Cuban and local health-care workers.

3   Interviews took place in January 2010 with students studying at Mbarara University, a medical school the Cuban government helped to establish in 1989.

4   Assuming return airfare to cost about $800 (maximum) for a flight in the Caribbean from Havana; rural area lodging at $150 per month; and the contract salary for a Cuban doctor working overseas at $150 per month, this is a very rough estimate.

Notes to Chapter 4

1   Paul Farmer's (2005) book *Pathologies of Power* helps to define and explain this term. Broadly understood, structural violence involves negative impacts against vulnerable populations that lead to increased risk, poor health, and loss of livelihood. Economic restructuring, lagging services, and displacement of peoples may not usually be thought of as the focus of violence, but they are imposing structures that can negatively affect a person's well-being.

2   The Henry Reeve Brigade is an emergency response brigade formed in 2005 to offer medical relief to victims of Hurricane Katrina in the US. Washington refused the Cuban offer. Subsequently the brigade was deployed to Central America and later to Pakistan in response to a devastating earthquake that killed 69,000 and displaced up to 3 million people. In Pakistan the brigade involved over a thousand Cuban personnel. They maintained operations for thirteen months, and the MINSAP offered a thousand medical scholarships to local youth from the affected region.

3 Otorhinolaryngologists are more commonly known as ear, nose, and throat specialists.

4 By this, I mean that medical education moved from a Eurocentric vision of medicine to one that emphasized advancements in health through technology, biotechnology, and advanced surgical procedures. I call this neocolonial in order to suggest that although other approaches to health and health care abound in the Americas, many of the traditional and indigenous approaches to health care were discredited in the pursuit of scientific advancement in medicine.

5 A great deal of scholarship connecting individual health to social and economic determinants is done through identifying trends between populations and place. Epidemiology plays a major role in making these connections; however, more evidence-based studies are sought within the Cuban curriculum to make direct connections between socio-environmental health vectors and health trends.

6 Coppelia is a famous open-air ice cream parlour that is tremendously popular among Cubans for dishing out high-quality ice cream in Cuban national pesos. As ELAM students have national student cards, they, too, get to enjoy the ice cream in national pesos, whereas tourists would have to line up in the foreign currency line and pay twenty-six times the price for the same product.

Notes to Chapter 5

1 This figure is based on interview data gathered in Sachas in 2006.

2 This claim is based on fieldwork conducted in Maharashtra, India, in 2011.

3 In health, proximal care usually refers to care that is up close and involved. The Cuban and Venezuelan programs operate in this sense by placing health workers in the community and by having direct and involved relations with people's health needs. As well, there is specific attention to the social determinants of health within their programs.

4 Distal care is the antithesis to proximal care. In public health, this can be understood as the state having minimal involvement with an individual's needs. Instead of dedicated programs and services offered to patients, there is a tendency to rely on market forces and individual behaviour in handling health troubles.

5 Integrated family medicine is the preferred term for this specialization, although it could be considered close to community medicine as the trainees work in rural settings and practise medicine in the community at the *consultorio* level. Since 2005, ELAM graduates are able to work alongside Cuban brigade workers in countries such as Haiti and Guatemala.

6 Hutten-Czapski (1998) found that many contractual or forced-service medical postings are disastrous. Physicians are often frustrated from the experience, and marginalized communities have a continuous stream of new physicians merely serving their time rather than establishing long-term practices.

REFERENCES

Aid Facts on Haiti. (2011, June). *Canada Haiti Action Network.* Retrieved from http://canadahaitiaction.ca/content/aid-facts-haiti-june-2011

Alemañy Pérez, E. J., Otero Jacinta, I., Borroto Cruz, R., & Fernández, G. (2002). El pensamiento de Fidel Castro Ruz sobre el modelo del especialista en medicina general integral. *Revista Cubana Educacion Medica Superior, 16*(3), 231–48.

Aluwihare, A. P. R. (2005). Physician migration: Donor country impact. *Journal of Continuing Education in the Health Professions, 25*(1), 15–21.

Álvarez Sintes, R. (2001). *Temas de medicina general integral: Vol 1. Principales afecciones del individuo en los contextos familiar y social.* La Habana, Cuba: Editorial Ciencias Médicas.

Anderson, B. (2006). *Imagined communities: Reflections on the origin and spread of nationalism* (Rev. ed.). London, England: Verso.

Anderson, M. (2009, July 17). Update on Dr. Luther Castillo & the Honduran coup. *Social Medicine.* Retrieved from http://www.socialmedicine.org/2009/07/17/latin-american-social-medicine/update-on-dr-luther-castillo-the-honduran-coup/

Angeles, G., Trujillo, A., & Lastra, A. (2007). Is public health expenditure in Ecuador progressive or regressive? *International Journal of Public Policy, 2*(3/4), 186–216.

Archer, N., Moschovis, P., Le, P., & Farmer, P. (2011). Perspective: Postearthquake Haiti renews the call for global health training in medical education. *Academic Medicine. 86*(7), 889–91.

Astor, A., Akhtar, T., Matallana, M. A., Muthuswamy, V., Olowu, F., Tallo, V., & Lie, R. (2005). Physician migration: Views from professionals in Colombia, Nigeria, India, Pakistan, and the Philippines. *Social Science & Medicine, 61*, 2492–500.

Asturizaga Rodriguez, D. (1996). *Situacion del servicio social rural obligatorio en Bolivia.* Revised paper originally presented at the workshop El Servicio Social en Medicina en America Latina, Washington, DC.

Atun, R., Pothapregada, S. K., Kwansah, J., Degboste, D., & Lazarus, J. (2011). Critical interactions between the global fund-support HIV programs and the health system in Ghana. *Journal of Acquired Immune Deficiency Syndromes, 57*(2), S72–S76.

Barber Fox, M., & Barber Gutiérrez, E. (2000). La fisiología del problema de la correlación entre lo biológico y lo social. *Revista Cubana Educacion Medica Superior, 14*(2), 163–70.

Becker, H. S. (1977). *Boys in white: Student culture in medical school.* New Brunswick, NJ: Transaction Books.

Bhorat, H., Meyer, J., & Mlatsheni, C. (2002). Skilled labour migration from developing countries: Study on south and southern Africa. *International Migration Paper 52.* Cornell University. Retrieved from http://www.ilo.int/public/english/protection/migrant/download/imp/imp52e.pdf

Blakeley, R. (2006). Still training to torture? US training of military forces from Latin America. *Third World Quarterly, 27*(8), 1439–61.

Bloch, B. (2009). Washington's double standard on Cuba: Havana as a spurious 'state sponsor of terrorism.' *COHA.* Retrieved from http://www.coha.org/washington's-double-standard-on-cuba-part-i-cuba-as-a-"state-sponsor-of-terrorism"/

Bloom, G., & Standing, H. (2001). Human resources and health personnel. *Africa Policy Development Review, 1*(1), 7–19.

Bosch Valdés, F. (1999). La medicina tradicional y natural en Cuba. *RESUMED, 12*(1), 3–6.

Boulet, J. R., Norcini, J. J., Whelan, G. P., Hallock, J. A., & Seeling, S. S. (2006). The international medical graduate pipeline: Recent trends in certification and residency training. *Health Affairs, 25*(2), 469–77.

Bourgeault, I., Parpia, R., Oryeme, N., & Gulamhusein, H. (2010). *Keeping their health workers: Comparing source country approaches to self-sufficiency.* Paper presented at Canadian Society of International Health Conference, University of Ottawa. Contact ivy.bourgeault@uottawa.ca

Brelih, J., Branco Jefer, C., Castelman, B. I., Charniack, M., Christiani, D. C., Cicolella, A., … Yassi, A. (2005). Texaco and its consultants. *International Journal of Occupational and Environmental Health, 11*(2), 217–20.

Brotherton, S. (2012). *Revolutionary medicine: Health and the body in post-Soviet Cuba.* Durham, NC: Duke University Press.

Buchan, J., Kingma, M., & Lorenzo, F. (2005). International migration of nurses: Trends and policy implications. *Global Nursing Review Initiative, 5*, 1–33. Retrieved from http://www.icn.ch/images/stories/documents/publications/GNRI/Issue5_Migration.pdf

Bundred, P. E., & Levitt, C. (2000). Medical migration: Who are the real losers? *Lancet, 356*(9225), 245–46.

Burnett, J. (2010, January 24). Cuban doctors unsung heroes of Haitian earthquake [Radio transcript]. *NPR.* Retrieved from http://www.npr.org/templates/story/story.php?storyId=122919202

Campbell, B., & Marchildon, G. (2007). *Medicare: Facts, myths, problems, promise.* Toronto, ON: Lorimer & Company.

Canadians favour health care to U.S. system: Poll. (2009, July 10). *CTV.* Retrieved from http://www.ctv.ca/CTVNews/Health/20090710/health_care_090710/

Candib, L. (2004). Family medicine in Ecuador: At risk in a developing nation. *Families, Systems, & Health, 22*(3), 277–89.

Cardellá Rosales, L., & Hernández Fernández, R. (1999). *Bioquímica médica tomo I: Biomoléculas.* La Habana, Cuba: Editorial Ciencias Medicas.

Carrillo de Albornoz, S. (2006). US lifts immigration restrictions for Cuban doctors. *British Medical Journal, 333*, 411–12.

Castañeda, M. (2005, August 23). First graduation of the Latin American School of Medicine. *Granma International.* Retrieved from http://www.cubanismo.net/teksten_eng/gezondheid/graduation_elam.htm

Castro, F. (1967). *History will absolve me.* Havana, Cuba: Guairas.

Castro, F. (1982). Ética y educación ética de los trabajadores de la salud en la atención primaria. Retrieved from http://www.sld.cu/galerias/pdf/sitios/pdguanabo/etica_y_educacion.pdf

Castro, F. (1999, November 15). Key address by Dr. Fidel Castro Ruz, President of the Republic of Cuba, at the inauguration of the Latin American School of Medicine. Retrieved from http://www.cuba.cu/gobierno/discursos/1999/ing/i151199i.html

Castro, F. (2000, September 21). Speech at the Riverside Church in Harlem, New York City, NY. Retrieved from http://www.democracynow.org/2000/9/11/fidel_in_harlem

Cavender, A., & Albán, M. (1998). Compulsory medical service in Ecuador: The physician's perspective *Social Science & Medicine, 47*(12), 1937–46.

Chikanda, A. (2006). Skilled health professionals' migration and its impact on health delivery in Zimbabwe. *Journal of Ethnic and Migration Studies, 32*(4), 667–80.

Cockburn, A., St. Clair, J., & Silverstein, K. (1999). The politics of "natural" disaster: Who made Mitch so bad? *International Journal of Health Services, 29*(2), 459–62.

Cole, K. (1998). *Cuba: From revolution to development.* London, England: Pinter.

Constante, F. (2006, December 19). Hay un avance en los indicadores de Salud. *Expreso de Guayaquil.* http://expreso.ec

Contreras Díaz, J. (2006). Women at a disadvantage: Pollution in Quito, Ecuador. *Women & Environments International Magazine, 70,* 40–42.

Cooper, R. (2005). Physician migration: A challenge for America, a challenge for the world. *Journal of Continuing Education in the Health Professions, 25,* 8–14.

Country health profiles: Ecuador. (1998). *Pan American Health Organization.* Retrieved from http://www.paho.org/English/SHA/coredata/tabulator/newTabulator.htm

Country health profiles: Ecuador. (2006). *Pan American Health Organization.* Retrieved from http://www.paho.org/English/SHA/coredata/tabulator/newTabulator.htm

Cowley, C. (2006). Polemic: Five proposals for a medical school admission policy. *Journal of Medical Ethics, 32*(8), 491–94.

Cox, R. (2005). Gramsci, hegemony and international relations: An essay in method. *Millennium—A Journal of International Studies, 12*(2), 162–75.

Crutcher, S. (2006, August 14). "Hands off Cuba!" activists demand in Atlanta. *Atlanta Progressive News.* Retrieved from http://www.atlantaprogressivenews.com/news/0079.html

Cuba Health Profile. (2007). *Medical Education Cooperation with Cuba [MEDICC].* Retrieved from http://www.medicc.org/publications/cuba_health_reports/cuba-health-data.php

Cuban ladies in white march again. (2010, May 2). *BBC News.* Retrieved from http://news.bbc.co.uk/2/hi/americas/8657567.stm

Danielson, R. (1985). Medicine in the community. In S. Halebsky, & J. M. Kirk (Eds.), *Cuba, twenty-five years of revolution, 1959–1984* (pp. 45–61). New York, NY: Praeger.

Debuque-Gonzales, M., & Gochoco-Bautista, M. (2007). The Philippines: Ten years after the crisis. *IDS Bulletin—Institute of Development Studies, 38*(4), 72–95.

Delgado García, G. (1993). Facultativo de semana: Antecedente histórico del médico de la familia. *Cuadernos de Historia de la Salud Pública, 78,* 112–18.

Delobelle, P., Rawlinson, J., Ntuli, S., Malatsi N., Decock, R., & Depoorter, A. M. (2009). HIV/AIDS knowledge, attitudes, practices and perceptions of rural nurses in South Africa. *Journal of Advanced Nursing, 65*(5), 1061–73.

Department of Health (South Africa). (2006). *A national human resources plan for health to provide skilled human resources for healthcare adequate to take care of all South Africans.* Retrieved from http://www.doh.gov.za/docs/discuss/2006/hrh_plan/chapt2.pdf

Douglas, T. (1982). The future of medicare. Retrieved from http://healthcoalition.ca/archive/tommy.pdf

Dovlo, D. (2003, September 23). *The brain drain and retention of health professionals in Africa*. Report to Regional Training Conference on Improving Tertiary Education in Sub-Saharan Africa, Washington, DC. Retrieved from http://medact.org/content/health/documents/brain_drain/Dovlo%20-%20brain%20drain%20and%20retention.pdf

Ebrahim, S. H., Anderson, J. E., Correa-de-Araujo, R., Posner, S., & Atrash, H. (2008). Overcoming social and health inequalities among US women of reproductive age—Challenges to the nation's health in the 21st century. *Health Policy, 90*(2/3), 196–205.

Eckstein, S. (2009). *The immigrant divide: How Cuban Americans changed the U.S. and their homeland*. New York, NY: Routledge.

Edelstein, R., Reid, H., Usatine, R., & Wilkes, M. (2000). A comparative study of measures to evaluate medical students' performances. *Academic Medicine, 75*(8), 825–33.

Ehrbeck, T., Guevara, C., & Mango, P. (2008). *Mapping the market for medical travel*. New York: McKinsey & Company. Retrieved from http://www.cosmashealth.com/workspace/assets/uploads/McKinsey-MedicalTravel.pdf

Escuela Latinoamericana de Medicina. (n.d.). *Infomed*. Retrieved from http://www.sld.cu/sitios/elam/

Evans, T., Whitehead, M., Diderichsen, F., Bhuiya, A., & Wirth, M. (2001). Introduction. In T. Evans, M. Whitehead, F. Diderichsen, A. Bhuiya, M. Wirth . (Eds), *Challenging inequities in health: From ethics to action* (pp. 2–12). Oxford, England: Oxford University Press.

Falcoff, M. (2003). *Cuba the morning after: Confronting Castro's legacy*. Washington, DC: AEI Press.

Farmer, P. (2005). *Pathologies of power: Health, human rights, and the new war on the poor*. Berkeley, CA: University of California Press.

Farrow, A., Larrea, C., Hyman, G., & Lema. G. (2005). Exploring the spatial variation of food poverty in Ecuador. *Food Policy, 30*(5/6), 510–31.

Feinsilver, J. (1993). *Healing the masses: Cuban health politics at home and abroad*. Berkeley, CA: University of California Press.

Filipino doctors becoming nurses abroad. (2007, December 29). *UPI*. Retrieved from http://www.upi.com/Health_News/2007/12/29/Filipino-doctors-becoming-nurses-abroad/UPI-45281198963264/

Filou, E. (2011, February 4). In Africa, cancer is a burden that can no longer be ignored. *The Guardian*. Retrieved from http://www.guardian.co.uk/global-development/poverty-matters/2011/feb/04/cancer-africa-health-burden

Fitzgerald, F. S., (2000). The crack-up. In J. C. Oates & R. Atwan (Eds). *The Best American Essays of the Century* (pp. 139–53). Boston, MA: Houghton Mifflin.

Fleshman, M. (2001). Counting the cost of gun violence. *Africa Recovery, 15*(4), 1–3. Retrieved from http://www.un.org/en/africarenewal/vol15no4/154arms.htm

Font, M., & Larson, S. (Eds.). (2006). *Cuba in transition? Pathways to renewal, long-term development and global reintegration*. New York, NY: City University.

Franco, M., Kennelly, J., Cooper, R., & Ordúñez-Garcia, P. (2007). Health in Cuba and the millennium development goals. *Revista Panamerica de Salud Publica, 21*(4), 239–50.

Frank, M. (2005). Cedric Edwards, MD. First U.S. graduate of the Latin American Medical School. *MEDICC Review, 7*(8). Retrieved from http://www.medicc.org/publications/medicc_review/0805/mr-interview.html

Frank, M., & Reed, G. (2005). Doctors for the (developing) world. *MEDICC Review, 7*(8). Retrieved from http://www.medicc.org/publications/medicc_review/0805/spotlight.html

Frenk, J., Knaul, F., Vázquez-Segovia, L., & Nigenda, G. (1999). Trends in medical employment: Persistent imbalances in urban Mexico. *American Journal of Public Health, 89*(7), 1054–58.

Friedman, M. (1962). *Capitalism and freedom.* Chicago, IL: University of Chicago Press.

Galeano, E. (1992). *We say no: Chronicles, 1963–1991.* New York, NY: Norton.

Galeano, E. (1997). *Open veins of Latin America: Five centuries of the pillage of a continent.* New York, NY: Monthly Review Press.

Galeano, E. (2000). *The book of embraces.* New York, NY: W.W. Norton & Company.

Galeano, E. (2001). *Upside down: A primer for the looking glass world.* New York, NY: Picador.

Gapminder [Website]. (n.d.). Retrieved from http://www.gapminder.org

García Márquez, G. (2003). *Love in the time of cholera.* New York, NY: Vintage International.

Garrett, L. (2007). The challenge of global health. *Foreign Affairs, 86*(1), 14–38.

Gaye, P., & Nelson., D. (2009). Effective scale-up: Avoiding the same old traps. *Human Resources for Health, 7*(2). Retrieved from http://www.human-resources-health.com/content/pdf/1478-4491-7-2.pdf

Gever, J. (2011, September 13). Number of uninsured up another million. *Medpage Today.* Retrieved from http://www.medpagetoday.com/Washington-Watch/Washington-Watch/28488

Gill, L. (2004). *The School of the Americas.* Durham, NC: Duke University Press.

Giraldo, G. (2007). Cuba's piece in the global health workforce puzzle. *MEDICC Review, 9*(1), 44–47.

Giraldo, G. (2007, January 15). Studying medicine in Cuba: First impressions. *MEDICC Review.* Retrieved from http://www.medicc.org/cubahealthreports/chr-article.php?&a=1028

Gleijeses, P. (1996). Cuba's first venture in Africa: Algeria, 1961–1965. *Journal of Latin American Studies, 25,* 159–95.

Golden, T. (2003). Health care in Cuba. In I. Harrowitz & J. Suchlicki (Eds.), *Cuban communism 1959–2003* (pp. 303–7). Rutgers, NJ: Transaction Publishers.

Gorry, C. (2005). Joining forces to develop human resources for health. *MEDICC, VII*(8), 15–18.

Gramsci, A. (2006). The state and civil society. In A. Sharma & A. Gupta (Eds.), *The anthropology of the state: A reader* (pp. 72–81). London, England: Blackwell Publishing.

Guevara, E. (1997). Speech to medical students and health workers. In D. Dutchman (Ed.), *Che Guevara reader* (pp. 95–105). New York, NY: Ocean Press.

Hagopian, A., Thompson, M., Fordyce, M., Johnson, K., & Hart, G. (2004). The migration of physicians from sub-Saharan Africa to the United States of America: Measures of the African brain drain. *Human Resources for Health, 2*(17), 1–10.

Hallock, J. A., Seeling, S. S., & Norcini, J. J. (2003). The international medical graduate pipeline. *Health Affairs, 22*(4), 94–96.

Handal, A., Lozofil, B., Brelih, J., & Harlowl, S. (2007). Sociodemographic and nutritional correlates or neurobehavioral development: A study of young children in a rural region of Ecuador. *Revista Panamerica de Salud Publica. 21*(5), 292–300.

Harhay, M., & Munera Mesa, N. M. (2009). The challenge of the health worker migration crisis to health reform in the United States. *American Journal of Bioethics, 9*(3), 14–16.

Harper arrives in Haiti. (2010, February 15). *CBC News.* Retrieved from http://www.cbc.ca/news/world/story/2010/02/15/harper-haiti.html

Harvey, D. (2005). *A brief history of neoliberalism.* Oxford, England: Oxford University Press.

Heisler, M., Wagner, T., & Piette, J. (2005). Patient strategies to cope with high prescription medication costs: Who is cutting back on necessities, increasing debt, or underusing medications? *Journal of Behavioral Medicine, 28*(1), 43–51.

Hentschel, J., & Waters, W. (2002). Rural poverty in Euacdor: Assessing local realities for the development of anti-poverty programs. *World Development, 30*(1), 33–47.

Hernández, E. R. (1971). *Administración de salud pública.* La Habana, Cuba: Editorial Ciencia y Técnica.

Herrera Ramirez, D., & Garces, M. (2003). *Sistematización o insumos para el taller de nueve de agosto: Medicina familiar en el Ecuador* [*Systematic approach for the August 9th workshop: Family Medicine in Ecuador*]. Conference Proceedings. Paper presented at Medicine Familiar en el Ecuador, Quito, Ecuador.

Heynen, N. (2007). Crude chronicles: Indigenous politics, multinational oil, and neoliberalism in Ecuador. *Environment and Planning A, 39*(1), 237–38.

Hobsbawm, E. J. (1990). *Nations and nationalism since 1780: Programme, myth, reality.* Cambridge, England: Cambridge University Press.

Horas asignadas a las disciplinas de Salud Pública en el Plan de Estudios de Medicina. (n.d.). *Infomed.* Retrieved from http://aps.sld.cu/bvs/materiales/carpeta/carpeta.html

Houston, C. S. (2002). Steps on the road to medicare: Why Saskatchewan led the way. Montreal: McGill–Queen's University Press.

Huergo, C. C. (2007). Concepción Campa Huergo, President & General Director, Finlay Institute [Interview]. *MEDICC Review, 9*(1), 11–13. Retrieved from http://www.medicc.org/mediccreview/index.php?issue=6&id=58&a=vahtml

Huish, R. (2009). How Cuba's Latin American School of Medicine challenges the ethics of physician migration. *Social Science and Medicine, 69*(3), 301–4.

Huish, R., & Kirk, J. M. (2007). Cuban medical internationalism and the development of the Latin American School of Medicine. *Latin American Perspectives, 34*(6), 77–92.

Huish, R., & Kirk, J. M. (2009). Cuban medical internationalism in Africa: The threat of a dangerous example. *The Latin Americanist, 53*(3), 125–39.

Huish, R., & Lovell, W. G. (2008). Under the volcanoes: The influence of Guatemala on José Martí. *Cuban Studies, 59*(1), 25–43.

Huish, R., & Spiegel, J. (2008). Integrating health and human security into foreign policy: Cuba's surprising success. *International Journal of Cuban Studies, 1*(1), 1–13.

Hurtig, A. K., & San Sebastián, M. (2004). Incidence of childhood leukemia and oil exploitation in the Amazon basin of Ecuador. *International Journal of Occupational and Environmental Health, 10*(3), 245–50.

Hutten-Czapski, P. (1998). Rural incentive programs: A failing report card. *Canadian Journal of Rural Medicine, 3*(4), 242–47.

Indrayan, A. (2008). *Measure of mortality: Maternal and adult mortality.* New York, NY: Chapman & Hall.

Jochnick, C., & Zaidi, R. (1994). Rights violations in the Ecuadorian Amazon: The human consequences of oil development. *Health Human Rights, 1*(1), 82–100.

Jochnick, C., Normand, R., & Zaidi, R. (1994). *Violaciones de derechos en la Amazonía Ecuatoriana: Las consequencias humanas del desarrollo petrolero.* Quito, Ecuador: Ediciones Abya-Yala.

Johnson, P. (2006, June 1). Despite 'el bloqueo,' Americans go to Cuban medical school. *Final Call News.* Retrieved from http://www.finalcall.com/artman/publish/article_2548.shtml

Joint letter on publicly funded health care. (n.d.). *CAW Canada.* Retrieved from http://www.caw.ca/en/sectors-joint-letter-on-publicly-funded-health-care.htm

Kearns, R. (1994). Putting health and health care into place: An invitation accepted and declined. *The Professional Geographer, 46*(1), 111–15.

Keeble, A. (2000). *Con el espíritu de los maestros ambulantes.* Melbourne, Australia: Ocean Press.

Kimerling, J. (2001). Corporate ethics in the era of globalization: The promise and peril of international environmental standards. *Journal of Agricultural & Environmental Ethics, 14*(4), 425–55.

King, M. L. (1966, March 26). Speech given to the Medical Committee for Human Rights. Chicago, IL.

Kirby, J. B. (2008). Poor people, poor places and access to health care in the United States. *Social Forces, 87*(1), 325–55.

Kirigia, J. M., Gbary, A. R., Muthuri, L. K., Nyoni, J., & Seddoh, A. (2006). The cost of health professionals' brain drain in Kenya. *Biomedical Central Health Service Research, 6*(89). Retrieved from http://www.biomedcentral.com/content/pdf/1472-6963-6-89.pdf

Kirk, J. M., & Erisman, M. H. (2009). *Cuban medical internationalism: Origins, evolution and goals.* New York, NY: Palgrave Macmillan.

Labonte, R., Packer, C., Klassen, N., Kazanjian, A., Aplan, L., Adalikwu, J., ... Zakus, D. (2006). *The brain drain of health professionals from sub-Saharan Africa to Canada.* Kingston, Ontario, Canada: Queen's University.

Larrea, C., & Kawachi, I. (2005). Does economic inequality affect child malnutrition? The case of Ecuador. *Social Science & Medicine, 60,* 165–78.

Latin American School of Medicine—How to apply. (2007). *Medical Education Cooperation with Cuba [MEDICC].* Retrieved from http://www.medicc.org/ns/index.php?s=54&p=10

Leavitt, M. (2008, December 12). *Increased role of health diplomacy in U.S. foreign policy.* Paper presented at the Global Health Policy Center Speaker Series, CSIS—Center for Strategic and International Studies, Washington, DC.

Lema, C., McCoy, D., Morton, P., Rowson, M., Salvage, J., & Sexton, S. (Eds.). (2007). *Global health watch 2005-2006: An alternative world health report.* London, England: Zed Books.

Lewis, S., Donaldson, C., Mitton, C., & Currie, G. (2001). The future of health care in Canada. *British Medical Journal, 323,* 926–29.

Lipson, D. (2001). The World Trade Organization's health agenda. *British Medical Journal,* *323,* 1139–40.

Lorenzo, F., Galvez-Tan, J., Icamina, K., & Javier, L. (2007). Nurse migration from a source country perspective: Philippine country case study. *Health Services Research,* *42*(3), 1406–18.

Lovell, W.G. (2000). *A Beauty That Hurts: Life and Death in Guatemala.* Toronto: Between the Lines

Macintyre, K., & Hadad, J. (2002). Cuba. In B. Fried & L. M. Gaydos (Eds.), *World health systems: Challenges and perspectives* (pp. 445–63). Chicago, IL: Health Administration Press.

Maingot, A. (2006). Bridging the ideological divide: Cuban doctors for Caribbean recognition. *Focal Point, 5*(4), 4.

Marchildon, G. (2005). Private insurance for medicare: Policy history and trajectory in the four western provinces. In C. Flood, K. Roach, & L. Sossin (Eds.), *Access to care, access to justice: The legal debate over private health insurance in Canada* (pp. 429–53). Toronto, Ontario, Canada: University of Toronto Press.

Marimón Torresm, N., & Martínez Cruz, E. (2010). Evolución de la colaboración médica cubana en 100 años del Ministerio de Salud Pública [Evolution of the Cuban medical co-operation during one hundred years of existence of the Ministry of Public Health]. *Revista Cubana de Salud Pública. 36*(3), 254–62.

Martí, J. (1961). Emerson. In *Obras completas* (Vol. 19) (pp. 351–56). La Habana, Cuba: Editorial Nacional de Cuba.

Martí, J. (1963). Nuestra América. In *Obras completas* (Vol. 7) (pp. 98–102). La Habana, Cuba: Editorial Nacional de Cuba.

Martí, J. (1999). Our America. In D. Shnookal & M. Muñiz (Eds.), *José Martí reader: Writings on the Americas* (pp. 111–20). New York, NY: Ocean Press.

Martin, R. (2009, November). Who killed Canada's education advantage? A forensic investigation into the disappearance of public education investment in Canada. *The Walrus,* 22–27.

Martineau, T., Decker, K., & Bundred, P. (2002). *Briefing note on international migration of health professionals: Leveling the playing field for developing country health systems.* Retrieved from http://www.mpdc.es/components/com_mtree/attachment .php?link_id=106&cf_id=39

Matrícula. (n.d.). *ELAM.* Retrieved from http://www.elacm.sld.cu/matricula.html

Mayor Lorán, J. (2007, July 25). A graduating class for humanity. *Granma International.* Retrieved from http://www.granma.cu/ingles/2007/julio/mier25/A-graduating -class-for-humanity.html

McCoy, D., Chand, S., & Sridhar, D. (2009). Global health funding: How much, where it comes from and where it goes. *Health Policy and Planning, 24*(6), 407–17.

McLea, H. (2011, July 4). Regulate health costs: Motsoaledi. *The Sunday Times.* Retrieved from http://www.timeslive.co.za/thetimes/2011/07/04/regulate-health-costs-motsoaledi

MEDICC Review Staff. (2005). Profiles in commitment: Conversations with ELAM students. *MEDICC Review, 7*(8). Retrieved from http://www.medicc.org/ publications/medicc_review/0805/mr-features.html

Medicina natural y tradicional. (n.d.). *Infomed.* Retrieved from http://www.sld.cu/sitios/ mednat/

Mendez, I., Hill, R., Clarke, D., Kolyvas, G., & Walling S. (2005). Robotic long distance telementoring in neurosurgery. *Neurosurgery. 56(3)*, 434–40.

Migration resources: Brain drain resources—Introduction. (n.d.). *South African Migration Programme.* Retrieved from http://www.queensu.ca/samp/migrationresources/braindrain/

Miles, A. (1998). Science, nature and tradition: The mass-marketing of natural medicine in urban Ecuador. *Medical Anthropology Quarterly, 12*(2), 206–25.

Millman, J. (2011, January 15). New prize in cold war: Cuban doctors. *Wall Street Journal.* Retrieved from http://online.wsj.com/article/SB10001424052970203731004576045640711118766.html

Montaner, C. A., & Ramonet, I. (2007). Was Fidel good for Cuba? A debate between Carlos Alberto Montaner & Ignacio Ramonet. *Foreign Policy* (158), 56–58.

Morgenthau, H. (1985). *Politics among nations: The struggle for power and peace.* Boston, MA: McGraw-Hill.

Moyo, D. (2009). *Dead aid: Why aid is not working and how there is a better way for Africa.* New York, NY: Farrar, Straus and Giroux.

Mullan, F., & Epstein, L. (2002). Community-oriented primary care: New relevance in a changing world. *American Journal of Public Health, 92*(11), 1748–55.

Multari, G., Gallo, F. R., & Fiorentini, C. (2011). Dal veleno dello scorpione cubano Rophalurus junceus: Un prodotto presentato come antitumorale. *Notiziario dell'Istituto Superiore di Sanitá. 24*(11), 3–6.

Muntaner, C., Armada, F., Chung, H., Mata, R., Williams-Brennan, L., & Benach, J. (2008). Venezuela's Barrio Adentro: Participatory democracy, south–south cooperation and health care for all. *Social Medicine, 3*(4), 232–46.

Muntaner, C., Salazar, R. M. G., Benach, J., & Armada, F. (2006). Venezuela's Barrio Adentro: An alternative to neoliberalism in health care. *International Journal of Health Services, 36*(4), 803–11.

Muntaner, C., Salazar, R. M. G., Rueda, S., & Armada, F. (2006). Challenging the neoliberal trend—The Venezuelan health care reform alternative. *Canadian Journal of Public Health–Revue Canadienne de Santé Publique, 97*(6), 119–24.

Nussbaum, M. (2003). Capabilities as fundamental entitlements: Sen and Social Justice. *Feminist Economics, 9*(2/3), 33–59.

Nye, J. S. (2004). *Soft power: The means to success in world politics* (1st ed.). New York, NY: Public Affairs.

Oficina Nacional de Estadísticas. (2007). *Habitantes por médico y estomatólogo.* La Habana, Cuba: Autor.

Ogilvie, L., Mill, J. E., Astle, B., Fanning, A., & Opare, M. (2007). The exodus of health professionals from sub-Saharan Africa: Balancing human rights and societal needs in the twenty-first century. *Nursing Inquiry, 14*(2), 114–24.

Operación Milagro ha devuelto la vista a más de 300 000 personas. (2006, June 26). *Granma International.* Retrieved from http://www.granma.cu/espanol/2006/junio/mier21/milagro.html

Orbinski, J. (2008). *An imperfect offering: Humanitarian action in the twenty-first century.* Toronto, Ontario, Canada: Doubleday.

Padarath, A., Chamberlain, C., McCoy, D. Ntuli, A., Rowson, M., Loewenson, R. (2006). Health personnel in southern Africa: Confronting maldistribution and brain drain. *Medact.* Retrieved from http://www.medact.org/content/health/documents/brain_drain/Padarath%20et%20al.%20-%20Medact-HST-Equient.pdf

Padron, L. (2003). Cuba's national traditional and natural medicine program. *MEDICC Review, 5*(1). Retrieved from http://www.medicc.org/mediccreview/articles/mr_50.pdf

Parikh, R., Antoniello, P., Arole, S., & Thakkar, P. (2008). The Jamkhed model: Income generation programs, health policies and sustainability. *Journal of Investigative Medicine, 56*(1), 125–26.

Pathman, D. E., Fowler-Brown, A., & Corbie-Smith, G. (2006). Differences in access to outpatient medical care for black and white adults in the rural south. *Medical Care, 44*(5), 429–38.

Peet, R., & Hartwick, E. R. (2009). *Theories of development: Contentions, arguments, alternatives* (2nd ed.). New York, NY: Guilford Press.

Pena, S., Ramirez, J., Becerra, C., Carabantes, J., & Arteaga, O. (2010). The Chilean rural practitioner programme: A multidisciplinary strategy to attract and retain doctors in rural areas. *Bulletin of the World Health Organization, 88*(5), 371–78.

People's Health Movement, Medact, & Global Equity Gauge Alliance. (2008). The health-care sector. In E. Hansson et al. (Eds.), *Global health watch 2: An alternative world health report* (pp. 35–101). London, England: Zed Books.

Pérez López, J. (2006). The Alice in wonderland economy. *Focal Point, 5*(1), 2.

Physician database. (2009). *Canadian Institute for Health Information.* Retrieved from http://www.cihi.ca/CIHI-ext-portal/internet/EN/document/spending+and+health+workforce/workforce/physicians/hhrdata_npdb

Plato. (1987). *Plato's Republic.* (F. Cornford MacDonald, Trans.). New York, NY: Garland.

Pogge, T. (2008). *World poverty and human rights* (2nd ed.). Cambridge, England: Polity Press.

Powell, C. L. (2004). *Commission for assistance to a free Cuba: Report to the president.* Washington, DC: US Department of State.

Presno Labrador, C. (2004). 20 years of family medicine in Cuba. *MEDICC Review, 6*(2). Retrieved from http://www.medicc.org/publications/medicc_review/1104/pages/spotlight.html

Proceso docente educativo en la atención primeria de salud. (n.d.). *Infomed.* Retrieved from http://aps.sld.cu/bvs/materiales/carpeta/carpeta.html

Professores. (n.d.). *Infomed.* Retrieved from http://www.sld.cu/sitios/elam/

Puckett, J. (1997). The Basel Ban: Triumph over business as usual. *Basel Action Network.* Retrieved from http://ban.org/about_basel_ban/jims_article.html

Puertas, B., & Schlesser, M., (2001). Assessing community health among indigenous populations in Ecuador with a participatory approach: Implications for health reform. *Journal of Community Health, 26*(2), 133–47.

Ramírez de Arellano, B. (2007). Patients without borders: The emergence of medical tourism. *International Journal of Health Services. 37*(1), 193–98.

Reed, G. (2000). Challenges for Cuba's family doctor-and-nurse program. *MEDICC Review, 2*(3).Retrieved from http://www.medicc.org/publications/medicc_review/II/primary/sloframe.html

Reinhardt, U. (2006). President Bush's proposals for healthcare reform—New plan offers 'consumer empowerment' through rationing by socioeconomic class. *British Medical Journal, 332*, 314–15.

Resources: The case for medicare. (2010). *Doctors for Medicare.* Retrieved from http://www.doctorsformedicare.ca

Ribeiro Galardo, A., Arruda, M., D'Almeida Couto, A., Wirtz, R., Lounibos, P., & Zimmerman, R. (2007). Malaria vector incrimination in three rural riverine villages in the Brazilian Amazon. *American Journal of Tropical Medicine and Hygiene, 76*(3), 461–69.

Ritter, A. (2006). "La revolución energética" generates a "quick fix". *Focal Point, 5*(5), 2.

Ritter, A. (2010). Shifting realities in special period Cuba. *Latin American Research Review, 45*(3), 229–38.

Robertson, R., Castro, C., Gomez, L. C., Gwynne, G., Tinajero Baca, C. L., & Zschock, D. (1991). Primary health services in Ecuador: Comparative costs, quality and equity of care in Ministry of Health and rural social security facilities. *Social Science & Medicine. 32*(12), 1327–36.

Rodwin, M. (1995). *Medicine, morals, and money: Physicians conflicts of interest.* Oxford, England: Oxford University Press.

Roeser, T., (2007, June 23). All in the (gasp!) family. *Chicago Daily Observer.* Retrieved from http://www.cdobs.com/archive/syndicated/all-in-the-gasp-family/

Rojas Ochoa, F. (2003). La enseñanza de la salud pública a estudiantes de medicina en Cuba. *Revista Cubana Educacion Medica Superior, 17*(2). Retrieved from http://www.bvs.sld.cu/revistas/ems/vol17_2_03/ems01203.htm

Rojas Ochoa, F. (2004). Origins of primary health care in Cuba. *MEDICC Review, 6*(2). Retrieved from http://www.medicc.org/publications/medicc_review/1104/pages/cuban_medical_literature.html

Roman, P. (2003). *People's power: Cuba's experience with representative government* (Updated ed.). Lanham, MD: Rowman & Littlefield.

Rosell Puig, W., & Paneque Ramos, E. (2007). Evolución histórica de la enseñanza de la anatomía en Cuba. *Educacion Medica Superior, 21*(3). Retrieved from http://bvs.sld.cu/revistas/ems/vol21_3_07/ems09307.html

Rosell Puig, W., Dovale Borjas, C., & Gonzáles Fajo, B. (2005). Orden lógico de estudio de las características morfofuncionales de los sistemas orgánicos y de sus componentes. *Educación Médica Superior. 20*(2). Retrieved from http://scielo.sld.cu/scielo.php?pid=S0864-21412006000200004&script=sci_arttext

Roy, J. (2006). Cuba: The role of the international community. *Focal Point, 5*(8), 5.

Rubel, A. J. (1990). Compulsory medical service and primary health care: A Mexican case study. In J. Coreil & J. D. Mull (Eds.), *Anthropology and primary health care* (pp. 137–53). Boulder, CO: Westview Press.

Russell, P., & Sossin, L. (2009). *Parliamentary democracy in crisis.* Toronto, Ontario, Canada: University of Toronto Press.

Said, E. W. (1979). *Orientalism.* New York, NY: Vintage Books.

Samb, B., Evans, T., Dybul, M., Atun, R., Moatti, J., Nishtar, S., ... Wright, A. (2009). An assessment of interactions between global health initiatives and country health systems. *Lancet, 373,* 2137–69.

San Sebastián, M., & Hurtig, A. K. (2004a). Oil exploitation in the Amazon basin of Ecuador: A public health emergency. *Revista Panamericana de Salud Pública [Pan American Journal of Public Health], 15*(3), 205–11.

San Sebastián, M., & Hurtig, A. K. (2004b). Cancer among indigenous people in the Amazon basin of Ecuador, 1985–2000. *Revista Panamericana de Salud Pública [Pan American Journal of Public Health], 16*(5), 328–33.

San Sebastián, M., & Hurtig, A. K. (2005). Oil development and health in the Amazon basin of Ecuador: the popular epidemiology process. *Social Science & Medicine. 60*(4), 799–807.

San Sebastián, M., & Hurtig, A. K., Breilh, J. & Peralta, A. Q. (2005). The people's health movement: Health for all now. *Revista Panamericana De Salud Pública [Pan American Journal of Public Health], 18*(1), 45–49.

Sanchez, G. (2006). *Barrio Adentro and other social missions in the Bolivarian revolution.* Sydney, Australia: Ocean Press.

Saney, I. (2004). *Cuba: A revolution in motion.* London, England: Zed Books.

Sariol, J. (2005). ¿Profesor ideal? En busca del eslabón perdido. *Alma Mater.* Retrieved from http://www.almamater.cu/sitio%20nuevo/sitio%20viejo/webalmamateruniver -sidad/paginas/profesor.htm

Sawyer, S. (2004). *Crude chronicles: Indigenous politics, multinational oil, and neoliberalism in Ecuador.* Durham, NC: Duke University Press.

Schenarts, P., Love, K., Agle, S., & Haisch, C. (2008). Comparison of surgical residency applicants from US medical schools with US-born and foreign-born international medical school graduates. *Journal of Surgical Education, 65*(6), 406–12.

Schweller, R. (1996). Neo-realism's status quo bias: What security dilemma? *Security Studies, 5*(3), 90–121.

Scott, S. V. (2004). Is there room for international law in realpolitik?: Accounting for the US 'attitude' towards international law. *Review of International Studies, 30*(1), 71–88.

Shah, A. (2006, April 16). Brain drain of workers from poor to rich countries. *Global Issues.* Retrieved from http://www.globalissues.org/article/599/brain-drain-of-workers -from-poor-to-rich-countries

Sideridis, K., Canario, D., & Cunha, B. A. (2003). Dengue fever: Diagnostic importance of a camelback fever pattern. *Heart & Lung, 32*(6), 414–18.

Siemionow, M., & Gordon, C. (2010). Overview of guidelines for establishing a face transplant program: A work-in-progress. *American Journal of Transplantation, 10*, 1290–96.

Sierra, G., Campa, H., Varacel, N., Garcia, I., Izquierdo, P., Sotolongo, P., . . . Terry, M. H. (1991). Vaccine against Group B Neisseria Meningitidis: Protection trial and mass vaccination results in Cuba. *NIPH Annals. 14*(2). Retrieved from http://www.finlay .sld.cu/publicaciones/tomo1/T1-01.PDF

Sims, H., & Vogelmann, K. (2002). Popular mobilization and disaster management in Cuba. *Public Administration and Development, 22*(5), 389–400.

Sinclair, S. (1997). *Making doctors: An institutional apprenticeship.* Oxford, England: Berg.

Six months after the earthquake: Time to build public health care in Haiti. (2010). *MEDICC.* Retrieved from http://www.medicc.org/ns/index.php?s=79

Snyder, J. (2009). Is health worker migration a case of poaching? *American Journal of Bioethics, 9*(3), 3–7.

Spiegel, J., & Yassi, A. L. (2004). Lessons from the margins of globalization: Appreciating the Cuban health paradox. *Journal of Public Health Policy, 25*(1), 85–110.

Steger, M. & Roy, R. (2010). *Neoliberalism: A very short introduction.* Oxford, England: Oxford University Press.

Steinbrook, R. (2006). Private health care in Canada. *New England Journal of Medicine, 354*, 1661–64.

Stelnick, A. H., Swiderski, D., Fornai, A., Gorski, V., Korin, E., Ozuah, P., . . . Selwyn, P. A. (2008). The Residency Program in Social Medicine of Montefiore Medical Center:

37 years of mission-driven, interdisciplinary training in primary care, population health, and social medicine. *Academic Medicine, 83*(4), 378–89.

Stephens, S. (2012, April 17). Summit of the Americas—Flashback and fast forward. *Huffington Post.* Retrieved from http://www.huffingtonpost.com/sarah-stephens/cuba-doctors_b_1424736.html

Stevenson, M., Williams, A. P., & Vayda, E. (1988). Medical politics and Canadian medicare: Professional response to the Canada Health Act. *Milbank Quarterly. 66*(1), 65–104.

Stewart, W. (2004). *The life and political times of Tommy Douglas.* Toronto, Ontario, Canada: McArthur & Company.

Summers, L. (1991, December 12). Subject: GEP [Internal e-mail memo]. *The World Bank.* Retrieved from http://www.jacksonprogressive.com/issues/summersmemo.html

Suzarte, M. S. (2007, March 25). Bringing health to the world. *Granma International.* Retrieved from http://www.granma.cu/ingles/2007/marzo/juev22/12elam-i.html

Talati, J. J., & Pappas, G. (2006). Migration, medical education, and health care: A view from Pakistan. *Academic Medicine, 81*(12), S55–63.

Thaver, I. H., Harpham, T., McPake, B., & Garner, P. (1998). Private practitioners in the slums of Karachi: What quality of care do they offer? *Social Science & Medicine, 46*(11), 1441–49.

The Andes have Cuban doctors. (2012, February 18). *Cubaheadlines.com.* Retrieved from http://www.cubaheadlines.com/2012/02/18/34600/the_andes_have_cuban_doctors.html

The Declaration of Alma-Ata: The International Conference on Primary Health Care, Alma-Ata, USSR. (1978). Retrieved from http://www.searo.who.int/LinkFiles/Health_Systems_declaration_almaata.pdf

The priority given to health in the Cuban system. (n.d.). *CubaMinRex.* Retrieved from http://www.cubaminrex.cu/English/61CDH/Complete%20texts/ HealthCare.htm

Tomlinson, K. (2008). Doctor overbilling needs scrutiny: Ontario Auditor. *CTV News.* Retrieved from http://www.ctvnews.ca

Tong, R. (2001). Towards a feminist global bioethics: Addressing women's health concerns worldwide. *Health Care Analysis, 9*(2), 229–46.

Ugalde, A. (1984). Where there is a doctor: Strategies to increase productivity at lower costs. The economics of rural health care in the Dominican Republic. *Social Science and Medicine, 19,* 441–50.

United Nations Human Development Program. (2006). *Human development report 2006.* Retrieved from http://hdr.undp.org/en/

Valdés Moreno, J., Cardellá Rosales, L., Rojas Palacios, G., & Gómez Álvarez, A. M. (2002). Determinación de variables nutricionales y metabólicas en recién nacidos de bajo peso. *Revista Cubana investigaciones biomedica, 21*(4), 235–40.

Venezuelan doctors protest plans to bring Cuban medical staff. (1999, April 15). *Cubanet News.* Retrieved from http://www.cubanet.org/CNews/y99/apr99/15e1.htm

Waitzkin, H., & Iriart, C. (2001). How the United States exports managed care to developing countries. *International Journal of Health Services, 31*(3), 495–505.

Warren, J., & Carlisle, K. (2004). *On the side of the people: A history of labour in Saskatchewan.* Toronto, Ontario, Canada: Canadian Committee on Labour History.

Werner, D. (1978). *Where there is no doctor: A village health care handbook.* Palo Alto, CA: Hesperian Foundation.

Whitten, N. E. (2004). Indians, oil and politics: A recent history of Ecuador. *Hispanic American Historical Review, 84*(3), 555–57.

Wilkinson, R. G. (1996). *Unhealthy societies: The afflictions of inequality.* London, England: Routledge.

Wilkinson, S. (2008). Cuba's tourism boom: A curse or a blessing? *Third World Quarterly, 29*(5), 979–93.

Woodford, P. (2006). Free Cuban med school trains US docs: Expert argues it's more than a Fidel Castro publicity stunt. *National Review of Medicine, 3*(3). Retrieved from http://www.nationalreviewofmedicine.com/issue/2006/02_15/3_policy_politics 04_3.html

World Bank. (2012). *Migration and remittances factbook 2011.* Washington, DC: Author.

World Health Organization [WHO]. (1946) *Preamble to the Constitution of the World Health Organization as adopted by the International Health Conference.* New York, NY: Archives of the United Nations.

World Health Organization [WHO]. (2006). *The world health report: Working together for health.* Retrieved from http://www.who.int/whr/2006/en/

World Health Organization [WHO]. (2007). *World health survey results.* Geneva, Switzerland: Author.

Xaba, J., & Phillips, G. (2001). *Understanding Nurse Emigration. Final Report. Trade Union Research Project.* Pretoria, South Africa: Democratic Nursing Organisation of South Africa.

York, G. (2010, February 1). Maternal mortality: Why it's a crisis. *Globe and Mail.* Retrieved from http://www.theglobeandmail.com/

Younger, S. (1999). The Relative Progressivity of Social Services in Ecuador. *Public Finance Review. 27*(3), 310–52.

INDEX

A

Act for Free Maternity and Infant Services (Ecuador), 124–25. *See also* childbirth and pregnancy; Ecuador; infant; maternity wards

acupuncture training at ELAM, 95, 101. *See also* Latin American School of Medicine (Escuela Latinomericana de Ciencias Médicas) (ELAM)

Afghanistan: absence of gender equality and education in, 6; life expectancy compared with Canada and Swaziland, 6; maternal mortality in, 6; support for military action in, 14. *See also* Asia; Canada; global South, 14; life expectancy; maternal; Swaziland

Africa: absence of public health clinics in, 152; critical health-care worker shortage in, 61, 63, 76; Cuban medical brigades working in, 4–5, 154; death from diarrhoea in West, 113; internal migration of health-care workers to South Africa, 16, 63–64; enrollment at ELAM of people from, 80; extent of global burden of disease, 76; external migration from, 7; insufficient quantity of health-care personnel in sub-Saharan, 77; insufficient training of health-care workers for, 7; participation in Operación Milagro, 58; students at ELAM from, 80; sub-Saharan, 5, 77; Venezuelan funding of Cuban ophthalmological services for, 57. *See also* Angola; Burundi; Cuban medical brigades; Ethiopia; The Gambia;

Kenya; Latin American School of Medicine (Escuela Latinomericana de Ciencias Médicas) (ELAM); Liberia; Libya; Malawi; maternal; migration of health-care workers; Operación (or Misión) Milagro; Organization of African Unity; public health care; Swaziland; Tanzania; Uganda, West African medical brigades formed by ELAM graduates; Zimbabwe

aid and philanthropic health-care efforts: cooperation as better alternative to, 18, 71; cooperation between Cuba and United States as means of delivering satisfactorily, 151; domestic as preferable over foreign, 79; funding from European Economic Union, 141–43; inadequacy of as health-care solution, 2, 3, 5, 6, 12, 23, 32, 18, 79, 114; invalid narrative concerning, 14–15; in Haiti after 2012 earthquake, 75; limited commitment of Canadian outreach, 18; short-term medical brigades, 12; tendency to focus on specific and manageable diseases, 2, 15–16. *See also* Bill & Melinda Gates Foundation; Cuba; global North; primary care; private health care; public health care; William J. Clinton Foundation; United States

AIDS. *See* HIV/AIDS

ALBA. *See* Bolivarian Alliance for the Peoples of Our America (Alianza Bolivariana para los Pueblos de Nuestra América) (ALBA)

Haiti; Henry Reeve Emergency
Response Medical Brigade (Henry
Reeve Brigade); Honduras; Latin
America; Latin American School of
Medicine (Escuela Latinomericana de
Ciencias Médicas) (ELAM); migration of health-care workers; Pakistan;
pharmaceuticals; sanitation; solidarity; Soviet Union, effects on Cuba of
collapse of; United States; Venezuela;
West African medical brigades
formed by ELAM graduates
Cuban medical internationalism,
ix–x, 9–13, 30, 35; as alternative to
medical tokenism, 17–18; benefits
for foreign policy of, 11, 150; as
challenge to narratives of war
and health-care provision, 14–15;
as challenge to private health-
care systems, 19; compared with
Canadian humanitarian efforts, 32; as
convergence of trends in public health
and foreign policy, 157ch1n2; creation
and extension of, 46–49; definition
of 2, 157ch1n2; economic benefits
of, 9, 11, 72; ethics of, 148, 155; as
geopolitical strategy, 11, 149, 155;
in a country's best interests 15–17;
increase since 2003 of, 10; José Martí
as philosophical guardian of, 34, 81;
lessons for medical education, 149;
lessons to be drawn from, 17, 149;
management and development of, 12;
as means to reach needs of poor, 3, 9,
11–12, 149, 155; as means of realizing
human right, 26–29; motivations of,
3, 4, 8, 19; national self-sufficiency
as main goal of, 84; nationalism as
pertaining to, 14–15, 81; Operación
Milagro as example of, 54, 57–60, 68,
71; opposition to the compartmentalized of health services, 4; pan-
Americanism as pertaining to, 81;
as planned strategy of international
outreach, 4; as practised in Ecuador,
113–148; remuneration bonuses of
programs, 60–61; solidarity as basis

for medical, 15; support from global
South for, 19; as symbol of soft power,
2, 3, 17, 149, 150, 153; uniqueness of,
4; values taught at ELAM of, 111–12;
148, 149, 155; as work-in-progress, 3,
155. See also Alma-Ata (health care
for all); Canada; Cuba; definition of;
Ecuador; global South; Latin America;
Latin American School of Medicine
(Escuela Latinomericana de Ciencias
Médicas) (ELAM); Martí, José;
nationalism; Operación (or Misión)
Milagro; pan-Americanism as basis
for solidarity; primary care; private
health care; public health care; private
health care; solidarity; theory of soft
power
Cuban Medical Professional Parole
Program (CMPP), 69–70, 108, 133,
152. See also migration of health-care
workers
Cuban Women's Federation (FMC), 38.
See also Cuban medical brigades
Cuenca (Ecuador), 119, 135, 137; medical
school at, 130. See also Ecuador;
pesticides

D
Dalhousie University (Canada), 82. See
also Canada; Nova Scotia
Day, Brian, 25. See also Canadian Medical
Association; private health care
debt relief and repayment, 18, 66, 70, 78,
115, 157ch1n6. See also Haiti; Haitian
earthquake; Philippines
Declaration of Alma-Ata (health care for
all). See Alma-Ata (health care for all)
definition of: anti-model of health
care, 126–27; backward innovation, 157ch1n3; Cuban medical
internationalism, 2, 157ch1n2;
distal care, 159ch5n4; forward
innovation, 157ch1n3; health, 76;
health-care worker, 75; humanitarian
doctors, 146; humble and needy,
90; medical tourists, 56; medical
traveller, 55, 56; neoliberalism, 77;

organizational changes, 81; popular epidemiology, 120; proximal care, 159ch5n3; socioeconomic structural changes, 81; structural violence, 158ch4n1; stunting, 120; tokenism, 157ch1n5. *See also* cost-benefit analysis as basis for health care in Ecuador; Cuba; Cuban medical internationalism; epidemiology, including epidemiological; Ecuador; Latin American School of Medicine (Escuela Latinomericana de Ciencias Médicas) (ELAM); La Joya de los Sachas; Ríos Montt, Efrín; neoliberalism; McKinsey & Co., report by; medical tourism; poaching, concept of; structural violence; Venezuela; World Health Organization (WHO)

dehydration in infants, 114. *See also* infant

dengue, 1, 2, 33. *See also* mosquitoes; potable and non-potable water

dentists: opposition to Medical Care Act by, 24; participation in Cuban program for public rural health care, 37; volunteers as part of NGO health brigade, 143. *See also* Canada; Cuba; Cuban medical brigades; La Joya de los Sachas; Medical Care Act

diabetes, 58; diabetic, 142, 143

diarrhoea, 37, 38, 113, 120, 123

Dr. Gustavo Aldereguía Lima (hospital) (Cienfuegos, Cuba), 93–94, 105. *See also* Latin American School of Medicine (Escuela Latinomericana de Ciencias Médicas) (ELAM); maternity wards

Doctors Without Borders (Médecins Sans Frontières) (MSF), 23, 79. *See also* Cuban medical brigades

doctor–patient ratio of: Canada, 6, 60–61, 76; Cuba, 9–10, 27, 33, 36, 40, 43, 45, 76, 105; The Gambia, 47; Haiti, 77; Havana (city), 46; Havana (province), 46; East Timor, 83; Ecuador, 7, 76, 126; Japan, 27; Malawi, 6, 19, 77; Nepal, 77; Pakistan, 76; South Africa,

61, 76–77; Soviet bloc nations, 27; Switzerland, 76; United Kingdom, 27; United States, 6, 76. *See also* Canada; Cuba; East Timor; Ecuador; The Gambia; Haiti; Havana (city); Havana (province); Japan; Malawi; nurse–patient ratio; Pakistan; South Africa; Switzerland; United Kingdom; United States

Donde no hay doctor (*Where There Is No Doctor: A Village Health Care Handbook*) (Werner), 114, 116

Douglas, Tommy, 23–24, 25, 26. *See also* primary care; Saskatchewan

drinking water. *See* potable and non-potable water

E

East Timor: ELAM scholarships for youth from, 83, 84; doctor–patient ratio of, 83; population displacement of, 83; Henry Reeve Emergency Response Medical Brigade in, 84. *See also* Asia; Cuban medical brigades; doctor–patient ratio of; global South; Henry Reeve Emergency Response Medical Brigade (Henry Reeve Brigade); Latin American School of Medicine (Escuela Latinomericana de Ciencias Médicas) (ELAM); Ministry of Foreign Affairs (Ministerio de Relaciones Exterior) (MINREX); Ministry of Public Health (Ministerio de Salud Publica) (MINSAP) (Cuba)

Ecuador, medical education in, 127–35; *año rural* of, 126–27, 136, 137–38, 139, 141, 143–44, 147, 148; class sizes of, 128; compulsorily medical services, problems with, 130; curricula and foci of, 127; lack of spaces to specialize as part of, 128–29, 135, 139; limited number of residencies of, 128; pressure to students to specialize with, 127, 130, 134, 135; focus on clinical care in urban centres, 130; graduates of, 127; pediatrics, including pediatricians; public and private schools teaching, 127; student attitudes

graduates of, 133–34; role in training global health workforce, 83–84; role of Cuban embassies in recruitment for, 88–90; role of IFCO in American applications to, 89, 90; salaries of graduates of, 153; Sancti Spíritus (campus), 86; scholarships to, 83, 84, 86–87, 107, 123, 146; shifts in student population, 86–87; specialization at, 133; student enrollment at, 29; student evaluations of curriculum, 101–3; student life at, 103–6; student population of, 9, 29, 80, 84, 85, 86–87; student recruitment at, 88–90; student response to, 101–3; suitability of Ecuador as point of study of ELAM graduates, 116; TNM as part of curriculum of, 95–96; 122; traditional and natural medicine (*medicina verde*) (TNM) as part of curriculum, 95–96, 121–22, 123–24; use of doctor-nurse teams, 100–101; Venezuela, increased student population from, 87; Villa Clara (campus), 85; Werner, David, 114, 116; West African medical brigades formed by ELAM graduates, 154; work against perceived undersupply of global physicians, 116. *See also* Africa; Antigua; Argentina; Barrio Adentro (into the neighbourhood); Belizean students at ELAM; Brazil; Bush, George W., administration of; Caracas; cardiovascular; Castro, Fidel; Chile; Cienfuegos; Costa Rica; Cuba; Cuban embassy in; Cuban medical brigades; Cuban medical internationalism; definition of; Dr. Gustavo Aldereguía Lima (hospital); East Timor; Ecuador; El Salvador; Eloy Alfaro Brigade (Brigada Eloy Alfaro); embargo on Cuba by United States; epidemiology, including epidemiological; family doctors; Front of Multidisciplinary Professional Graduates; global North; global South; Guatemala; Haiti; Haitian earthquake;

Harper, Stephen; Havana (city); health insurance; Henry Reeve Emergency Response Medical Brigade (Henry Reeve Brigade); Honduras; hospitals; indigenous peoples; Internationalist Federation of Health (Federación Internacionalista de Salud) (FIS); Interreligious Foundation for Community Organization (Pastors for Peace) (IFCO); La Joya de los Sanchas; Latin America; Leavitt, Michael; Martí, José; maternity wards; Mbarara; Medical Education Cooperation with Cuba (MEDICC); medical education; medical tourism; Mexico; National School of Public Health (Escuela National de Salud Pública) (ENSAP); neoliberalism; Nicaragua; nurses; ophthalmology; pediatrics, including pediatricians; Panama, Paraguay; paraphysiology; physiology; Peru; pharmacology; physiology; primary care; private health care; public health care; Quito; salaries of; School of the Americas; shamans (*colundrenos*); Sintes, Álvarez; solidarity; South Africa; Soviet Union, effects on Cuba of collapse of (*Periodo Especial*); surgery; tuberculosis; *Themes in Integral General Medicine* (*Temas de Medicina General Integral*); traditional and natural medicine (*medicina verde*) (TNM); United States; Uruguay; use of doctor-nurse teams; Venezuela; volunteerism and volunteers (*brigadistas*); Werner, David; World Health Organization (WHO); Zamora
Leavitt, Michael, 17. *See also* Bush, George W., administration of; theory of soft power
leprosy, reduction in Jamkhed (India), 8; in Cuba, 38. *See also* Cuba
leukemia, 120–21. *See also* cancer
liberalism. *See* neoliberalism
Liberia, infant mortality rate of, 43–44. *See also* Africa; global South

of, 61, 149; from Cuba, 27, 69–70,
72, 151, 152; from Cuba to Ecuador,
153; from Cuba to South Africa, 30;
defences of, 62; of Ecuadorian medical
residency students to Chile, 16, 128;
encouragement by United States State
Department, 69–70; ethics of choice
of participation in, 71–72; from global
South to global North, 16; of medical
technicians from Ecuador to Chile,
128; moral platform of, 61, 67; of
medical residents from Ecuador to
Columbia, 128; of nurses from South
Africa, 62–63; from Pakistan, 76; by
poor in Ecuador, 119; reasons for,
61–63, 65–67, 78; from Philippines,
65–66, 151–52; from South Africa,
62–65, 72; to South Africa from
Kenya, Malawi, Tanzania, and
Zimbabwe, 63–64; to United States,
32, 65–66, 69, 151, 152; supposed
benefits of, 60–62; from Venezuela,
68. *See also* Africa; Australia; Barrio
Adentro; Canada; Caribbean; Chile;
Colombia; Cuba; Ecuador; Ecuador,
medical education in; global North;
global South; Kenya; Malawi; New
Zealand; nurses; Pakistan; Philippines;
Saskatchewan; South Africa; Tanzania;
United Kingdom; United States;
Venezuela; Zimbabwe
Millennium Development Goals Fund, 53
Ministry of Foreign Affairs (Ministerio
de Relaciones Exterior) (MINREX)
(Cuba), 16, 83, 84, 123. *See also* East
Timor; Pakistan
Ministry of Public Health (Ecuador), 135,
136; coverage of population by, 125;
denial of hospital rights to *médico
general básico*, 137; description of
auxiliary health-care posts by, 126;
expectation of students to seek
specialization and residency, 130;
increased use of free provisions
provided by, 125; obligatory service
for Ecuadorian medical students
working for, 128; operation of AIDS/

HIV and tuberculosis campaigns, 145;
provision of free services to pregnant
women and newborn children,
124–25; rules for granting of public
licences by, 128; screening of ELAM
applicants by, 146. *See also* Act for
Free Maternity and Infant Services;
childbirth and pregnancy; Ecuador;
HIV/AIDS; Instituto Ecuatoriano de
Seguridad Social; Latin American
School of Medicine (Escuela
Latinomericana de Ciencias Médicas)
(ELAM); *médico general básico*;
tuberculosis
Ministry of Public Health (Ministerio de
Salud Publica) (MINSAP) (Cuba),
36, 46, 85, 96–97; effects of embargo
by United States on health care,
41, 42, 46; ELAM student needs
and services accommodated by, 80;
encouragement of development
and implementation of alternative
medicines, 96, 122; establishment
of country-specific schools by, 106;
expansion of health-care workers
medical education placements in the
1990s, 28–29, 43; foreign scholarship
opportunities offered by, 83, 84,
158ch4n2; insistence on traditional
childbirth, 38; offer of free training
for specialization by, 133; publication
on intranet of articles by, 82; quoted,
82; reconsideration of *policlinicos*,
44; support of Cuban health workers
for outreach and primary care, 146;
survey of medical students conducted
by, 101. *See also* childbirth and
pregnancy; East Timor; Pakistan;
policlinicos (specialty clinics); Soviet
Union, effects on Cuba of collapse of;
embargo on Cuba by United States;
traditional and natural medicine
(*medicina verde*) (TNM)
Ministry of Welfare (Cuba), 38
MINREX. *See* Ministry of Foreign Affairs
(Ministerio de Relaciones Exterior)
(MINREX)

primary care; salaries; Southeast Asia; University of Manila; University of the Philippines; wait times

physiology, 99–100, 124; morphophysiology (*morfofisiologia*), 84; paraphysiology, 127, physiologists, 91, 99. *See also* Cuban health care; Latin American School of Medicine (Escuela Latinomericana de Ciencias Médicas) (ELAM)

Plato, quoted, 27

poaching, concept of, 61–62, 70. *See also* definition of; migration of health-care workers

policlinicos (specialty clinics), 44, 97; absence of resources to improve, 41; Alamar, 39; insufficient community impact of, 39; as means to remove pressure from hospitals, 45; as merging of levels of care at community level, 44; placement of doctors and nurses outside of, 40; responsibilities of, 38–39, 45. *See also consultorios* (consultation rooms); family doctors; hospitals; Ministry of Public Health (Ministerio de Salud Publica) (MINSAP)

polio, eradication in Cuba of, 38

postnatal care, 38. *See also* childbirth and pregnancy

potable and non-potable water, 1, 17, 18, 22, 33, 38, 42, 120, 144; *See also* dengue; Ecuador, epidemiology, including epidemiological; Havana; India; malaria; mosquitoes; petroleum, including oil waterborne infections; Zamora

poverty: as source of crime, 52; in global South, 52; relationship to structural ethics of inequality, 152. *See also* global South

Powell, Colin, 108. *See also* Bush, George W., administration of

pregnancy. *See* childbirth and pregnancy

Premio Anual de la Salud (award), 91

primary care, 1, 15; absence in Ecuador of government stated support for, 131; anticipated failure in Philippines to support primary care system, 65; BHTs as responsible for first stage of, 44; commitment in Cuba and Venezuela to, 117; comparative needs between countries for, 70; contribution of Canada to, 32; Cuban encouragement of and model for, 3, 4, 16, 18, 26, 27, 35, 36; Cuban provision in Caracas of, 67; Cuban training of foreign doctors in, 80; difficulty of ELAM graduates in Ecuador to provide, 146; effects of collapse of Soviet Union on Cuban system of, 40, 41; encouragement by Cuban medical internationalism of, 17–18, 32; encouragement by Tommy Douglas, 24; global rejection of preventative, 20; as goal of Cuba's foreign cooperation, 84; higher workloads for Cuban doctors practising in, 59; history in Cuba of, 36; importance of appreciation of non-Western approaches to health, 96; introduction in Cuba of, 27–29; as means of addressing basic health indicators, 18; inability in Ecuador to afford or obtain, 121–22, 131; low status in Ecuador of, 127, 146; as means of individual and societal empowerment, 29; medical tourism as undermining, 55, 57; as part of Cuban and ELAM mission and curriculum, 82, 83, 95, 108, 112; as part of Operación Milagro, 18; possible limitations on humanitarian aid to provide, 79; proven Cuban ability to train doctors of, 59; provision through Cuban clinics of, 37; reflected in Cuban medical internationalism, 46; shift from *consultorios* to *policlinicos*, 45; student reaction at ELAM to course in, 101; in *Themes in Integral General Medicine* (*Temas de Medicina General Integral*), 95; through Internationalist Federation of Health (Federación

also aid and philanthropic health-care efforts; Cuba; doctor–patient ratio of; Haiti; Michigan, global North; Honduras; Latin American School of Medicine (Escuela Latinomericana de Ciencias Médicas) (ELAM); migration of health-care workers; life expectancy; nurses; Operación (or Misión) Milagro; Philippines; salaries of; School of the Americas; solidarity; South Africa

Universidad Central del Ecuador, 89, 127–28, 130, 148. *See also* Ecuador; Ecuador, medical education in; Quito

University of Havana (Cuba), 27, 35; medical school of, 35. *See also* Cuba; Latin American School of Medicine (Escuela Latinomericana de Ciencias Médicas) (ELAM)

University of Manila (Philippines), 66. *See also* nurses; Philippines

University of the Philippines, 66. *See also* Philippines

Uruguay, 9, 86, 94, 104. *See also* global South; Latin America

USMLE. *See* United States Medical Licensing Exam (USMLE)

V

vector-borne infections, 53
venereal diseases, 38
Venezuela: Barrio Adentro, 67–71, 87; economic and political benefits afforded Cuba by, 47; Gross Domestic Product of, 68; literacy campaigns in, 57; migration of health-care workers from, 68; missions with Cuba, 57; participation with Cuba in Operación Milagro and other health-care missions, 3, 10, 57–60, 61; proximal versus distal responses to health-care risks, 117; provision of petroleum to CARICOM countries, 69; reintegration plan for ELAM graduates, 133; sponsorship of eye surgeries, 57–58, 59–60. *See also* Barrio Adentro; Bolivarian Alliance for the Peoples

of Our America (Alianza Bolivariana para los Pueblos de Nuestra América) (ALBA); Caracas; Caribbean; Caribbean Community (CARICOM); Cuba; definition of; eyes; Latin America; Latin American School of Medicine (Escuela Latinomericana de Ciencias Médicas) (ELAM); migration of health-care workers; nationalism; Operación (or Misión) Milagro; petroleum, including oil

volunteerism and volunteers (*brigadistas*), 23; in Barrio Adentro, 68, 70; Cuban, 11, 70; by IFCO in American applications to ELAM, 89, 90; post-Revolution medical volunteerism in Cuba, 37; in La Joya de los Sachas, 143. *See also* Barrio Adentro; Cuba; Interreligious Foundation for Community Organization (Pastors for Peace) (IFCO); La Joya de los Sachas (Ecuador); Latin American School of Medicine (Escuela Latinomericana de Ciencias Médicas) (ELAM)

W

Wagner, Guillermo, 131
wait times: in Canada, ix, 32; in Cuba, 45; in global North, 54; in Philippines, 115. *See also* Canada; Cuba; global North; Philippines
war and violent conflict: perception of economic benefit from, 14; shifts in life expectancy as result of, 52. *See also* life expectancy
water, drinking or potable. *See* potable and non-potable water
waterborne infections, 53. *See also* potable and non-potable water
Werner, David, 114, 116. *See also* Latin American School of Medicine (Escuela Latinomericana de Ciencias Médicas)
West African medical brigades formed by ELAM graduates, 154. *See also* Cuban medical brigades; Latin American School of Medicine (Escuela